Cutting Class

Cutting Class

Socioeconomic Status and Education

Edited by
Joe L. Kincheloe and
Shirley R. Steinberg

Rowman & Littlefield Publishers, Inc.
Lanham • Boulder • New York • Toronto • Plymouth, UK

ROWMAN & LITTLEFIELD PUBLISHERS, INC.

Published in the United States of America
by Rowman & Littlefield Publishers, Inc.
A wholly owned subsidary of
The Rowman & Littlefield Publishing Group, Inc.
4501 Forbes Boulevard, Suite 200, Lanham, Maryland 20706
www.rowmanlittlefield.com

Estover Road
Plymouth PL6 7PY
United Kingdom

British Library Cataloguing in Publication Information Available

Library of Congress Cataloging-in-Publication Data

Cutting class : socioeconomic status and education / edited by Joe L.
  Kincheloe and Shirley R. Steinberg.
    p. cm.
  ISBN-13: 978-0-8476-9117-3 (cloth : alk. paper)
  ISBN-10: 0-8476-9117-9 (cloth : alk. paper)
  ISBN-13: 978-0-8476-9118-0 (pbk. : alk. paper)
  ISBN-10: 0-8476-9118-7 (pbk. : alk. paper)
    1. Children with social disabilities—Education—United States.
  2. Poor—United States. 3. Educational equalization—United States.
  4. Education—Social aspects—United States. I. Kincheloe, Joe L.
  II. Steinberg, Shirley R., 1952–
  LC4091.C88 2007
  302.43—dc22   2007001482

Printed in the United States of America

⊗™ The paper used in this publication meets the minimum requirements of
American National Standard for Information Sciences—Permanence of.
Paper for Printed Library Materials, ANSI/NISO Z39.48-1992.

Contents

Part I

INTRODUCTION: THE NATURE OF CLASS, SOCIOECONOMIC CONTEXT, AND CRITICAL PEDAGOGY

CHAPTER 1

Cutting Class in a Dangerous Era:
A Critical Pedagogy of Class Awareness

Joe L. Kincheloe and Shirley R. Steinberg

In the last years of the first decade of the twenty-first century, educators observed the appalling results of a right-wing reeducation of the public, an imperial pedagogy of race, gender, and class that works best by feigning the irrelevance of class in the social, political, and educational spheres. The word *class* will rarely pass the delicately pursed lips of the neoliberals and neoconservatives who now control the sociopolitical and educational world. About the only time one hears them speak the term is in response to a critical analysis of the growing disparity of power and wealth and the suffering it inflicts on the poor around the world. "There they go again," the right-wing talking heads repeat on script, "trying to scare everyone with their pathetic use of class warfare." Such rhetoric works to position expressions of concern for poverty and human suffering as somehow dangerous and traitorous acts worthy only of punishment. A social cosmos where such concerns can successfully be represented in such a way is not a sane place to live—indeed, it's a world gone mad. A critical pedagogy of class awareness challenges this world, exposing the reality of class stratification in the contemporary globalized society and analyzing its impact on schooling in general and teachers and students in particular.

In the new world in which we now live governments owned by private interests work to shield dominant power from accountability. Concurrently, their educational institutions with their standardized curricula promote political cynicism and conformity. Democracy as a concept atrophies in such an ideological matrix, as disparity trumps justice, corporate earnings take precedence over human needs, and the future becomes simply another commodity to be subjected to the logic of the unfettered market. (We will use the terms *ideology* and *ideological* frequently in this book. Ideology defined in a critical theoretical manner involves the construction of knowledge, the making of meaning, and the production of affect that supports dominant power.)

Even among those who criticize such macroarrangements, among those who speak out against racism, gender, and sexual bias there remains a blindness to class bias and the everyday microdynamics of classism. Thus, the poor face a double whammy of sorts: they are screwed by a structural system designed to pamper the needs of the wealthy while suffering the indignities of class at a lived, microlevel on a daily basis. The editors and authors of *Cutting Class* are concerned with both social levels, with the class pain they evoke. Thus, particular chapters focus on the macrostructural dimensions of class bias and their impact on education, while others focus on the microlevel of lived existence, the autobiographical-phenomenological aspects of education and its intersection with issues of socioeconomic class.

Along with issues of racism, sexism, and homophobia, issues of class are often ignored in classrooms. But unlike racism, sexism, and homophobia, class oppression has few advocates who "call it out," who provide workshops and seminars to help fight against it. As bad and exploitative as some of the $10,000-per-day workshops can be around issues of racism and sexism, for example, this might once in a while be viewed as a blessing. But, unfortunately, the silence about class tyranny usually works to extend the damage, to deepen the pain. Without conversation the public is unaware of the grotesque—and growing—disparity of wealth in the United States and other Western societies.

When such absences are combined with the cutting of socioeconomic class from everyday school and media conversations, a school and political environment is created that presents a worldview so bizarre to students from lower socioeconomic backgrounds that the concept of education, of being educated, becomes meaningless. "What world are these people living in?" my southern Appalachian friends and I (Joe) asked when school leaders and teachers would paint pictures of our school and world devoid of class differences. With such unrealistic portraits of the society in which we lived swimming in our heads, we found it difficult to take anything they said very seriously. In my adulthood I interact with students from poor backgrounds who express in their own unique ways the same sentiments. I intellectually and emotionally understand their dismissive attitudes toward schooling. Teachers who understand such class dynamics and work to empathize with and touch the lives of such students are, in my book, heroic figures.

THE FAUX CLASSLESS SOCIETY— RIGHT-WING STYLE: THE CONTEMPORARY CORPORATIZED POLITICS OF KNOWLEDGE

One of the great phenomena of our era is that right at the time inequality is increasing, when the difference in per-pupil expenditures for well-to-do and poor kids is expanding, the topic for all intents has been erased from school curricula, teacher education, and the social unconsciousness. No doubt, many social, cultural, psychoanalytical, and political-economic forces have come together to cut class from these domains—cutting class is an extremely complex operation. Of course, we use the word *class* incessantly—but in a different context and discursive universe than we are using it in *Cutting Class*. One would be hard pressed to watch a sporting event on television without the commentator proclaiming one player "a class act." It is not uncommon to hear news commentators or gossip television hosts speak of the low-class or classless behavior of a particular celebrity. For example, "Michael Moore's classless injection of politics into the Oscar ceremony was an insult to the Academy," *Entertainment Tonight* TV personalities proclaim to millions of viewers. "50 Cent is a classless thug," other commentators tell us. Examples abound. The use of "class" in this context contributes to the cutting of conversations about and explorations of socioeconomic class oppression and its effects on schooling, work, health, and human well being in general.

Such use of *class* creates a situation where many individuals don't know what we're talking about when we use *class* in a way that involves social rankings, power relationships, and an axis of oppression. America, as many have argued, is a classless society. George Herbert Walker Bush elevated this sentiment to a quasi-official article of American faith in the 1992 election in response to criticism of policies that allowed for the loss of millions of factory jobs and middle-management positions. Such a position set Bush and other right-wing politicians up to represent those who did employ the term in the sense used here as radical class warriors, Marxists, or other undesirables. This, along with many other right-wing actions over the last thirty years in particular, has worked to make it déclassé to talk about class. Such successful efforts made it far easier to recover policies, rebuild structures, and cultivate attitudes that allowed the wealthy more privilege and the unrestricted right to rule.

In the world-gone-mad, authentic compassion—not the media-friendly, duplicitous "compassionate conservatism" of George W. Bush—is the province of naïve weaklings. Real men and their women get what they can no matter who it hurts or what damage is done to the social and ecological fabric. In such a society greed comes to be viewed as good, while generosity is represented as a drag on the economy. "Don't talk about class and economic oppression to me, dude, I'm getting mine while I can." And amazingly all of this has taken place in a time of renewed religious fervor and the rise of Christian influences on the political fabric, on the market-driven ideological position that most zealously promotes the cutting of class awareness from public discourse and action. It is, indeed, a strange world (hooks 2000; Aronowitz 2003; Brantlinger 2003; Quan 2004). This is a book about that bizarre sociopolitical and educational landscape.

Much of the contemporary educational conversation, especially the discourse of No Child Left Behind (NCLB) and test-driven curricula, takes place in a discursive space where there is no connection between what happens in schools and the other major institutions in a society. The notion that drives our work and *Cutting Class*—that schools, classrooms, students, teachers, etc. are located within and shaped by society at large—has been erased through a very carefully planned process. We must admit that we find it difficult to accept that we live in a world where many people have been induced to believe that a child's dire poverty makes little difference in her educational life. But various analyses of the rhetoric of the public conversation about education and schooling seem to indicate the reality of such a perspective. Again, our difficulty accepting that this has happened is amplified by our observation of a class war being waged against the poor of the world by transnational corporations and their political allies. Class has played a

central role in every society, but with the technological and communication innovations of the last century that function has morphed and intensified. Indeed, the ability of capital to regulate workers and shape information and, thus, consciousness has never been more pronounced
(Bruner 1996; Zweig 2004).

Students of education understand that nothing we're asserting here is
remotely new. W. E. B. DuBois (1973) articulated these insights over a
century ago; John Dewey (1916) pointed out the tendency for the
United States and other nations to promote unique modes of selfishness
that undermine democracy and democratic education; George Counts
(1978) warned us about the impact of class on education during the
Great Depression and beyond; and C. Wright Mills (1956) laid out a
treatise on power and class in the conservative 1950s. These are just a
few of the scholars who have asserted such positions over the last
century—and, of course, there were many who warned us of the dan-
gers of class stratification and inequality in previous centuries. A critical pedagogy of class awareness takes its cue from these and many
other thinkers and educators from societies around the globe. In this
multilogical, multicultural, and multiperspectival context, such a view
of education maintains that we must build relations of solidarity among
the poor, working people, educators, those oppressed by race, gender,
and sexuality, and our students. In this context we must learn the ways
that class intersects with these other domains, in the process discerning
how class bias and oppression plays out even among those who are intellectually aware of inequality and exploitation.

HISTORICALLY CONTEXTUALIZING CONTEMPORARY
CLASS OPPRESSION

Part of the explanation of why Western societies—the United States in
particular—continue to ignore the admonitions of so many about the sociocultural and educational damage of class oppression involves what
Aaron Gresson (2004) calls the recovery movement. While we have
written with Gresson about this topic in many other books and articles,
it is worth mentioning again here in a class context. The last 150 years
have in many ways been marked by insurrections against various forms
of domination: racial, colonial, gender, sexual, and class in particular. A

key goal of any critical pedagogy of class awareness in the twenty-first century involves developing a historical understanding of these insurrections, their successes and failures, and dominant power blocks efforts to "recover" the power perceived to be lost to the challengers. This effort to recover dominant power has reached its apex in the last three decades. It is only in this zeitgeist of recovery that the belief that poverty and education are unrelated could be successfully propagated. Only with a metahistorical consciousness can we begin to understand how cutting class from the world's consciousness fits with a larger effort to promote regressive, oppressive, and antidemocratic political and educational activities.

The recovery movement cannot be appreciated outside of an understanding of European colonialism and economic development over the last 500 years—and over the last 100 years the American reformulation of these dynamics. Though it would rarely be heard in the mainstream world that cuts class, the sociopolitical, philosophical, psychological, and economic structures constructed by the last 500 years of Euro-American colonialism have a dramatic everyday effect on education. After several centuries of exploitation the early twentieth century began to witness a growing impatience of colonized peoples with their sociopolitical, economic, and educational status.

A half millennium of colonial violence had convinced Africans, Asians, Latin Americans, and indigenous peoples around the world that enough was enough. Picking up steam after World War II, colonized peoples around the world threw off colonial governmental strictures and set out on a troubled journey toward independence. Poor laboring people worked during the same time to secure the right to unionize and bargain collectively. In numerous industrial societies exploited workers gained work benefits and social protections—for example, social security—that helped move them toward the possibility of a more economically secure future.

European colonial powers and their corporate allies, however, were not about to give up lucrative socioeconomic and colonial relationships so easily. With the United States leading the way, Western societies developed a wide array of neocolonial strategies for maintaining the benefits of colonialism. This neocolonial effort continues unabated and in many ways with a new intensity in an era of transnational corporations and the "war on terror" in the twenty-first century. With globalization, corporate power wielders are able to regulate labor in new and effective ways that trash previous worker rights and protections, in the process increasing their profit margins and executive salaries to levels unimaginable only a few years ago.

Understanding these historical power dynamics and their influence is central to the metahistorical consciousness of our critical pedagogy of class awareness. Indeed, though most Americans are not aware of it the anticolonial rebellion initiated the liberation movements of the 1960s and 1970s that shook the United States and other Western societies. The civil rights movement, the women's movement, and the gay rights movement all took their cue from the anticolonial struggles of individuals around the world. For example, Martin Luther King Jr. wrote his dissertation on the anticolonial rebellion against the British led by Mahatma Gandhi in India. King focused his scholarly attention on Gandhi's nonviolent colonial resistance tactics, later drawing upon such strategies in the civil rights movement.

By the mid-1970s a conservative counterreaction—especially in the United States—to these liberation movements was taking shape with the goals of "recovering" what was perceived to be lost in these movements (Gresson 1995, 2004; Kincheloe, Steinberg, Rodriguez, and Chennault 1998; Rodriguez and Villaverde 2000; Kincheloe 2006). Thus, the politics, cultural wars, and educational and psychological debates, policies, and practices of the last three decades cannot be understood outside of these efforts to "recover" white supremacy, patriarchy, heterosexual "normality," Christian dominance, the European intellectual canon, and class privilege with its unregulated power of capital.

These are some of the most important defining macroconcerns of our time, as every social and educational issue is refracted through their lenses. Any view of education and class conceived outside of this framework becomes a form of ideological mystification. This process of ideological mystification operates to maintain present dominant-subordinate power relations by promoting particular forms of meaning making. In this colonial context ideological mystification often involves making meanings that assert that non-European peoples and the poor of all backgrounds are incapable of running their own political and economic affairs and that colonialism and a paternalistic capitalism *was* an effective way of taking care of these incapable peoples.

Contemporary standardized, test-driven, psychologized education is enjoying great support in the twenty-first century because, in part, it plays such an important role in recovering what was perceived to have been lost in the anticolonial and labor liberation movements. One of the educational dimensions of what was perceived to have been lost involves the notion of Western or white and middle, upper-middle- and upper-class intellectual supremacy. No mechanism works better than intelligence/achievement testing and school-performance statistics to "prove" Western and upper-class supremacy over poor people and racially and ethically diverse individuals around the world. Positivistic psychometricians operating in their ethnocentric domains routinely proclaim the intellectual superiority of Western white middle and upper class people. Statistically, white students perform better in schools than nonwhite students, the economically privileged better than the poor. Richard Herrnstein and Charles Murray (1994), for example, write unabashedly that the average IQ of African peoples is about seventy-five and that the reason the poor remain poor is that they are not as intelligent as their economic superiors.

By the 1970s, right-wing educational policy was directly connected to the larger recovery movement, as it sought to eliminate the anticolonial, antiracist, antipatriarchal, and class-conscious dimensions of progressive curriculum development. Understanding the way some educators were using education to extend the goals of the worldwide anticolonial movement and the race, gender, and class liberation movements in particular, right-wing strategists sought to subvert the public and civic dimensions of schooling. Instead of helping to prepare society for a socially mobile and egalitarian democracy, education in the formulation of the right-wing recovery redefined schooling as a private concern. The goal of this private concern was not to graduate "good citizens" but to provide abstract individuals the tools for socioeconomic mobility.

By the 1970s, with the emergence of this ideology of recovery, the very concept of government with its "public" denotations began to represent the victory of minorities, the undeserving poor, and concerns the inequities of race, class, gender, and colonialism. "Big government" began to become a code phrase for anti-upper-middle-class white male social action in the recovery discourse. Indeed, in this articulation it was time to get it off "our" backs. Thus, privatization became more than a strategy for organizing social institutions. Privatization was the ostensibly deracialized, declassed term that could be deployed to signify the recovery of white, upper-middle-class patriarchal supremacy. In the same way the word *choice* could be used to connote the right to "opt out" of government mandated "liberal" policies. Like good consumers, "we" (those people with traditional values) choose life, privatized schools, the most qualified job applicants, and Christian values over the other "products."

Thus, in this historical context we can better understand the right-wing use of NCLB as a legal tool to reconfigure the federal government's role as the promoter of equality and diversity in the educational domain. Though it was promoted as a new way of helping economically marginalized and minority students, such representations were smokescreens used to conceal its mission of recovery of traditional forms of dominant power. In this power context NCLB is quite cavalier about the inequity between poor and well-to-do school districts and even schools within particular districts. The right-wing public discourse about education has successfully erased questions of race and class injustice from consideration. The fact that 40 percent of children in the United States live in poor or low-income conditions is simply not a part of an educational conversation shaped by the rhetoric of recovery. The understanding that students who are upper-middle-class and live in well-funded school districts have much more opportunity for academic and socioeconomic success than students from poor contexts is fading from the public consciousness in the twenty-first century.

The realization that inequality is deemed irrelevant even when we understand that socioeconomic factors are the most important predictor of how students perform on high-stakes standardized tests is distressing. In this context we begin to discern that in a system driven by such high-stakes tests, it is not hard to predict who is most likely to succeed and fail. In the name of high standards and accountability, the recovery project scores great victories. "We can't let these 'incompetents' get by with such bad performance," right-wing ideologues righteously proclaim. "It degrades the whole system." As they cry their crocodile tears for poor and marginalized students in their attempt to hide their real agenda and garner support of naïve liberals for their educational plans, they concurrently support deep cuts in any programs designed to help such students.

During the George W. Bush presidency, for example, Americans have witnessed cuts in food stamps, Temporary Assistance for Needy Families, nutrition programs for children, childcare, the enforcement of laws for child support, child health insurance, and the Low-Income Home Energy Assistance Program. And this does not include the education programs that help poor and marginalized students targeted for termination in the coming years. The privatization-based voucher programs proposed as means of helping students from poor families avoid failing schools and gain access to a higher quality education do not work. The price of attending many private schools, especially the elite ones, is more costly than the worth of the meager voucher. Most students from poor families even with their vouchers will still not be able to afford private education, not to mention meeting the high standardized-test-score requirements such schools require. Such issues are, of course, not typically a part of the truncated public conversation about vouchers and private schooling. They have too much to do with class.

GROWING INEQUALITY AND
THE REEMERGENCE OF CLASS ANALYSIS

Obviously, people in contemporary society talk about money all the time—but they generally do *not* talk about socioeconomic class. Wherever class questions emerge from this money talk, dominant ideology is well prepared to stop it in its tracks. Capitalism, the dominant story asserts, creates meritocratic societies where individuals rise or fall on the basis of their intelligence and willingness to work. In this formulation, class segregation does not exist and education is a reliable vehicle for socioeconomic mobility. In addition, the dominant ideology—in the United States in particular—also contends that any inequality that does exist is overridden by the fact that poorer people in the United States are much better off than the vast armies of the poor in Latin American, Asia, and Africa. How can the American poor complain when they live a regal existence compared to the rest of the world?

What is referred to as a meritocracy falls short on many levels:

- socioeconomic resources must be evenly dispersed
- the funding of schools as well as the conditions of different schools must be relatively equivalent
- students should have equal access to high-quality teaching and learning
- the curriculum must have cultural relevance for all groups of students
- the educational system must make sure that the system does not operate to simply extend privilege to the privileged and the marginalization of the marginalized
- school leaders and teachers are well qualified to identify and disrupt long-standing cycles of poverty and school failure found among particular groups of individuals

We are nowhere near these markers of a level socioeconomic and educational playing field. And, unfortunately, with the political landscape that now exists in the United States and other Western states, the outlook for change in the short term is not good. With the prevailing politics of corporate controlled knowledge more and more people, especially the young and the poor, identify with concerns and needs of the upper class. The media with its endless parade of programs about the daily trials and travails of the upper class and advertisements that induce the poor to buy into a set of consumption-based values work to quash class consciousness. Wars of empire such as America's Iraq fiasco are designed to deploy patriotism to repress awareness of class oppression. But luckily, history is fickle and often the darkest hour comes just before the dawn. Indeed, because of the misguided nature and foolish execution of the Iraq War, more individuals around the world and even in the United States have come to understand the structural dimensions of empire, global economics, and international class oppression. Given the cutting of conversation about class in media and schools, this new understanding on the part of many people is a cause for great hope, a demonstration of people's ability to resist power and its manipulations.

It's hard to find hope for race, gender, sexual, and class justice as we write this in the middle of the second term of the George W. Bush

administration—a time when antagonism toward the civic and egalitarian features of public education grounds official school policy. If an
educational or social policy in this context fails to extend the cause of
transnational capital, the power and best interests of the privileged, the
ends of corporatization, the effort to privatize education and other traditional public services, and the privileged position of the children of
the white well-to-do, it is relegated to the dumpster of history. As
transnational corporations compete with one another for access to new
locales with lower labor costs that operate to increase corporate profits while lowering the wages of workers in North America, Europe,
and the particular country that previously possessed the lowest labor
costs, the workforce realizes they are left no options. They must form
truly international labor unions with members from the United States,
Canada, Australia, the United Kingdom, Latin America, Southeast
Asia, India, Indonesia, and, eventually, China and Africa.

Such international unions would increase wages concurrently and
proportionately. This would challenge employers' threats to meet wage
increases with factory closings and moves to cheaper labor sources. A
critical pedagogy of class awareness promotes attentiveness to these
macroissues, as it works to make sure that corporate leaders can no
longer pit workers from one nation against workers from another one.
In a time marked by passionate fights over Mexican and other Latin
American immigration into the United States, one of many actions necessary to address the problems emerging from a situation involves the
uniting of U.S., Canadian, Mexican, and other Latin American labor
movements. Unified workers from different countries could stand up to
multinational corporations, the World Trade Organization (WTO), the
World Bank, and the International Monetary Fund (IMF). Critical pedagogy must be one of many movements that help forge alliances connecting labor organizations, environmental groups, social justice col-
lectives, communications workers and researchers, and educators.

Hurricanes Katrina and Rita in 2005 helped promote awareness of
the class segregation and vulnerability of the poor. The poor—the poor
African American population in particular—of New Orleans was dev-
astated by Hurricane Katrina with an indifferent and incompetent response from local, state, and federal governments. Images of poor people at the Superdome trapped in the flooded city, refused escape to

neighboring towns shook some Americans out of their racial and class blindness. In some cases images from Katrina-devastated New Orleans led individuals to study other poor communities in "affluent" America. What they found is that in city after city and in many rural areas poverty-stricken people have been abandoned, left to fend for themselves for the scraps thrown out by the prosperous.

On the other end of the socioeconomic continuum live the affluent in gated communities where they operate to protect their property and class interests. Individuals entering these communities who look poor and/or nonwhite are quickly removed. Because of the sociocultural, political-economic, and educational policies promoted by the right wing, these disparities continue to grow. The United States and other Western nations become more and more lands of extremes—and absolutely nothing good can come from such disparity. When a chief executive officer (CEO) of a corporation makes about fifty times the salary of the average worker—not counting stock options—something is amiss. With the welfare reform passed during the Clinton administration and extended by the Bush administration, we find that the most poor are worse off as evidenced by huge increases in the number of people seeking refuge in emergency shelters for the hungry and the homeless (Hooks 2000; Hartman 2002; Aronowitz 2003; Brantlinger 2003; Piven 2004; Quan 2004).

A central dimension of right-wing social and educational policy in contemporary Western societies involves the repugnant effort to discern inadequacy of some form in the poor and socially marginalized. This deficitism drives contemporary schooling. At the level of lived reality, we find it difficult to deal with this elitist, condescending mode of being. As educators, parents, friends, researchers, and citizens, we must work to control our anger toward those who work to construct the "inferiority" of their fellow human beings. Indeed, a key aspect of the foundation on which dominant power rests involves its ability to name particular groups and individuals as substandard.

The right-wing misinformation engine continuously turns out ideological-charged data that constructs the emotion-laden belief that the socioeconomic, cultural, and educational playing field is level. Thus, all people who don't succeed in school or work, fail because of their personal inadequacy—not a stacked and marked social deck. In this context corporations have worked hard to blame any economic problems on worker inferiority—to divert accountability from bad economic policy or managerial blunders. In this world other people's children are screwing up the schools, immigrants are ruining our society, and the poor and the nonwhite just don't have the same values as "we" do.

In what is becoming a twenty-first century, media-promoted, neo-feudal form of social stratification, a critical pedagogy of class awareness makes sure that such a growing inequality is a central concern of educators. Because of the extremism of particular right-wing leaders, free marketers, and class elitists of various stripes, a conversation about class oppression is beginning to reemerge in isolated locales in Western societies and around the world. The neoconservative effort to construct an American sociopolitical, economic, and military empire combined with its transnational corporate allies has been so repugnant to millions of people in North America and around the world that resistance movements are taking shape. We find a new interest in such issues when we speak around North America and impassioned support when addressing audiences in Brazil, Latin America, Spain, Portugal, Korea, and other locales. If such neocolonial, imperial, deficitist, and elitist policies continue to be pursued by the United States and its allies, resistance movements will continue to grow. Such crass inequality between nations and within nations cannot continue to exist without dramatic consequences.

UNDERSTANDING THE NATURE OF INEQUALITY

Critical pedagogy (see Kincheloe 2004 for an introduction) is dedicated to the creation of a more just world. With this foundation it seeks to help students and other individuals develop analytical, ethical, cognitive/intellectual tools to identify the insidious modes of oppression that undermine the quality of so many people's lives. In a critical pedagogy of class awareness, transformative scholars work to expose the ideologies that demonize the poor and challenge oppressive dominant cultural ways of seeing and being. With its literacy of power it identifies power relationships, how schools deploy such power against the poor, how transnational corporations create worldwide conditions for the oppression of the have-nots, and how these macro-micro dynamics intersect to create the most "powerful power" ever. With these understandings it is more prepared to fight oppressive dominant power in ways that help the poor at the political, social, psychological/cognitive, and educational levels.

At the political level a critical pedagogy of class awareness helps build coalitions and allies to engage in political struggles against those groups who promote political-economic policies harmful to the poor. At the social level it helps individuals understand the way representations of the rich and the poor, the white and the nonwhite, the colonizers and the colonized operate to shape consciousness in ways that reward the privileged and punish the marginalized. At the psychological/cognitive level it helps people appreciate the ways that Eurocentric, class-biased science uses reductionistic, decontextualized ways of producing knowledge to paint the poor and marginalized as undeserving and incompetent in a variety of fields. IQ tests that fail to account for one's family's educational background and relationship to learning are great examples of the ways dominant power works to "prove" the incompetence of the poor. And, of course, too many schools operate to build hostile, exclusive environments for the poor in which they are made to feel as outsiders who don't belong.

As a critical pedagogy works to understand inequality, it concurrently works to build a vision for a more just society—a happier, more erotic, and less consumption- and status-based world where people build new forms of relationships based on generosity, fairness, and intellectual curiosity. Even in the Western past we see evidence of social reforms that addressed class oppression, and when we look to non-Western and indigenous societies we find literally hundreds of insights to inform our vision of less class-stratified, more connected and life affirming social and educational institutions. In contemporary societies, however, this vision quest, this search for new and better ways of being, seeing, teaching, and learning have been represented as frightening and ill-considered acts of dangerous radicals. Those in power typically dismiss such attempts to construct new visions as a colossal waste of time, far removed from the everyday needs of classrooms—impractical. The development of vision as referenced in this critical pedagogy of class awareness is an effort to help us all become more attentive to our world, our surroundings, to the pain of those in need.

Nothing, I believe, could be more directly related to the everyday life of the class—nothing could be more practical.

This dismissal of the importance of vision—what some call theorizing—is a profoundly important dimension of the class oppression of dominant hegemonic power. "There may be some problems with what we do in education," they tell us, "but there's really nothing we can do about it. It's just the way the world is." In a positivistic world where measurable quantities—no matter how important the measurable qualities actually are, for example the ability on a test to underline adjectives—take on an almost mystical magnitude, the hidden factors that help shape the world are seen to be of little consequence. A critical pedagogy of class awareness is by nature irrelevant in such a cultural context because so many of its concerns are invisible to the naked eye. The political-economic structures, ideological constructs, hegemonic strategies, cultural capital, cognitive assumptions, and discursive practices that shape class oppression are not typically visible in everyday experience. Here it is the difficult, frustrating, conflict-producing task of critical pedagogy: to perform the magic of bringing the invisible to visibility.

If this were not enough, it is also the job of such a pedagogy to convince one's audience that such factors are important—indeed, their invisibility in everyday life gives them the power to perform their diabolical feats under the radar of consciousness. In other words, individuals are not aware that these agents of dominant power are attempting to shape their view of the world, of the privileged and the poor, all the while developing mechanisms to clandestinely dictate the electoral and governmental processes. And it's not too hard to understand that such a *covert* process works best in the domain of consciousness construction and political control.

If one knows that she is being manipulated or the democratic agencies of her society are being subverted, defense mechanisms are immediately deployed. Many readers may as they read these words find themselves rejecting them out of hand, because they are aware that we are writing to persuade them of something they don't presently believe. Though it is against the principles of a critical pedagogy, if we were to hide our agenda it might be easier for some readers to swallow. To operate in that way, however, would be to sell our pedagogical souls to the devil and to become propagandists who are no better than dominant power wielders attempting to insidiously shape our perspectives for their own personal gain. Critical educators dealing with class cannot tiptoe around the tulips of class power and the agents who wield it. They have to name names, identify who has the power and how they are using it, and point out who is getting hurt and how. Such tasks—especially in contemporary society—rarely win them Miss Congeniality awards. Even with their allies in gender, sexual, racial, and ability-related justice movements, they have to point out the class insensitivity that may be found in such groups. At the same time, they listen carefully and humbly and take heed when gender, sexual, ability-related, or other groups point out their own insensitivities in these domains.

Thus, advocates/practitioners of a critical pedagogy of class awareness work to become experts on the multidimensionality of inequality. In this task they seek to engage in a new form of scholarly work that leaves behind the egocentric dimensions of becoming the leading "competitor" in a field of study. Such scholarly work is based on an ethic of cooperation and the building of synergistic learning communities. Scholars and their students work together with a variety of community-based allies to understand class in relation to diverse forms of oppression, to develop new interpretations and insights into the complex processes of inequality, and to formulate intellectually sound and pragmatic forms of resistance to such tragic realities. A good example of such work involves resistance that is grounded on an understanding of the intersection of class bias with racism. The value of this work, for example, for students of class oppression becomes profoundly clear when such scholars ask why there is so little class consciousness in the United States.

While there are many factors that contribute to this phenomenon, certainly a central force involves the historical presence of racism in American society. Racial divisions within the working and lower classes consistently undermined efforts to construct working-class politics—white racism negated any sense of class solidarity that could spark resistance to class exploitation. A critical pedagogy of class awareness understands the omnipresence of race and class in all dimensions of social and educational life. When individuals tell me that "we're all white at this school, there's no need for racial analysis," we know immediately how much such insight is needed in such a setting. The same is true with class. We've had students in master's level teacher education courses tell us that class didn't matter much at their school—"most everyone is middle class." Class inscribes all dimensions of social life and such inscriptions make a huge difference in what happens in classrooms. When race intersects with class—as it always does—the impact of invisible socioeconomic and cultural structures becomes even more acute.

Indeed, at the macro level this intersection of race and class is so profound that it has produced and is continuing to produce racialized political-economic systems. Moreover, racialized class structures shape all classrooms and every student's educational experience. We see this in student vocational decisions, teacher perceptions of the intent of students' actions from different racial/class backgrounds, and a plethora of other phenomena. In the political domain we observe poor and working-class men giving their political support to right-wing parties promoting policies that subvert their class interests. Here race intersects with class in a way that induces white poor people to identify themselves more by race than by class. When political operatives can evoke such reactions with appeals to the white poor around issues of affirmative action, illegal immigration, gay marriage, patriotism, school prayer, a macho foreign policy, and other so-called wedge issues, they ensure the perpetuation of class oppression—and for that matter racism, gender bias, and homophobia (May 1993; Fernandez-Balboa 2004; Fletcher 2004; Lustig 2004; Teitelbaum 2004; Quan 2004).

In this context class membership and identification become far more complex than once thought. While one's relationship to the means of production is undoubtedly important, class membership and identification are multidimensional and often contradictory. Registers of emotion and affect play far more of a role than rationalistic theories assumed. Thus, the poor can react negatively to many working-class movements' identification with gay and lesbian rights, in the process associating movements for social change that are in their own fiscal interests with "gayness." Their emotion-based homophobia in this situation may induce them to identify politically with more heterosexist, dominant masculinity-based interests. Such individuals may not be able to overtly articulate their register of affect, their feelings on this matter, but the power of such emotions shapes their ideological consciousness.

Thus, class membership and identification come to involve psychoanalytical dynamics, basic assumptions about the world, views of success and failure, self-image, the way people present themselves to the world, and so on. Thus, in *Cutting Class* we understand that individuals are not simply members of the working class or the upper class. With the above dynamics in mind we appreciate the fact that working-class people are also shaped by forces of race, culture, gender, sexuality, religion, physical ability, age, and many other factors. Class, therefore, is central to who we are and our relationship to institutions such as education—but it is not deterministic. Because of this complexity we shape and we are shaped by numerous social dynamics. If we are to understand education—teaching and learning specifically—we must appreciate the ways these factors influence the process.

TEACHERS NEED TO UNDERSTAND THE CENTRALITY OF CLASS IN THEIR TEACHING

A critical pedagogy of class awareness is irrelevant in education if teachers do not intellectually embrace it and emotionally embody it in their everyday work in the classroom. I (Joe) often write (see Kincheloe 2003) about the concept of critical ontology—that is, ways of being in the world that are aware of our social construction and our relational identity. In a critical ontology, learning involves not just an epistemological (having to do with knowledge) act of committing data to our memory; instead it becomes an ontological (having to do with being, in this case what it means to *be* human) act where learning actually changes who we are—it modifies our relationship to the world and other people. In our critical pedagogy of class, teachers must understand the sociopolitical construction of their own selfhood, their own class location, and the ways such a class placement shapes their view of the world, the purpose of school, and their students. A critical pedagogy of class insists that teachers become agents of socioeconomic and political change, who reconfigure their own class identity in relation to their students and their curriculum.

In this context, they would not view students from a class lower than theirs as social inferiors or their students from a class higher than theirs as social superiors. Instead, they would use their class insights to understand their own reactions to students from different classes and to help develop curricula that meet the needs of these different students. Such class-sensitive teachers would understand the ways that class — and other sociocultural factors — shaped different students' relationship to school and how such dynamics construct different needs at different times in their educational lives. Every aspect of schooling and teaching is affected by these class issues and can make the difference between whether school is a painfully negative experience or a positive, empowering experience for students oppressed by class. In this context we get down to the nuts and bolts of how education relates to living, breathing young people. A critical pedagogy of class awareness is not some arcane, abstract concept but one that matters to teachers, students, and the society at large in the most profound ways possible.

In a world and in specific societies that are becoming more class divided a critical pedagogy of class awareness becomes more important with every passing day. Of course, teachers did not generate these tragic macrostructural conditions that pathologically play themselves out at the political and educational systemic levels, the school level, and in their classrooms. Yet, they must face the consequences of class-biased policies every day. Even though political and educational leaders know full well that there is a strong relationship between students' socioeconomic class position and how well they do in schools, issues of class are typically ignored in the public and professional conversation about education. This cutting of class from pedagogical dialogue allows for the wide disparity between curriculum and teaching styles employed for students from differing socioeconomic classes.

Few individuals in the twenty-first century are around to challenge the overwhelmingly divergent quality of education students from different classes receive. One of the rare times that class is referenced in an educational context is in the negative comments are made about poor and working-class people. We have attended, taught, and conducted research in clique-dominated schools in the process, observing the hurt and pain of those students coming from economically poor

backgrounds. In the same contexts we've watched economically privileged students in the "popular" crowd talk with teachers and school
leaders about the inferiority of and annoyance caused by the presence
of students from the lower socioeconomic class. Such realities take us
back to the previously referenced deficitism.

My (Joe) childhood friend Larry Dillon, from the rural, poor,
southern Appalachian Mountains of rural east Tennessee of the 1950s
was viewed as an irredeemable school failure because he—like
countless other students from economically poor backgrounds—was
deemed to have come from an inferior family. As long as such deficit-
laden beliefs about Larry and his family persisted, I'm not sure what
he could have done to reverse his educational fortunes. He was condemned to school hell before he completed his first lesson—just another victim of deficitism. Larry carried the cross of his family's "inferiority" right into the school door and sat there holding it from the
first grade until his eventual "escape" from his class-inscribed school
prison. The fact that he was a brilliant and multitalented child was totally irrelevant to his school experience. The ideological ways that
educator social consciousness had been insidiously shaped blinded
people to Larry's talents—they saw only a poorly dressed little boy
who spoke nonstandard mountain English, and didn't appear to be especially interested in learning.

One of the ideological ways that educators are induced to see the
world and their students involves the "happy consciousness construction" to which they are subjected. In this sociopolitical shaping of subjectivity, individuals are led to believe that school is an unequivocally
"good" thing that will consistently operate to assist worthy individuals
and the society at large. Indeed, in this construction this benevolent institution with an equitable and just environment does not hurt students—
it is an impartial social tool waiting for those with the ability and motivation to use it for their personal benefit. Thus, those educators who,
unquestioning, accept this ideological cargo are much more likely to
"succeed" in many school systems than those who question it. Those
who don't question such perspectives protect the status quo by divorcing
macrostructures of inequality from everyday classroom life. Of course,
those who do question the dominant ideological view of inequalities of

all types often find themselves punished for speaking out against or acting in opposition to such hurtful practices.

The punishments dealt out in such contexts are justified in bizarre and misleading ways. When we and many, many other educators are punished for our words or actions in opposition to class and other types of oppression taking place in the institutions in which we teach, we are always shocked by the nefarious motives ascribed to our deeds. Keeping issues of social justice—class justice in particular—on the everyday agenda of schools is a rigorous and often lonely undertaking. A critical pedagogy of class awareness promotes teachers as rigorous scholars and adept researchers who are agents of anticlassism and other forms of oppression. As such agents, critical teachers learn to teach all students in ways that address their personal needs and idiosyncrasies as well as the forces that crush their dreams and aspirations. To say the least, this is not the type of pedagogy being promoted in the United States and many other Western societies in the contemporary era (Cochran-Smith 2000; Crebbin 2001). In this context, for many people social justice has become a word with negative and disreputable connotations. Those who often oppose a language of social justice and socially just political and educational policies resent the criticisms of corporations implicit in the concept.

We have actually had such corporate-identified people in audiences to which we have spoken rush the stage with physical assault on their mind. One audience member during a speech to a group of teachers jumped out of his seat, shouting over and over as he ran toward Shirley, "I didn't come here to hear corporations bashed." He had to be physically restrained. Critical educators have to be emotionally ready for such reactions to those who connect macroclass dynamics with the everyday lives of students in schools, school purpose, the curriculum, and other pedagogical matters. In this process the point of a critical pedagogy of class awareness is to name the ways such class subjugation takes place. Contrary to the beliefs of many, such teaching is not designed to position the poor as some helpless set of victims but to help everyone involved understand the ways that education can facilitate lower socioeconomic-class students' efforts to become more and more resilient to oppression.

DEVELOPING A MULTIDIMENSIONAL AWARENESS OF CLASS THWARTS THE EFFORT TO CUT CLASS FROM THE EDUCATIONAL CONVERSATION

Critical theorists and critical pedagogical scholars have maintained for decades that in hyperreality (contemporary technological, electronic, image and information saturated, power-driven societies), corporate knowledge producers help create a social amnesia, a loss of connection with history and one's own historical formation. In this context power wielders find it much easier to cut class from the public conversation—talk about schooling in particular. In this formulation class does not and never did play a role in shaping macrosocial structures and individual microcosms. Thus, class oppression—along with, as always, racial, gender, sexual, and religious subjugation—is a central concern of a critical pedagogy of class awareness. In this hyperreal context power becomes more powerful and the racialized corporatism of contemporary Western societies exerts a greater impact on public discourse and other dimensions of "public education." Even outside the boundaries of this hyperreal power few people want to talk about class—and when proponents of critical pedagogy do they can find themselves severely punished.

Too often we have worked with individuals who pay great lip service to abstract notions of social justice, who, around lived issues of class, exhibit startling hierarchical and demeaning behaviors. Class issues are not merely academic; they are visceral. They kick us in the guts, exposing previously hidden dimensions of our identities. Right-wingers often score big points with their audiences when they speak about the "elite left-wingers" who talk a good game about social justice but don't like to be associated with poor people. Having been one of those poor people, I (Joe) instinctively understand such an argument. Those of us who come to academia from the "outside" know the sting of exclusion from the clique of those connected to elite institutions, the discourse community of particular scholars, and—for those of us who want to research and write about these matters—personal relationships with publishers and other guardians of "official knowledge." We know the disillusion that comes when we understand that a person who speaks and writes so eloquently about matters of injustice treats those below him or her in the hierarchy with contempt. Such actions on the part of elite academics profoundly damage the effort to construct a more just society and educational system.

Such actions push many people with backgrounds like mine (Joe) to embrace a right-wing ideology and affectively bond with the dominant ideology around social, political, and educational issues. "To hell with these two-faced, condescending hypocrites," numerous individuals have told me, "I don't need to be around people like that who think they're better than me." And with such raw feelings, they dismiss anyone in academia who would speak to inequality. This is but one of numerous factors that help us to understand the disconnection between poor and working-class people from larger movements for social and economic justice. Such a disconnect is tragic in its consequences, as poor and working people around the world are dissociated from class awareness and the insight it provides into a way out of the unfairness and hopelessness they face. Indeed, such dissociation exacerbates the social amnesia and lack of awareness of class that allow the already egregious disparity of wealth, hope, and power between peoples to intensify. It is a hegemonic vicious circle.

No good can come of such a situation. Advocates of critical pedagogy have their work cut out to overcome the damage caused by this constellation of factors. In this one context we can begin to understand the complexity of contemporary class politics. Class consciousness and class identification are not merely economic matters. Instead, they are much more complex as social and cultural factors come into the mix, adding emotional and affective dimensions to the process. In this context social theories such as Pierre Bourdieu's (1989) notion of cultural, social, and symbolic capital emerge. In this framework a critical pedagogy of class awareness better understands the complexities of studying class and teaching with knowledge of the effects of socioeconomic class in the twenty-first century.

In the quagmire of socioeconomic class complexity, our critical pedagogy of class awareness works feverishly to cut through the thick underbrush of forces that subvert class awareness and dedication to socioeconomic justice (Aronowitz 2003; Fletcher, Jr. 2004; Jensen 2004). As knowledge of class is erased, teachers—especially those from the white middle class—fail to appreciate the psychic turmoil many students from marginalized backgrounds must face as they attempt to use schooling for socioeconomic mobility. Such students are often looked at by their peers as sell-outs who think they're too good to stay where they are. Concurrently, their new associates may look at them with class condescension and exclude them from full membership in the domain of the educated.

For many who have sought and achieved mobility via education, life after school can be a very lonely place. Many times such individuals sense that they fit nowhere—they know no one who can empathize with their predicament. In this context we begin to realize that schools as they are presently situated as institutions of dominant culture demand that students must "kill" their poor or working-class selves and adopt the cultural capital and values of the upwardly mobile middle class. Obviously, many students refuse to commit class suicide and opt out of education. Educators, educational psychologists, and other educational professionals often view this understandable existential choice as students:

- having a bad attitude
- being uninterested in learning
- being slow or having low intellectual aptitude
- lacking motivation
- being socially maladjusted
- coming from bad families

Anyone teaching, administering a school, or contemplating a career in education who doesn't understand the difficult choices marginalized students face needs to gain awareness of these class (and, of course, racial and cultural) dynamics. Critical pedagogy insists that an important dimension of teacher education and public knowledge about schooling involve an understanding of the complexity of crossing class boundaries and the role this hurdle plays in the pedagogical process. With this in mind our critical pedagogy of class awareness refuses to equate being educated with being middle-class or white or Christian for that matter. Critical pedagogues see no conflict between remembering where one comes from, maintaining close relationships with one's longtime friends and family, and becoming a highly educated person.

Often class values and racial/cultural ways of being are so closely tied to educational success that educational success is impossible without the previously referenced class suicide. Although I (Joe) have been an academic-researcher-writer for over three decades, I still hold on dearly to many of the Southern Appalachian Mountain values of my childhood.

While working to escape grotesque forms of racism, gender, sexual, and religious biases that went along with my cultural heritage, I (Joe) still embrace the humility, value of friendship, loyalty, egalitarianism, contempt for pomposity, loud laughter, and disdain of competition that could be found among the rural poor of the region. I find, many times, that I am profoundly uncomfortable with the competitive, bourgeois, consumption-based, status-driven, and low-affect orientations of many of those I stumble upon in academia. In my encounters with students from the lower socioeconomic classes, I use these values to make contact with, understand, appreciate, and teach such students. In many circumstances students and other academics from such a background become my best friends. In such contexts we can develop powerful pedagogies—relevant in the lives of individuals no matter what their class background—grounded on an understanding of who we were, who we are in the present, and who we want to become. Such a personalized critical pedagogy understands that learning and identity are directly related. We cannot gain a rich comprehension of pedagogy unless we understand that all acts of learning change our identities. In a critical pedagogy teachers and students carefully monitor these changes.

A LITERACY OF POWER GROUNDS AN AWARENESS OF CLASS

Dominant power has traditionally dictated that despite the fact that democratic impulses always exist in educational institutions, schools have historically not been what one could categorize as democratic institutions. As school operates to privilege the privileged and marginalize the marginalized, it provides so-called scientific proof of the superiority of the middle and upper classes. Academic credentials grant such classes a certificate of their superiority to the poor and racially marginalized. A diploma from an elite private school, as we all know, is worth far more than one from a school from a lower-class neighborhood. Not only do different schools provide significantly different symbolic capital and status to graduates, but throughout educational history diverse schools and school districts are separated by divergent access to funding. Thus, different schools provide wildly different levels of socioeconomic opportunity to their attendees. Add to these traditional disparities the gross inequalities constructed by the globalized, corporatized political economy of the contemporary era with its hegemonic politics of knowledge, and it is easy to see that the engines of inequality have never been more efficient.

With the unleashing of the unregulated free market over the last twenty-five years, entry level jobs for high school graduates are found more and more in the nonunion service sector. Such jobs, of course, are marked by low pay, long work hours, dangerous worksites, and few benefits. Companies such as Wal-Mart and McDonald's (see Kincheloe's *The Sign of the Burger: McDonald's and the Culture of Power*, 2002) make sure that no union activity is tolerated in their outlets. In light of the jobs that are available for high school graduates in the contemporary era, we understand how using economic gain as a motivation for poor kids to graduate from high school might be less than successful. The fact that high school graduates face such a bleak economic future in such corporations is unacceptable in so-called democratic societies (DeFreitas and Duffy 2004; McLaren 2006).

In this corporate context, critical pedagogy's literacy of power around issues of class becomes profoundly important to what we are attempting to accomplish in *Cutting Class*. The rise of corporate power over the last three decades, a critical pedagogy of class awareness maintains, does not simply signal bad business behavior but a deeper structural problem. Westerners and other peoples around the world are going to have to think about the institutional relationship between enormous aggregations of capital and the ways such financial power affects institutions of government, media and knowledge production, and education. It doesn't take a genius to appreciate the myriad ways that corporations can dictate governmental decisions, determine the knowledge that is produced and disseminated, and lay out the purpose, curriculum, teaching methods, and evaluation procedures for schools. In the last years of the first decade of the twenty-first century, we can clearly see concentrated capital attempting to accomplish all of these tasks. To speak of contemporary politics, the sociocultural role of media in shaping consciousness and identity, and education without reference to such power is to ignore the elephant droppings on the dining table.

Such corporate work is ideological as it tries to shape the sociopolitical perspectives of people around the world so they will accept the right of concentrated capital to manipulate policies in ways that enhance its ability to make money. This "right to profit," they argue, "is in everybody's best interest." Of course, in the process they fail to point out the growing disparity of wealth within and between nations. Thus, a critical pedagogy of class awareness has to be aware of several things at once—the power of capital:

- to mold the actions of various institutions around the world
- to shape ideological consciousness, how people think about power and politics
- to exacerbate the disparity of wealth between the "haves" and the "have-nots"
- to construct educational policy and purpose
- to fashion schools that serve the interests of corporations and the middle/upper-middle/upper class
- to perpetuate the inequality between "poor" schools and "rich" schools
- to undermine actions to eliminate the obstacles socioeconomically poor children have to face in the educational process.

While issues surrounding class are intensely complex—the meaning of class, multiple identities vis-à-vis class identity, the role of class in social theory, pedagogy, and class, and so on—there does exist a bifurcation globally between those with inordinate power and those devoid of socio economic capital. An understanding of complexity should never interfere with our awareness of this egregious disparity of wealth and opportunity and our ethical duty to challenge and undermine such an unacceptable state of affairs. Thus, while globalization and empire building are in this historical period reshaping class structures at an international level, dramatic changes in the class dimensions of everyday life in schools are observable. And while the mutations at the international level do not dictate what happens in individual classrooms, such macro-forces do exert a profound effect on individual teachers and students.

The U.S. attempt, for example, to administer the socioeconomic and political world order has to have a citizenry complete with a warrior class willing to go along with such a tall order (Tabb 2004; Panitch 2004). Education, thus, takes on a special role in this imperial, transnational profit-making enterprise. It is not surprising that at a time that citizen consent is so important, standardized curricula with well-defined ideological boundaries permeate the nation's schools. Indeed, any efforts to open up the curriculum to diverse points of view, perspectives from other peoples, even other cultural ways of being and religious perspectives are met with excessive resistance (see our *The Miseducation of the West: How Schools and the Media Distort Our Understanding of the Islamic World*). As we wrote this book, we were amazed by the lengths to which power wielders would go to regulate the curriculum that would discourage any questioning of American motives in world affairs and geopolitical struggles.

A PEDAGOGY FOR A RECONCEPTUALIZED CLASS STRUGGLE

Of course, we are encouraged—despite operating in the heart of imperial darkness—by the antiglobalization movement and its understanding of these political-economic and class-related dimensions of prevailing transnational power. Too often, however, the movement has focused on international organizations such as the World Trade Organization (WTO) and the World Bank to the exclusion of the imperial state and the myriad of ways—including education and knowledge control—such entities serve the needs of the political-economic and military empire. A critical pedagogy of class awareness seeks to work with those who recognize these dynamics to expand the scope of their understanding and actions. We seek to forge alliances with union leaders, political operatives, and educators from around the world. In addition, we support the class-related protests and activism of many young people against sweatshops, unfair wages in global markets, and one-sided economic development policies.

Thus, our critical pedagogy of class awareness supports a new class struggle that is:

- never separated from issues of race, gender, sexuality, and religion
- constantly aware of the complexity of class identity in contemporary society
- always sensitive to the different ways class issues operate in diverse situations
- forever conscious of the danger of determinism when dealing with political-economic structures and class oppression
- continuously on notice that humans have agency and can devise ingenious ways to subvert the imperializing power of macrostructures of capital and class elitism.

The twenty-first-century class struggle supported by our critical pedagogy identifies with the poor and those marginalized by race, gender, sexuality, and religion. Indeed, the poor are closer to the soul of the universe, and are revered at least in the scriptures of the world's religions. In Christianity, it is amazing that the logic of capital with its use of race, gender, and sexual prejudices has co-opted many of the faithful into a belief that religion and dominant power are partners in the oppression of the poor and other marginalized groups. This Christo-fascism is an influential and dynamic force in contemporary class politics. Individuals coming from Christian backgrounds should be key allies in our class struggle, not enemies who support the oppression of the poor. Our critical pedagogy of class awareness seeks an ecumenical form of liberation theology that seeks wisdom from and an alliance of the world's religious peoples. In such a movement individuals would unite around all religions' and spiritual traditions' expressed concern for the poor and the oppressed. Aided by this ecumenical liberation theology, critical pedagogy's class struggle is grounded on what Paulo Freire called a radical love. In this context it offers a daily critique of dominant power and its impact on the poor around the planet—a critique that leads to particular forms of action in the political-economic, cultural, and educational spheres.

Also shaping critical pedagogy's class struggle is the concept of economic citizenship for the entire world's people. All workers in all organizations should have a say in directing the organization. Economic citizenship in the critical sense moves far beyond the kind of input found in ornamental worker empowerment programs where employees can choose what day to hold the company picnic. Such citizenship demands a living wage, workplace safety, and health and retirement benefits—all features of work that are quickly disappearing from the economic stage. Any critical pedagogy of class is grounded on these principles of economic citizenship, as students study the causes of poverty and inequality and what one can do to address them. They understand the way that concentrated capital uses its power to affect government policy about issues such as, say, pollution and environmental destruction. They examine the neoliberal arguments that corporate pollution is a private matter and that corporations have the right to operate freely without public interference.

Economic citizens/students learn that schooling is never a neutral institution. School and its curriculum are always vulnerable to the meddling power of capital with its ability to shape knowledge and consciousness in ways that coincide with its best interests. With these understandings, students are better equipped to evaluate the ideological inscriptions of what they learn. Indeed, economic citizens are empowered to use their minds in the workplace and to reject modes of workplace organization and sociopolitical arrangements that skew the distribution of wealth. Economic citizens, students learn, are scholars who are aware of the power of concentrated capital to produce meanings and deliver "truth" in institutions other than school such as the media and religious organizations.

This ability to make meaning and deliver truth is just as important in the twenty-first century as ownership of the means of production of goods and services. It has taken countless hours of information management and public relations planning to convince a large percentage of people in Western societies to support a political-economic system that provides one group with material prosperity while most people around the world do without. Economic citizens refuse to buy into this snake oil economics and politics of knowledge. A critical pedagogy grounded on this new class struggle moves beyond calls for justice to an endorsement of new arrangements of social, cultural, political-economic, and educational power. Such new matrices of power enable people from all classes, all races, genders, sexual orientations, religious backgrounds, and geographic places to play a central role in shaping social institutions, producing knowledge and making meaning, determining whose stories and perspectives become part of the official histories of our era, and constructing a future with opportunity for everyone.

With these ideals in mind, proponents of the new class struggle operating in a critical pedagogical context, help inform people around the world of just who is responsible for the growing disparity between the haves and have-nots (Aronowitz 2003; Defreitas and Duffy 2004; Quan 2004). Of course, U.S. and other Western transnational corporations help create these mind-boggling lopsided political-economic conditions. Exxon, just one of thousands of these corporations, for example, made $36 billion in profits in 2005. In the spring of 2006 the company's retiring CEO, Lee Raymond, was awarded a $400 million retirement package. Leaders of other corporations receive similar retirement packages in addition to their multimillion dollar annual salaries (Newell 2006). People in Western societies need to know such information and the way such corporate activities produce and perpetuate poverty in all parts of the world. A critical pedagogy of class awareness stands ready to make such information public.

AN EVOLVING CRITICALITY: CRITICAL PEDAGOGY'S NEW UNDERSTANDING OF CLASS

Critical pedagogy—especially a critical pedagogy of class awareness—can never remain static, can never rely on traditional ways of explaining ever-changing social, cultural, and political-economic phenomena. In this context we are profoundly concerned with tracing an evolving criticality that studies the ways new times evoke new manifestations of power, new consequences, and new ways of understanding and resisting them. Concurrently this evolving criticality devises new social-economic arrangements, new institutions, and new forms of selfhood (see Kincheloe 2004, 2005 for a detailed delineation of an evolving criticality). A central dimension of an evolving criticality involves the effort to avoid essentialism—the belief that a set of unchanging properties (essences) delineates the construction of a particular category. Thus, an essentialist view of class maintains that classes in the time of

Karl Marx were constructed and operated in the same way they are in the contemporary era.

With our notion of an evolving criticality in mind we begin to lay the foundations for an updated, complex, and pragmatic understanding of class. Understanding the interconnection of all people, a critical complex notion of class insists that class can never be separated from other axes of power including race, gender, sexuality, religion, geographic place, relationship to colonialism, etc. One's class-position relationship to capital is profoundly affected by, say, one's perception of issues of sexuality. Many working-class heterosexual men in the contemporary era feel uncomfortable engaging in protests over class exploitation because they associate protest against the status quo with not being within the boundaries of dominant masculinity, of being queer. Thus, their sense of sexuality profoundly affects their relationship to class. Thus, one's class politics in this example are more shaped by affective dynamics than material forces. A working-class heterosexual man's *feeling* about his own sexuality and the threat of homosexual others may contribute as much or more to his class politics and ideology as his socioeconomic position. Critical pedagogues are very sensitive to such issues, as they shape the nature of the educational strategies they use to teach such individuals about class.

In this complex context, a critical pedagogy of class awareness has to pay special attention to the concepts of hegemony and ideology and how they operate around these issues. An evolving criticality focused on class is intensely concerned with the need to understand the various and complex ways that power operates to dominate and shape consciousness. Power, critical pedagogues have learned, is an extremely ambiguous topic that demands detailed study and analysis. A consensus seems to be emerging among criticalists that power is a basic constituent of human existence that works to shape both the oppressive and productive nature of the human tradition. Indeed, we are all empowered and we are all unempowered, in that we all possess abilities and we are all limited in the attempt to use our abilities. This means that a lower socioeconomic class person may find himself/herself in localized positions of power around issues of race, gender, and sexuality. "I may be poor," such a man might say, "but I'm not taking that shit from a woman"—thus invoking his patriarchal power of men over women.

The focus here, of course, is on critical theory's traditional concern with the oppressive aspects of power. An important aspect of critical-ity, however, focuses on the productive aspects of power—its ability to empower, to establish a critical democracy, to engage marginalized people in the rethinking of their sociopolitical role (Apple 1996, 1999; Fiske 1993; Macedo 1994, 2006; Nicholson and Seidman 1995). In the context of oppressive power and its ability to produce inequalities and human suffering, Antonio Gramsci's notion of hegemony is central to critical pedagogy. Gramsci understood that dominant power in the twentieth century was not always exercised simply by physical force but also through social psychological attempts to win people's consent to domination through cultural institutions such as the media, the schools, the family, and the church. Gramscian hegemony recognizes that the winning of popular consent is a very complex process and must be researched carefully on a case-by-case basis.

Students and researchers of power, educators, sociologists, all of us are hegemonized as our field of knowledge and understanding is struc-tured by a limited exposure to competing definitions of the sociopolit-ical world. The hegemonic field, with its bounded social and psycho-logical horizons, garners consent to an inequitable power matrix—a set of social relations that are legitimated by their depiction as natural and inevitable. "There will always be poor people," many are fond of say-ing. "There's nothing we can do about it." In this context critical re-searchers note that hegemonic consent is never completely established, as it is always contested by various groups with different agendas—human beings always have the agency to overcome the structures of power. To pursue its hegemonic agenda dominant power learns to use the racism, homophobia, and misogyny of many white, lower socio-economic-class men to secure their consent to right-wing political eco-nomic policies. Whenever, for example, the neoconservatives in George W. Bush's administration sensed they were losing favor with working-class men for their larger sociopolitical, economic, and impe-rial policies, they would bring out the specter of gay marriage and ho-mosexual rights to regain their consent. Unfortunately, such a hege-monic strategy enjoyed great success.

Critical pedagogues also understand that the formation of hegemony cannot be separated from the production of ideology. If hegemony is the larger effort of the powerful to win the consent of their "subordinates," then ideological hegemony involves the cultural forms, the meanings, the rituals, and the representations that produce consent to the status quo and individuals' particular places within it. The set of ideas that helps maintain existing unequal power relations is what we are referring to here as ideology. Understanding and making use of insights into ideology vis-à-vis hegemony moves critical educators beyond explanations of domination that have used terms such as propaganda to describe the way media, political, educational, and other sociocultural productions coercively manipulate citizens to adopt oppressive meanings. An evolving critical theory endorses a much more subtle, ambiguous, and situationally specific form of domination that refuses the propaganda model's assumption that people are passive, easily manipulated victims.

Our critical pedagogy of class awareness operating with an awareness of this hegemonic ideology understands that dominant ideological practices and discourses shape our vision of reality. Thus our notion of hegemonic ideology leads to a nuanced understanding of power's complicity in the constructions people make of the world and their role in it. Such awareness corrects earlier delineations of ideology as a monolithic, unidirectional entity that was imposed on individuals by a secret cohort of ruling-class czars. Understanding class domination in the context of concurrent struggles among different classes, racial and gender groups, critical students of ideology explore the ways such competition engages different visions, interests, and agendas in a variety of social locales. These venues—film, TV, popular music, sports, and so on—were previously thought to operate outside the domain of ideological struggle (Steinberg 2001).

With these notions of hegemony and ideology secure in our consciousness, we can begin to understand that dominant power can generally avoid the use of force to regulate poor people. Increasingly in the empire building of the Iraqi War and the aggressive U.S. and British foreign policy accompanying it, the use of force to protect geopolitical and transnational capital is deployed. But even the neoconservative imperialists are beginning to understand that there is a price, a blowback, to such violence—the insurgency in Iraq, for instance. It is so much easier to convince those who would interfere with the needs of capital that they are lesser beings in need of the help of those above them on the great hierarchy. IQ tests play this role so well within the United States and other Western societies. Such bogus evaluation instruments teach poor and other marginalized peoples that they are in unenviable positions not because of unjust social arrangements but because of their individual inferiority. "How can this not be true?" they ask, "science proves it." Dominant groups use such hegemonic ideological mechanisms to make social and economic hierarchies appear natural—not the creation of a particular domineering power bloc.

Power, critical pedagogues have learned, comes in many different forms and manifestations. Because of this we know that a class struggle that does not take issues of race, gender, sexuality, religion, geographic place, and other concerns into account is doomed to fail. Class struggles are not immune from racism, gender bias, homophobia, anti-Semitism, and Islamophobia—and if these exclusionary practices are not subverted by a larger commitment to understanding diverse forms of power and a multidimensional effort to work for justice, the movement will fail (May 1993; Brantlinger 2003). Failure is exactly what has resulted when movements based on biological identities have separated themselves from other movements of marginalized peoples—class included (Aronowitz 2003). In these movements difference between peoples around the axes of race, class, gender, sexuality, religion, geographical place, and so on. is not seen as a manifestation of strength but as a form of incompatibility. "How can a straight woman ever understand the suffering of a gay man?" we've heard activists ask one another. The multidimensional critical pedagogy of class doesn't ask these types of questions. Instead it asks how can people from different backgrounds work together to help overcome oppression of any form? It learns from difference, positioning it as a resource not a liability.

A MULTILOGICAL UNDERSTANDING OF CLASS AND IDENTITY: NEW INSIGHTS INTO CRITICAL PEDAGOGY

While it is important that we are aware of an individual's or a group's class location, it is equally crucial that we understand that identity is shaped by multiple dynamics. While class location is a key factor, people also identify themselves by race, gender, sexual preference, nationality, region, etc. Advocates of a multilogical class struggle, a multilogical critical pedagogy understand that knowledge producers, curriculum developers, teachers, and students perceive the world from a center located within themselves, shaped by the social and cultural context in which they operate, and framed by languages and discourses that contain within them tacit views of the world. As they dig deeper into the contexts surrounding the construction of knowledge and education, analysts sensitive to complexity and multilogicality find that students from different racial, ethnic, gender, and class locations will relate to schooling in different ways. If students who operate far from the middle-class, white, English-speaking mainstream are not provided assistance by insightful teachers, they will be the victims of culturally insensitive, decontextualized, and monological pedagogies.

These students will not fail to meet monological academic expectations because of some inability or lack of intelligence but because of a set of forces unleashed by their relation to what is often labeled the "common culture." When political and educational leaders use the term *common culture* in a positivist (an epistemological position that values objective, scientific knowledge produced in rigorous adherence to the scientific method—in this context knowledge is worthwhile to the extent that it describes objective data that reflect the world) way, the more those students who fall outside of its boundaries will fail. One of the key aspects of positivism is that it decontextualizes knowledge. In the case in question positivist analysts refuse to account for the impact an individual's contextual background exerts on his or her school achievement. If a gay student from a lower socioeconomic-class background with parents who never made it through the seventh grade and is bullied at school because he is a "fag" performs poorly in school, it has at least as much to do with the contextual factors than with some positivist notion of his academic ability or IQ.

Educators who understand contextual complexity appreciate the notion that Western culture is not a homogeneous way of life but a domain of difference shaped by unequal power relations. They understand that social and educational analysts and professional practitioners must act on an appreciation of the multiple ways these differences shape people's relationships to various institutions, education in particular. If everyone is seen as a part of some narrow articulation of a common culture, then those who don't fit the mainstream criteria will find themselves looking into the society's institutions as unworthy outsiders. Critical pedagogues understand these multilogical social tendencies and make sure that steps are taken to include everyone in a diverse, democratic, high-quality education (Apple 1996; Kincheloe and Steinberg, 1997).

The way these factors play out in the everyday life of school is multidimensional, complex, and always significant. When classroom instruction is driven by positivistic standards with their memorization of fragmented factoids, the same pedagogical actions take place repeatedly without regard for who succeeds and who fails—in particular, what social groups succeed or fail over time. A creative way of merely *delivering* content, no matter how ingenious it may be, still works to produce much the same results as long as the epistemological assumptions are the same. Thus, to avoid falling into these age-old traps, critical teachers must understand both the social context that shapes learners and the epistemological context that molds the way knowledge is constructed and educational goals are forged in the classroom. Such contextual awareness provides teachers with a monitoring system that allows them a cognizance of the multidimensional effects of their pedagogy.

In our context of multilogicality, critical teachers must understand not only the way these social factors play out educationally, but also which aspects of a student's multiple identity are operating to help shape a student's—or another teacher's or administrator's—reaction to a particular situation. The influence of class, whether it be on sociopolitical structures, identity, or behavior in a specific circumstance, never appears in some untainted, monolithic form but rather in relationship to race, gender, cultural, sexual, and many other dynamics. While all students in an urban school in Toronto may, for example, come from lower socioeconomic backgrounds, their racial and cultural differences may also play a particularly important role in understanding trouble between two particular ethnic groups.

Class is not irrelevant in understanding why a particular fight broke out, as the causes can only be understood in class's relation to these other factors. A view of class that sees it only involving the ownership of the means of production is not especially helpful when it comes down to making sense of what happens in the everyday life of education and other social institutions. The fight at the Toronto school is still a manifestation of class, but our point is that human behavior is never that simple. Thus, class dynamics are multidimensional questions of power, not simple questions of who owns property and the means of production of goods and services. When we witness the recovery of white supremacy, patriarchy, homophobia, religious hatred, and colonialist impulses, we begin to understand that economic disparity always manifests itself in relation to these forces. Class, in our multi-logical conceptualization, always exists in a multidimensional space. When we miss this complexity, critical pedagogues provide an impoverished view of the effects of class—a perspective on the important role of unequal power relations in education and other domains that seems unconvincing to many.

School battles over what is acceptable fashion, what music is considered worthy of inclusion in the curriculum, how particular speech patterns are positioned in school also signal the complexity of the interaction of class with other social axes of power—race, ethnicity, gender, sexuality, and so on. As we begin to understand that class is more about power than income, it becomes easier for us to identify who holds power, how it is used, and the ways people are affected by it. The term *power bloc* indicates that power is never stable, that there is no permanent "ruling class." In this volatile context power is always involved in struggles where alliances between diverse groups are formed around particular issues: e.g., neoliberal proponents of empire and transnational capital unite with fundamentalist Christians around issues of sexuality and "traditional values" to gain the fundamentalists' consent to neoliberal, geopolitical, and economic policies. Depending on the issues dominating the day, alliances will form and disintegrate and power blocs will come and go.

With this notion of ever-changing power blocs, critical pedagogy encounters complexity theory, thus making the possibility of leading a successful class struggle even more complicated. In educational politics we see this same alliance producing a curriculum that merges the teaching of Eurocentric knowledge and fundamentalist Christian interests such as the teaching of creationism and neoliberal concerns with a preparing an unquestioning workforce for the empire. Such modes of schooling are particularly hard on the poor, as they are prepared to accept their lot in life—and give their consent to working in low-paying, low-skill jobs often after serving in the military. The school and other social organizations help win their consent to engage such dangerous and low-status work by strategically deploying the ideology of nationalistic patriotism.

"It's my duty to go to Iraq," many soldiers tell us, "I'm fighting for America's freedom." In this way class antagonisms and the emergence of class consciousness are quashed. This, of course, is not a seamless process—many students from diverse classes refuse to accept the ideology and resist it in a variety of ways in and out of school. While the power of power has intensified, the human spirit refuses to be crushed. Although people—sensing something is wrong—continue to exercise their agency, there is a great need for a critical pedagogy of class awareness to help them coordinate and direct their efforts. Thus, a critical pedagogy becomes more important than ever before on this complex, hegemonized landscape.

INTO THE QUAGMIRE: NO UNIFORM IDENTITIES, NO FIXED AND UNIVERSAL STRUCTURES

There is no simple, homogeneous working class. Thus, class analysis is never some facile task of slotting individuals into tidy groups. With race, class, gender, sexual, and religious differences, massive diasporas from diverse parts of the globe, and the power of transnational capital reshaping relationships among the world's peoples, the notion of identifying an uncomplicated working class fades into the ether. The reality—as W. E. B. Du Bois (1973) maintained a century ago—that race continues to play a profound role in everyday life ensures that no simple, united notion of the working class exists. Racial divisions make sure that an individual's political interests cannot be determined from her place in the economic structure. Just because a person is working-class and belongs to union doesn't mean that her politics will fit progressive efforts to enhance economic opportunity and bring about a more equitable distribution of wealth.

Similarly, just because a person owns a corporation doesn't mean that she will support an extreme free-market position with its accompanying efforts to build a political-economic empire (Brantlinger 2003;

Lustig 2004; Zweig 2004). Thus, simple deterministic class theories are often misleading and move concerned people to act in ways that may not be particularly helpful to students from socioeconomically poor backgrounds in their efforts to succeed academically. When such deterministic perspectives deem students and other individuals to be passive entities who are at the mercy of structural forces, great harm can be done. We have heard individuals who adhere to such theories argue that "school reform cannot take place until the revolution comes"—that nothing can be done for students from poor backgrounds until a just and equitable society is established. In such a context we have just condemned generations of marginalized students to a life without allies.

In this context we have to develop a new understanding of sociopolitical and economic structures. Of course, structures exist and exert an often covert influence on everyday affairs in contemporary society. Nevertheless, such entities are ever-shifting and are the result of particular alliances that promote specific interests of one group of people against another group. "Class happens" as a variety of factors come together as a group of individuals begin to verbalize a set of interests that arise as a result of their experiences individually and in common. Thus, in a way class is enacted. Employing the enactivist insights of Umberto Mautarana and Francisco Varela (1987), we can begin to understand the way that class structures are not simply molded into place in a particular way but are enacted. In the enaction of these class structures, material realities and one's placement in relation to capital play an essential role but so do emotional considerations, gut feelings, and other psychoanalytical and tacit dimensions of human thought. These enactivist dimensions induce sociology, cultural studies, critical pedagogy, and other disciplines to focus more on the nonrational dimensions of class. Thus, many factors shape class structures, identity, and effects that are rarely studied in these disciplines.

With these ideas in mind twentieth- and twenty-first-century class structures of dominant capital used affect and desire to win the consent of people to the power of the capital. The compliance of particular individuals in Western societies to class politics of consumer capitalism was not simply a rational choice but involved their desire for particular consumer items. "I'll not challenge the status quo power structure," many people *felt*, "if I can live in this neighborhood and own this boat."

Thus, around material realities and affective dynamics, class structures were enacted by human players. These structures continue to be enacted in ever-changing ways, as new players interact in new ways. Thus, in an enactivist understanding of class, one always has to monitor the new ways class structures "play out." Our critical pedagogy of class awareness is dedicated to tracing this evolutionary process.

In this critical enactivist context (Kincheloe 2005), we present a fallibist notion of class—it is fallibist in the sense that we know that what we say today about the nature of class structures and class effects may not be relevant in 2021. Hopefully, with this fallibility in mind, our critical pedagogy of class awareness can provide insights about class structures, class struggles, class identity, and the multiple ways class impacts teaching and learning. We do not claim final answers to such questions, simply because we do not believe such answers exist in such a zone of complexity. For example, as craft knowledge declined with the rise of industrialization and traditional knowledges of production were overtaken by machines designed and operated by engineers and technicians, where did such a new category of workers fit on the traditional "class grid"? In the late twentieth and twenty-first century diaspora of educated workers from Asian and other areas of the world, where do, say, computer specialists from such areas fit the time-honored framework? How does their class position intersect with race, religion, national origin, or immigration status to produce their social power? These are questions that illustrate the inadequacy of many traditional ways of constructing class. Of course, in the contemporary they are central questions that educators must face.

A key dimension of a critical, complex, and enactivist understanding of class involves appreciating its historical contingency—it understands its own production at a particular historical place and time as well as the historical construction of class (Aronowitz 2003; Tabb 2004). This allows us to get beyond the reductionism of one-dimensional explanations of class, of seeing it from only the perspective of North America or from a patriarchal standpoint. While we understand, as previously referenced, the recovery of the power of capital over the last thirty years, we are simultaneously aware that "recovery" is only one dimension of a complex appreciation of class and its impact on education in the twenty-first century. The critical pedagogy of class awareness advocated here pushes us to always look for new contexts from which to explore class. Our search for class understanding is never ending, as dominant groups in grander historical context come and go.

The neoliberal, empire building, exploitive, class elitist power bloc guided by the military-transnational-corporate-cultural-religious politicos in United States will eventually fade into history, a victim of its own greed, arrogance, and violence. A critical pedagogy of class awareness would like to see its passing sooner than later—but mark our words, it will disappear. Corporate power in its transnational arrangement with its nation-state directorates now prevails. At this point no class struggle led by a proletariat exists; but such a circumstance does not denote an end of history (the final triumph of capital) or a failure of the working class. Instead, new configurations of resistant power are emerging that may lead the battle against the oppression of neoimperial power. Students and young people in different parts of the world are devising ingenious modes of resistance to imperial power. The power of many socially conscious young men and women in hip hop to construct resistance movements is a manifestation of not only genius but great civic courage. A critical pedagogy of class awareness connects with such groups in the larger struggle for class, race, gender, sexual, and religious justice.

In this configuration of class and class theory, schools play a complex role. Schooling is no doubt not a panacea for class disparity; concurrently, schooling is not an impotent force unable to make a difference until the revolution comes. A critical pedagogy of class awareness attends closely to the limitations and the possibilities of schooling (Books 2001; McLaren 2000; Tabb 2004) Critical teachers have to understand the way class operates in order to develop curricula and ways of being a teacher that benefit students raised in poverty. Just as teachers can reinvent themselves with new understandings of class, students can create new identities in their encounter with critical pedagogy. This refers back to the previously mentioned critical ontology (Kincheloe 2003). A critical ontology in a critical pedagogy of class understands that self-production cannot be understood outside the context of power. In this context teachers engage a critical mode of hermeneutics (interpretation) and engage with curricular texts for the purpose of gaining a new level of self-understanding. This question of gaining insight into personal identity is not a call to narcissism; indeed, it is quite the opposite.

In this ontological context educators learn to understand the oppressive forces that shape them—especially in contemporary Western culture—so they can become less self-absorbed and individually oriented. In this context they learn to situate themselves historical and socially. In a socioeconomic-class context they address the impact of their class background. We have taught in too many places that viewed such analyses of students' class position as an absurd activity. Such schools were so tied into dominant culture's pathologization of people from lower socioeconomic-class backgrounds that they thought such a pedagogy was either useless because the poor are beyond help or humiliating because no one wants to admit to the disgrace being poor.

With knowledge of how class shapes the world and their lives both inside and outside of school, students are far better equipped to make conscious decisions about who they want to be and how they will deal with the ideological socialization processes of twenty-first-century electronic societies. In this context they identify and work to thwart the socioeconomic and cultural forces that undermine the efforts of poor and working-class students to use education for their own and society's benefit. Thus, while they have no consistent and universal blueprint for how to deal with class in the classroom, critical teachers use their class insights and their understanding of their students and their particular situations to develop a class-conscious curriculum.

CRITICAL PEDAGOGY CONNECTS WITH OTHER SOCIAL MOVEMENTS

A critical pedagogy of class awareness is constantly on the lookout for a new social/class movement to which it can connect. Of course one of the most important of these movements involves transformative labor movements. The critical unionism that I (Joe) have written about elsewhere (Kincheloe 1999) is concerned with the issues we have laid out here; it is interested in building class consciousness that understands class in relation to the other social dimensions discussed throughout this chapter. A critical unionism understands the complex class struggle and the politics of corporate power discussed here. Critical unions and critical pedagogy are made for one another. Working together they can better understand the nature of contemporary power with its ability to explain the world to the public in a manner conducive to extending the power of capital. Critical unions appreciate that they are up against an oppressor who has access to the media with its slick advertising and ideological apparatuses that operate to justify growing inequality. A critical unionism with the help of critical pedagogy and critical pedagogy with the help of a critical unionism helps workers, teachers, students, and other citizens gain alternative understandings of the world (Lakes 1994; Fletcher, Jr. 2004).

Of course, such alliances with other socioeconomic groups would have to include movements for social justice for those individuals suffering oppression of diverse varieties. Transformative changes in a critical, complex understanding of critical social theory come from the unity of diverse struggles for justice. In this complex context, the class struggle supported by critical pedagogy does not have a preconceived, final configuration—because of its multiplicity it is always open to innovation and rearrangement. Of course, this openness does not mean that anything goes—our critical unionism–critical pedagogy alliance is grounded on a larger transformative vision that opposes the transnational hegemony of migratory capital and supports international economic, labor, and educational solidarity. Critical pedagogy helps unions with issues involving the intersection of race, gender, culture, sexuality, religion, etc., and the impact of other factors on workers' total life experiences; unions help critical pedagogy understand the nuts and bolts of everyday working life and the obstacles to critical social vision. Both groups have much to learn from one another on a plethora of levels.

Especially in a time of immigrant bashing and blaming, a critical pedagogy of class awareness with its understanding of the relationship of workers in one country to those in others helps unions seek solidarity with working peoples around the world. The class consciousness that accompanies this view of foreign workers is an essential element in the reconceptualized class struggle of the contemporary era. Such a consciousness takes us all back to an understanding of the power of transnational concentrated capital and what it can do to us. No twenty-first-century class struggle can be successful without these understandings and the international worker-educator cooperation that accompanies them. Commentators such Lou Dobbs and Bill O'Reilly fan the flames of U.S. worker resentment and anger toward foreign workers both in their country and abroad. "Go back to China" or "Go back to Mexico," some U.S. workers scream at immigrant laborers, attributing their low pay and lack of benefits not to multimillionaire corporate leaders but to domestic and foreign workers often making less than subsistence wages.

The ability of corporate power wielders and their political allies in the White House and Congress as well as in state governments to deflect blame to the most aggrieved victims of concentrated capital is an amazing hegemonic act. Watching this process play out, we sometimes feel as if we're from another planet. How can Lee Raymond and the other corporate offenders get away with their fleecing of the working people of the world? Of course, the corporate-supported recovery movement is very influential in shaping misguided sentiments, as it fans the flames of ethnic and racial hatred residing just below the surface among many struggling workers. So often when we speak with such workers we find that their awareness of the working conditions and wages of workers in the globalized economy is lacking. A key role of a critical pedagogy of class awareness is to make known these realties and the suffering they cause such a large percentage of the world's population.

Critical pedagogy must now unite with other organizations in an international class movement that addresses the globalized, imperial strategies now employed to regulate and create a complacent workforce for transnational corporations. We can no longer allow nationalism with its crass notion of a patriotism that excludes "others" or race, gender, immigration, and religion to divide us. The divisions between the peoples of the world are used to "conquer" them for the purposes of profit and geopolitical power. In this context critical teachers and students work together with labor and other social organizations to force corporations and the governments that support them to honor the basic rights of working people: a fair wage, a right to have a say in the organization of the workplace, supervision of overtime, regulations against child labor, the right to organize a union, and so on. In addition, critical pedagogy must be an ally of labor in shaping the international trade agreements, making sure that these labor rights are extended to all workers in the world. Labor organizations must make sure than when workers in "developed" countries obtain better pay that workers in other countries get wage increases of similar proportions. This would help preclude the migration of capital to the lowest bidder in terms of wages.

Without such policies, a pay increase for workers in, say, Thailand, has resulted in a transnational corporation pulling up its operations and moving to Indonesia where wages are lower. In the contemporary neoliberal economic cosmos we see such migrations both within and between nations. The result, of course, is that everyone except the corporation and its political allies loses. A critical pedagogy of class awareness never forgets that a wide-ranging class struggle will never succeed by an exclusive focus on the relationship between people's association with the means of production and distribution of goods and services (Fletcher, Jr. 2004; Panitch, 2004; Quan 2004). Such a movement must understand and address the race, gender, sexual, and religious ideologies that preclude unity of marginalized peoples. If such issues are not addressed, workers from different countries will view one another not as allies but as competitors. Indeed, many workers from the most wealthy and developed nations will embrace a right-wing racist, sexist, homophobic, and religiously intolerant populism that will support their nation's imperial policies. The fact that such a reality now exists is a major contributor to human suffering around the world. A critical pedagogy of class awareness maintains that such a situation must end.

RANKING AND ORDERING LIKE NEVER BEFORE: CONSTRUCTING CLASS HIERARCHIES IN SCHOOL

The educational reforms of the last couple of decades are obsessed with ranking and ordering students. Students are ranked increasingly against race, class, and gender-inscribed norms that are not open to questioning or analysis—a tacit class bias. This ranking of students reflects the free market, neosocial Darwinist impulse to base all human endeavors on values of competition, deficitism, consumer choice, and the necessity of winners and losers. This logic assumes that the best and brightest will always emerge and the undeserving will be identified and punished. In this barbaric value structure, ethics such as cooperation, collaboration, and sharing are discarded like the bodies of crawfish at the end of a Louisiana fai-do-do. In a critical pedagogy teachers, students, and the public come to understand the choices—the value choices and assumptions about the nature and purpose of education—being made in contemporary education.

And the politicos directing contemporary education are doing a "good" job at their task—the two out of every five children living in poor or borderline poor conditions are facing severe obstacles at school. School districts in poor neighborhoods receive far less funding than their affluent counterparts and suffer because of it. The notion that schools are egalitarian institutions that can be used for social mobility for the marginalized is viewed by neoliberals as a relic of a primitive time when people believed in the efficacy and social practicality of socioeconomic mobility. Such "outdated" belief systems simply do not fit the needs of globalized capital, as like the alien green pudding in the movie *The Blob*, it spreads its ooze of standardization, privatization, and deregulation around the earth. Thus, class stratification and the injuries of class are not simply the result of haphazard incidence, but are shaped by conscious ideological beliefs and concrete political decisions. Influential people—power—make political-economic/educational decisions knowing full well what consequences lie ahead for the poor. Not merely do the poor lose, but by stacking the economic and educational deck for the affluent they gain from such arrangements (Brantlinger 2003).

Walk in any school in a poor neighborhood or in an impoverished rural community. One can quite quickly discern the impediments to learning in such venues—broken windows, no air conditioning, old textbooks, a preponderance of worn-out teachers, alienated and depressed students, stark classrooms, little technology, little regard for aesthetics, and so on. It is a testimony to the spirit of great teachers and resilient students that many of them carry on and engage in ingenious and important work in these hellholes. Corporate-funded, right-wing think tanks such as the Heritage Foundation, Fordham Foundation, the Manhattan Institute, and many other misinformation mills, sling pages of pseudoauthoritative pulp into the corporate-run information environment where it is dutifully reported by the mainstream press as truth—we certainly don't see the release of critical pedagogical information covered by television, radio, newspapers, and magazines.

Over and over such think tanks tell the public that elevated levels of poverty are natural in a "meritocratic" society. Indeed, high poverty and escalating school failure rates are "proof" that the system is working—the wheat is being separated from the chaff. Since poverty is, as the Heritage Foundation has argued, a result of not adhering to "traditional values," failing students from socioeconomically poor backgrounds are reaping the wages of sin. In this formulation we suppose they have to pay for the "sins" of their parents. John Calvin could not have been clearer about the fate of the "elect" and the "nonelect" than the neoliberal prophets of this era. In many ways Western societies are reverting to a previous era in European history where the poor were reviled to the point that they were often just locked up or made to wear a cloth badge indicating their state of poverty (Coles 2003).

In such a regressive era teachers are taught in the school reward system where good teaching is judged by the degree of control a practitioner has over poor or working-class students (Brawdy and Fernandez-Balboa 2004). Teaching in this conception is both a matter of authority and the best way to attain it. Intellectual dimensions of the work are viewed as somewhat silly, if not amusing. It's not how learned teachers might be or how much they understand the context in which school takes place, good teachers know how to deliver information, how to manage student bodies, and how to be good team players who execute the orders of their superiors. Indeed, as far too many great teachers have experienced, possessing a sharp intellect and a well-considered sense of educational purpose in an egalitarian, democratic society may be viewed as a threat to the smooth running of the pedagogical machine.

As Frankfurt School theorists such as Max Horkheimer (1982) argued decades ago, a class-stratified system demands multiple forms of authority-subordinate relations. Even the patriarchal system—where children's submission to paternal power readied them for their place in the stratified political-economic system—contributed to the perpetuation of class and other axes of oppression. Such preparation works so well, the Frankfurt School maintained, it often led the individual to give consent to tyrannical political leaders. This is one of the many reasons that in some Western societies—at this historical juncture the United States in particular—fundamentalist Christianity and right-wing politics have made such good bedfellows. The authoritarian rule following and patriarchal power of such fundamentalism dovetails nicely with the right-wing need to perpetuate and extend sociocultural and political economic hierarchies.

This is one of the ways that working-class and poor people are co-opted into the oppressive system. Resistance to the dominant culture "feels wrong," as submission to the father creates a psychological context for obedience. In addition, the race, gender, and sexual scapegoating of "dumb" non-Whites and immigrants, "pushy" feminists, and "perverted" homosexuals has consistently worked to win the consent of the working class and the poor to the purveyors of dominant power blocs. Add to this mix, the irrational patriotism fueled by Karl Rove-like political strategies such as perpetual war, corporate controlled media, the seduction of consumerism, and a standardized, authoritarian, ideologically controlled educational system and, voila, the recipe for social regulation is complete. Ranking and ordering of different individuals on scales based on ability, morality, normality, and so on, seems quite routine when one has granted their consent to existing power relations. In light of such formidable mechanisms of dominant power, the resistance of countless people to such well-organized disciplinary efforts is testimony to the power of human agency.

But the struggle between a powerful power and human agency is a vicious one. Schooling plays such an important role in the battle with its capacity to bestow justification for inequality—the affluent live in nice communities because they're smart; the poor live in dangerous 'hoods because they're thick as a brick. "Shuffle the deck and by next week the same people will be rich and the same dumb bastards will be poor," dominant ideology tells us—using the lexicon of the workaday world. As sorting mechanisms become more pervasive and their correctness more accepted, marginalized students possess less and less access to the type of education affluent students get. Instead of empathizing with the burdens with which socioeconomically marginalized students have to deal, Western societies have come to see them more as test score liabilities undermining the quality of our schools.

There are no excuses for not doing well in school, right-wing commentators and think tanks tell the public (Books 2001). All this talk about oppression and poverty affecting student academic performance, they tell us, does nothing but give so-called marginalized students an excuse for their failure. If such comments were the opening assertions in a defense of the intellectual abilities of marginalized students, we could appreciate where the speakers might be going. But, of course, such remarks are not meant as a defense of socioeconomically poor students. What is conveyed here is that such students have no excuses for their failure, aside from their own inadequacy. We have observed too many students from marginalized backgrounds who simply have no reason to value the types of experiences they encounter in school.

Such a lack of valuing has nothing to do with ability—out of school such students display phenomenal talent in domains where their interest level runs high. "Why learn this laundry list of data?" they ask. "It has no relevance to our lives and makes little sense." We empathize with such feelings. They demonstrate no lack of motivation, no deficiency in intellect, no default in character. Such dismissal of much of what happens in the name of instruction—especially in the Dark Ages of standardization—is simply a reasonable response to an illogical, fragmented, and ideologically distorted curriculum. When we speak to many so-called bad students, their ability to articulate compelling critiques of the contemporary state of schooling is obvious. Yet such students tell us over and over again that no one at school has ever attended to or cared about what they had to say. Having been ranked and ordered at the bottom, these students are the "untouchables" of contemporary education.

THE PREVAILING "WISDOM": THERE IS NO REASON TO HELP THE SOCIOECONOMICALLY MARGINALIZED

These are the human costs of free-market capital and the ideologies that accompany it. In many ways this market ideology and critical pedagogy come into direct conflict on the sociocultural, political-economic, and educational gridiron. Contemporary right-wing attacks on teacher education, teachers, and educational institutions are grounded on the conflict—although the right-wing assailants believe that teaching and learning are far more influenced by critical pedagogy than they actually are. Take the right-wing attack on multiculturalism, for example. If one is to believe the right-wing ideology producers, multicultural education is denying deserving white middle- and upper-middle-class students equal treatment in textbooks and access to educational resources and teacher attention (Cochran-Smith 2000). An examination (see Kincheloe and Steinberg 1997) of the influence of what is called multicultural education provides a significantly different picture.

In most schools the standards movement and test-driven programs that emphasize the memorization of "traditional knowledge"—for instance, white, male, middle- and upper-middle-class history/social science, literature, science, and culture—have long since purged multicultural impulses from classrooms. In schools that claim multicultural sensitivities, the teaching and learning and the curriculum that emerges in such contexts is anything but a threat to the dominance of privileged students and traditional knowledge. Indeed, democratic and egalitarian educational efforts in the right-wing discourse are nothing more than a vast waste of effort, time, and money. A deeper examination of the right-wing discourse reveals more. In the spirit of the recovery movement the free marketers and the political-economic potentates of empire know that a successful critical pedagogy presents a great threat to them and their covert profit-driven, exploitive agendas.

As advocates of critical pedagogy over the last quarter of a century, during the emergence and success of the recovery movement, we understand that the reaction to our calls for class, race, gender, and sexual justice has been at times explosive and fanatical. The death threats, the attempts at physical violence, the *ad hominem* attacks reveal a pathological fear of democratic political/pedagogical activities and efforts to resist dominant power and its logic of capital. Inseparable from this panic is a fear of the poor, the nonwhite, and the sexually different. "Why should educators be concerned with the needs of such people?" the right-wingers ask. "We should be focusing on controlling them so they don't undermine our way of life." In this context, even though affirmative action affects so few middle- and upper-middle-class white males, the reaction to such a policy has reflected the same volatility and fanaticism referenced above. To observe the fear, rage, and zealotry exhibited by economically privileged young white males at antiaffirmative action meetings is to gain insight into the sociopsychological depths of the emotions evoked by efforts to bring about a more just social order.

Consider this anger—it is aimed at the victims (and those who would work with them) of capital's efforts to assign the human expenses of profiteering to the poor. We often wonder if such anger comes from the status anxiety that such white men feel—the lurking suspicion in their consciousness or subconsciousness that they don't actually deserve their socioeconomic privileges. Race, gender, and sexuality interact with class in this situation to produce fascinating but disturbing behaviors by those operating from within the dominant culture. In the centuries that Westerners have colonized, exploited, and harmed peoples around the world, a collective guilt has emerged.

Fascinating are the ways the recovery movement has struggled to assuage such guilt. While class self-interest is intensely important in understanding the forces that shape schooling, we draw upon our Frankfurt School roots to again assert that economic explanations alone are insufficient to the task of studying power and its influence on human affairs in general, schooling in particular (Adorno and Horkheimer 1979; Horkheimer 1982). Class and culture are joined at the hip—and neither makes sense outside of the presence of the other. Thus, we must work to understand the psychic configuration of those in privileged positions, those who wield power in some way, of those who mandate the ideological "adjustment" of the young. A critical pedagogy of class awareness sees this as a key dimension of an emancipatory research agenda.

EQUAL OPPORTUNITY: TELL ME LIES, TELL ME SWEET LITTLE LIES

Western societies are increasingly class-segregated—as are their schools. And although the rhetoric of contemporary educational reforms is wrapped in the diaper of compassion and concern for the poor, test-driven, standardized educational policies make sure that the segregation of classes is expanded. The way the evaluation strategies mandated by reforms function plays an important role in dominant power's class warfare against the poor. With legislated directives to dramatically increase the number of tests given in schools, the number of students labeled failures has exploded. Such labeling operates as an excellent method of social control. With the imprimatur of scientific authority, marginalized students are taught that it is not the social order than is unfair—it is their own fault that they do not succeed. Growing inequality as manifested by growing prison populations, obliterated social services, cuts to public transportation, expanding numbers of uninsured people, shrinking access to health services, and so on, is in this ideological context justified and consequently accepted (Caputo-Pearl 2001; Karp 2002; Lustig 2004).

The great lie of socioeconomic mobility told by the supporters of the free global market is perpetuated in a plethora of ways. None is more perplexing than the public rejection of status hierarchies by many upper middle, highly educated individuals, yet their concurrent and thinly veiled craving for them (Brantlinger 2003). We have observed individuals in higher education who, embracing a critical pedagogy and publicly denouncing hierarchies, operate in their everyday lives on the basis of competition and status-driven motivations. In this context we return to Horkheimer's concern with people's psychic makeup to understand dominant power and emancipation from it. Though it is not kosher to speak of such topics, we are profoundly depressed about the way that individuals who give lip service to class justice and the need for democratic education fall into the same psychic trap of those working in transnational corporations and other organs of the empire.

With notable and inspiring exceptions many of those who espouse such progressive perspectives are notorious for treating those equal to or above them in the status hierarchy quite differently than those perceived to be below them. Too many times we have watched at an academic conference while the status anxious progressive scholar talking to us, concurrently looks around for someone higher in the status hierarchy. Sometimes in mid-sentence upon seeing the higher-ranking individual, the scholar will run to him to bask in the glow of being seen with someone of such an elevated rank. We find such behavior simultaneously depressing and humorous and wish for a day when such status-driven behavior disappears into the vapor trail left by the bourgeoisie.

So with the help of some of those who claim to be our ideological brothers and sisters, the purveyors of the great lie of social mobility continue to successfully ply their trade. These status seekers scramble for eminence, as the right wing employs numerous scams to enhance their privileged position. The use of school vouchers, for example, to win the consent of marginalized peoples—especially those of African and Latin descent—to extant power relations as well as allegiance to dominant power's capital driven education is a cynical ploy (Hartman 2002; Miner 2004). "Your children can attain access to the same schools attended and the high status enjoyed by the families of the affluent," right-wing politicos promise poor parents. All the while such covert ideological operatives know that the worth of one of their vouchers provides merely a small fraction of the funds needed to enter an elite private school. Labeling the fight for vouchers the "new civil rights movement," these deceptive operators make sure that politicians who are in league with dominant cultural, corporate, imperial interests maintain power.

There is nothing new about such a lie. In 1961 the head of the Educational Testing Service (ETS), Henry Chauncey, wrote that "objective" tests help the poor compete more equally with the privileged (Owen and Doerr 1999). If Chauncey were to be believed, the recent growth of the testing industry would have ushered in a new era of egalitarianism and socioeconomic mobility instead of its polar opposite. Indeed, the test-driven reforms of the first decade of the twenty-first century use social mobility and academic excellence as ideological sirens to enlist public support for what is really an attack on the lower class and other marginalized peoples. At the same time the right-wing reformers point to their concern with social mobility and academic excellence, they cut existing social and educational programs—counseling, nutrition, child health insurance, foster care, childcare initiatives to name merely a few—designed to help those most in need (Coles 2003).

Continued testing with its ranking and ordering of students is producing great resentment among those students and their families who are continuously relegated into substandard educational arrangements—special education and low-ability classes, for example. Such families see through the lies about social mobility and academic excellence, as they watch their children flounder in inequitable, restrictive, and dispiriting situations (Brantlinger 2003). Again, we understand how a student from a lower socioeconomic-class background would want to escape such a dismal situation. As we observe students in special education and low-ability school placements, we often see hopeless but talented young people who stare vacantly into space. To monitor what happens when a great teacher understands their potential or to watch such students operate in domains in which they are interested is to observe a magical process take place. Students who were previously staring vacantly into space become the masters of their universe, activists against injustice, poets, scientists, mechanics, carpenters, musicians, writers, and more. Right-wing reformers, however, refuse to see these dimensions of the students their socioeconomic policies squelch.

When all is said and done in the discursive universe of ranking and ordering, these kids are just the detritus of society—the white trash, the black youth with dangerous attitudes, the terror-prone immigrants from the Middle East, the knife-wielding Latinos, and the inscrutable indigenous students who are high from "huffing" gasoline. We have seen all of them stereotyped, ranked, ordered, and abused in educational systems around the Western world. In this century the class war has replaced the war on poverty. The standardized curricula, the control of teachers, the obsession with ranking and ordering—the norm in schools for the marginalized—are not employed nearly as much in schools for the elite. In such schools obsession with the basics gives way to electives that draw upon the interests of such students—an eighth grade course on popular music, instruction in Japanese in grade five, complexity theory in math for high school seniors, and courses for college credit throughout high school. As the rockers, Timbuk 3 so aptly put it: the future of such students is so bright they have to wear shades. The future is so bleak for marginalized students that many feel the need to brighten the atmosphere that surrounds them with narcotics. Again, given the circumstances—the climate of deceit—we understand such a choice.

DECONTEXTUALIZING CLASS: DESTROYING SOME OF THE BEST MINDS OF *THIS* GENERATION

Cutting class—class is irrelevant, many individuals from diverse social, ideological, and educational context contend. Cutting class—class consciousness is subverted by TV shows that identify with and promote upper-middle-class values. Cutting class—"it embarrasses poor students to talk about class, it's not a subject that should be addressed in school." Cutting class—"those who challenge corporate activity and a progressive income tax are waging class warfare against the rich and this must stop." As George W. Bush added to this concept, stressing the inclusivity and justice of his tax cuts for the rich: "Everybody gets a tax cut in my plan" (Third Presidential Debate between Al Gore and George W. Bush, 2000). Why, it would be unfair, Bush assures us, to give tax cuts to only the poor and the middle class.

Right-wing political leaders get by with such assertions because of our class illiteracy. When we have no understanding of the contexts that shape class and thus contemporary social, political, economic, and educational life, class warfare against the poor continues unabated. A critical pedagogy of class awareness works to engage students in finding and researching this contextual information. Consider the following:

- Creating a huge national debt allows political leaders to cut funds for programs designed to aid the poor as well as public education.
- The Internal Revenue Service (IRS) spends more time examining the tax returns of the working poor than on auditing corporate and affluent taxpayers (Piven 2004).
- Efforts to demonize, criminalize, and deport illegal immigrants help ensure that a politics of class identity among low-paid workers will not germinate.
- One's financial inheritance is the most trusted predictor of academic success (Ohanian 1999).
- Particular research methods subvert our understanding of why students from lower socioeconomic backgrounds often do poorly in schools (Foley and Voithofer 2003).

A basic dimension of right-wing decontexualization of class involves this last point. As many scientists and scholars from many fields have pointed out, over the last several years dominant power wielders have deployed science in circumscribed ways guaranteed to validate the power-driven dominant cultural agenda. This strategy is quite complex and it is easy to exclude the public from an understanding of how it works. The use of such a science for antidemocratic and antiegalitarian objectives has become extremely important in the contemporary class war being waged against the world's poor. In this context it is imperative that the public understands this politics of knowledge in order to defend democracy and access to public education.

One of these complex elements involves the ability to identify and trace the effects of ethnocentrism and class bias within the positivist research tradition in education. Positivism is an epistemological (having to do with the production of knowledge) position that values objective, scientific knowledge produced in rigorous adherence to the scientific method. In this context knowledge is worthwhile to the extent that it describes objective data that reflect the world. Over the past several decades, scholars of research have discerned numerous problems with the positivist position—problems, as previously mentioned, often having to do with decontextualizing the object of study. This decontextualization along with many other factors leads to the production of very misleading understandings of the world around us, about poverty and education and their interrelationship.

Thus, science is always ideological. It always operates in some type of relationship to power à la race, class, gender, sexuality, colonial location, and so on. One dimension of science's power is that it exercises its ideological authority covertly. This has moved many observers to maintain that power operates not *on* science but often times *through* science. It is politicized in the name of depoliticization (Harding 1998). Positivist science simply never calls attention to its generation within particular racial, gendered, and class contexts. For example, the values of the middle- and upper-middle-class and the way they shape scientific activity are simply not addressed in positivist research. This holds dramatic consequences for the poor in numerous areas, education included.

In this positivist view, "true knowledge" can only be produced by a detached, disinterested, external observer who works to ignore background (contextual) information by developing "objective" research techniques. Here researchers hold to a reductionistic view of human activities, believing that the world—the social world in particular—is quite uniform and consistent in its workings. Thus, using correct research procedures—usually quantitative in nature—educational researchers can identify what causes what. The idea that there is an infinite array of contextual variables that influence the process of teaching and learning is dismissed in this positivist framework. Thus, educators don't need to study class in the way the editors and authors of *Cutting*

Class are doing here. Instead, researchers use student testing to determine what curricula and what teaching methods improve test scores. It's quite simple, once such curricula and teaching methods are mandated and employed, student performance will improve. As we have written before, it doesn't matter if students are from Moose Jaw, Atlanta, or Manila, we use the same quantitatively "proven" methods to teach them. Context in positivism is worthless, a waste of time.

In the long course of human history, most great wisdom has not been constructed in this manner. A central dimension of the right-wing recovery movement in education involves this attempt to recover and reinstate the positivist mode of producing a narrow form of knowledge. If positivism is "recovered," then the efforts to recover race, gender, and class supremacy are profoundly enhanced. A more global insight with awareness of and respect for diverse ways of knowing, cultural humility, and an ecologically sustainable and ethical conception of progress is not on the positivist conceptual map. Positivism, in this context, is a monocultural way of seeing the world that emphasizes the knowledge produced by patriarchy, white Europeans, and individuals from the upper-middle and upper classes.

The test-driven standards movement of the last couple of decades provides a case study of this phenomenon. Student knowledge and skills that fall outside of the narrow boundaries measured by positivist educational researchers are deemed irrelevant. Thus, some of the most brilliant students of this generation slip through the decontextualized gates of positivist-driven education, because the basis of their genius fails to show up on standardized tests and is dismissed as irrelevant to the standardized curriculum. In the neopositivist contemporary landscape, therefore, old forms of class oppression are revitalized and new varieties are created. As previously noted, good teaching becomes a form of pedagogy that best regulates and controls those potentially dangerous marginalized students.

COUNTERING A PEDAGOGY OF CLASS OPPRESSION

The right-wing Heritage Foundation proudly performs its ideological role in the class war, producing knowledge about education that leads to policies that privilege the privileged and marginalize the marginalized.

The foundation's pedagogical panacea for moving students out of poverty involves destroying any remaining vestige of a progressive education that focuses on building tailored curricula around the specific needs of children—needs such as the problems caused by being poor that can undermine academic performance. Heritage researchers and policy makers have no use for a pedagogy that values context. Thus, they promote rote learning of basic skills, more standardized testing, the hiring of educational leaders who will not ask for better-funded schools and school districts, and the firing of teachers who don't buy into this Neanderthal curriculum. The purpose of this *Pedagogicus Neanderthalus*, Heritage Foundation leaders tell us, is to make sure that students from the lower socioeconomic classes master the "rigors of global competition" (Coles 2003). If we have done our research on the Heritage Foundation correctly, we understand what might be meant by the phase "rigors of global competition."

Such a notion has little to do with the intellectual empowerment of economically marginalized students and more to do with a form of social regulation that fits such students into low-status, low-paid, no-benefits type of jobs. The emphasis here is not on self- and social-transformation or intellectual development but more on learning to follow directions, to be a team player, and to ask few questions about issues of justice. This is not a form of democratic education, it's more a form of stupidification dressed in costume designed to look like rigorous, "world class" learning. Students engage in an imitation of serious learning as they spend their days memorizing data and learning test-taking procedures. In many cases when not engaged in this mindless test prep, students attend "test pep rallies" where nubile cheerleaders exhort them with chants and gymnastic floor shows to "make the school proud" and score high on tomorrow's state-mandated tests. Cheers include "three in a row . . . no, no, no"—referring to the test-taking tip that the same answer (either a, b, c, or d) in a multiple choice test will not be used three times in a row.

> Sharpen that pencil,
> Has to be a number two.
> Answer those questions,
> Now it's up to you

Buckle down devils,
We know that you can.
When we ace those tests,
We'll be the best in the land.

Yeah, go Blue Devils! We can have the highest test scores! Yeah! We're
number one. We're number one.

Business and corporate leaders from around the country join with the
Heritage Foundation and other right-wing think tanks to promote narrow, test-driven curricula. Such curricula make sure that students are
never exposed to critiques of national, dominant cultural, and corporate
institutions. Focus is diverted from analysis, interrogation, and dissec-
tion of social and political data, as emphasis is placed on the acquisition of ideologically charged bits and fragments of data that relate to
the tests. The education advocated in these plans creates a diversion
from exploring what it means to be a scholar, to engage in intellectual
inquiry, to ask questions about what education in a truly democratic society might look like. The purpose of such classrooms is to help graduate students imbued with an acceptance of the globalized economy
and their role in it. For poor children this means reminding them of
their academic deficiency and thus their personal responsibility for
their poor grades. If I'm incapable of high-level, abstract thinking,
many poor students assume, then I better take whatever job I can get.

Studies of curriculum find that students' socioeconomic class does
make a difference in the types of pedagogy they receive. Such differences position them to fail (See Kincheloe, *Toil and Trouble: Good
Work, Smart Workers, and the Integration of Academic and Vocational
Education* and *How Do We Tell the Workers: The Socio-Economic
Foundations of Work and Vocational Education* for more information
on the specifics of this process). As a dominant power-based schooling
attempts to incorporate lower- and working-class students into the
grand system of twenty-first-century capital, corporate-directed television provides images of the good life that everyone can attain. If the
poor can get just a little money and pay on credit, they can ease their
class pain by engaging in the ritual of consuming these objects. The
truth claims of the dominant culture and its educational system, the

poor are taught, are intellectually and morally superior to their own understandings.

If such a belief can be inculcated into the minds of the poor, then they will believe that existing power blocs deserve their exalted status. With fundamentalist churches now preaching a gospel of economic success, even old religious teachings about both the danger of wealth and the quest for wealth have fallen by the wayside. The church in its fundamentalist right-wing format becomes a great ally of the dominant culture in promoting the virtues of the free market and the justice of the stratified status quo. Such factors have cultivated the desire for wealth among communities of different class, racial, cultural, and religious composition (hooks 2000; Caputo-Pearl 2001; Carter, Howell, and Sheid 2001, Tabb 2004). Corporations have poured great amounts of money into marketing to children in the belief that such efforts would result not only in increased sales of the products being advertised, but such advertising would create a new group of consumers—individuals with a consciousness directed toward consumption as central to their lives (Steinberg and Kincheloe 2003).

Obviously, the development of a critical class consciousness is difficult in such a world. But people are not sheep—as argued throughout this chapter, individuals have the agency to reject what they hear and to act against oppression. As the intensity of the class war against the poor has intensified more and more people, students included, are aware of some of the issues addressed here. The anger harbored by many of these individuals will frighten people isolated in the mainstream, insulated by the corporate driven politics of knowledge. Indeed, the expansion of the market-driven empire around the planet is creating enemies willing to die to avenge their oppressors. If things do not change soon, greedy power wielders will reap bloody harvests from the seeds of class, race, cultural, and religious hatred they have sown.

So far, even with the displeasure many Western peoples have with their governments, most North Americans, peoples from the English-speaking world, and Europeans do not appreciate the degree of the damage that has been caused by these greedy political-economic, geopolitical, and culturally insensitive policies. What we fear is that the violent reactions—such as the riots in France in 2005—will push Western societies in a more right-wing direction. This is why a critical pedagogy of class awareness is so important in such a dangerous era. If we fail to understand the class, race, ethnic, religious, and other divisions separating the peoples of the world into unequal and oppositional camps, we face a dismal future. In the United States right-wing politicos have attempted to make such understandings and the peace-driven policies they support look like vicious anti-American, anti-Western ploys. In such proto-fascist perspectives, the issue of class inequality within and between nations is never broached. The "enemy," whether it is the radical Islamists, the socialist states of South America, or the immigrants of the multiple diasporas now taking place in the globalized world, is scum.

The fact that the North African and Middle Eastern Muslim immigrant youth who rioted in France were facing a 50 percent unemployment rate was not particularly relevant to the French government and many of the Western news outlets that covered the story. The right-wing reaction to such insurrection was crystallized by French Interior Minister M. Nicolas Sarkozy who referred to the rioters as *racaille*—a class-inscribed French term for riff-raff (San Francisco Independent Media Center, 2006). With existing neoliberal policies in place, these riots signify the beginning of new waves of violence against Western power blocs. Education has a choice. It can either continue to contribute to the injustice and alienation of the marginalized, or it can become a source of hope, belongingness, justice, and mobility. While many dedicated, brilliant teachers do great things for students from diverse backgrounds, they are salmon swimming upstream in ideological state institutions too often designed to regulate the "dangerous" poor. Critical pedagogy supports a complex, multidimensional, twenty-first-century class struggle designed to change the direction of contemporary repressive educational, sociocultural, and political-economic policies. We must succeed in this undertaking.

REFERENCES

Adorno, T. and M. Horkheimer (1979) *Dialectic of Enlightenment*. London: Verso.

Apple, M. (1996). Dominance and Dependency: Situating *The Bell Curve* within the Conservative Restoration. In J. Kincheloe, S. Steinberg, and

A. Gresson (eds.), *Measured Lies: The Bell Curve Examined*. New York: St. Martin's.

Apple, M. (1999). *Power, Meaning, and Identity: Essays in Critical Educational Studies*. New York: Peter Lang.

Aronowitz, S. (2003). *How Class Works: Power and Social Movement.* New Haven, Conn.: Yale University Press.

Books, S. (2001). Saying Poverty Doesn't Matter Doesn't Make It So. In J. Kincheloe and D. Weil (eds.), *Standards and Schooling in the United States: An Encyclopedia*. 3 vols. Santa Barbara, Calif.: ABC-Clio.

Bourdieu, P. (1989). *Distinction: A Social Critique of the Judgment of Taste*. Cambridge, Mass.: Harvard University Press.

Brantlinger, E. (2003). *Dividing Classes: How the Middle Class Negotiates and Rationalizes School Advantage.* New York: Routledge Falmer.

Brawdy, P. and Juan-Miguel Fernandez-Balboa (2004). Becoming a "Good Teacher": Thinking Critically about Teaching. In J. Kincheloe and D. Weil (eds.), *Critical Thinking and Learning: An Encyclopedia for Parents and Teachers*. Westport, Conn.: Greenwood.

Bruner, J. (1996). *The Culture of Education.* Cambridge, Mass.: Harvard University Press.

Caputo-Pearl, A. (2001). Challenging High-Stakes Standardized Testing: Building an Antiracist, Progressive Social Movement in Public Education. In J. Kincheloe and D. Weil (eds.), *Standards and Schooling in the United States: An Encyclopedia*. 3 vols. Santa Barbara, Calif.: ABC-Clio.

Cochran-Smith, M. (2000). The Outcomes Question in Teacher Education. Paper Presented at AERA, New Orleans.

Coles, G. (2003). Learning to Read and the "W Principle." *Rethinking Schools*, 17, 4. www.rethinkingschools.org/archive/17_04/wpri174.shtml

Counts, G. (1978). *Dare the Schools Build a New Social Order?* Carbondale, Ill.: Southern Illinois University Press.

Crebbin, W. (2001). The Critically Reflective Practitioner. www.ballarat.edu.au/~wcrebbin/TB780/Critreflect.html

DeFreitas, G. and N. Duffy (2004). Young Workers, Economic Inequality, and Collective Action. In M. Zweig (ed.), *What's Class Got to Do with It? American Society in the Twenty-First Century*. Ithaca, New York: Cornell University Press.

Dewey, J. (1916) *Democracy and Education.* New York: Free Press.

DuBois, W. (1973). *The Education of Black People: Ten Critiques, 1906–1960*. New York: Monthly Review Press.

Fernandez-Balboa, J. (2004). Emancipatory Critical Thinking. In J. Kincheloe and D. Weil (eds.), *Critical Thinking and Learning: An Encyclopedia*. Westport, Conn.: Greenwood.

Fiske, J. (1993). *Power Plays, Power Works*. New York: Verso.

Fletcher, Jr., B. (2004). How Race Enters Class in the United States. In M. Zweig (ed.), *What's Class Got to Do with It? American Society in the Twenty-First Century*. Ithaca, New York: Cornell University Press.

Foley, A. and R. Voithofer (2003). Bridging the Gap? Reading the No Child Left Behind Act against Educational Technology Discourses. www.coe.ohio -state.edu/rvoithofer/papers/nclb.pdf

Gresson, A. (1995). *The Recovery of Race in America*. Minneapolis: University of Minnesota Press.

Gresson, A. (2004). *America's Atonement: Racial Pain, Recovery Rhetoric, and the Pedagogy of Healing*. New York: Peter Lang.

Harding, S. (1998). *Is Science Multicultural? Postcolonialisms, Feminisms, and Epistemologies*. Bloomington: Indiana University Press.

Hartman, A. (2002). Envisioning Schools beyond Liberal and Market Ideologies. *Z Magazine*, 15, 7. www.zmag.org/amag/articles/julang02hartman .html

Herrnstein, R. and C. Murray (1994). *The Bell Curve: Intelligence and Class Structure in America*. New York: Free Press.

hooks, Bell (2000). *Where We Stand: Class Matters*. New York: Routledge.

Horkheimer, M. (1982). *Critical Theory: Selected Essays*. Trans. M. O'Connell et al. New York: Continuum.

Howell, S., V. Carter, and F. Schied (2001). (Ill)equipped for the Future: Standards and Adult Education. In J. Kincheloe and D. Weil (eds.), *Standards and Schooling in the United States: An Encyclopedia*. 3 vols. Santa Barbara, Calif.: ABC-Clio.

Jensen, B. (2004). Across the Great Divide. In M. Zweig (ed.), *What's Class Got to Do with It? American Society in the Twenty-First Century*. Ithaca, New York: Cornell University Press.

Karp, S. (2002). Let Them Eat Tests. *Rethinking Schools*. www.rethinkingschools.org/special_reports/bushplan/eat164.shtml

Kincheloe, J. (1995). *Toil and Trouble: Good Work, Smart Workers, and the Integration of Academic and Vocational Education*. New York: Peter Lang.

Kincheloe, J. (1999). *How Do We Tell the Workers? The Socio-Economic Foundations of Work and Vocational Education*. Boulder, Colo.: Westview.

Kincheloe, J. (2002). *The Sign of the Burger: McDonald's and the Culture of Power*. Philadelphia: Temple University Press.

Kincheloe, J. (2003). Critical Ontology: Visions of Selfhood and Curriculum. *JCT: Journal of Curriculum Theorizing*. 19, 1, 47–64.

Kincheloe, J. (2004). *Critical Pedagogy*. New York: Peter Lang.

Kincheloe, J. (2005). *Critical Constructivism*. New York: Peter Lang.

Kincheloe, J. (2006). The Southern Place and Racial Politics: Southernification, Romanticization, and the Recovery of White Supremacy. *Souls: A Critical Journal of Black Politics, Culture, and Society*, 8, 11.

Kincheloe, J. and S. Steinberg (1997). *Changing Multiculturalism.* London: Open University Press.

Kincheloe, J. and S. Steinberg (2004). *The Miseducation of the West: How Schools and the Media Distort Our Understanding of the Islamic World.* Westport, Conn.: Praeger.

Kincheloe, J., S. Steinberg, N. Rodriguez, and R. Chennault (1998). *White Reign: Deploying Whiteness in America.* New York: St. Martin's Press.

Lakes, R. (1994). Is this Workplace Democracy? Education and Labor in Postindustrial America. In R. Lakes (ed.), *Critical Education for Work: Multidisciplinary Approaches.* Norwood, N.J.: Ablex.

Lustig, R. (2004). The Tangled Knot of Race and Class in America. In M. Zweig (ed.), *What's Class Got to Do with It? American Society in the Twenty-First Century.* Ithaca, New York: Cornell University Press.

McLaren, P. (2000). *Che Guevara, Paulo Freire, and the Pedagogy of Revolution.* Lanham, Md.: Rowman & Littlefield.

McLaren, P. (2006). *Rage and Hope: Interviews with Peter McLaren on War, Imperialism, and Critical Pedagogy.* New York: Peter Lang.

Maturana, H. and Varela, F. (1987). *The Tree of Knowledge.* Boston: Shambhala.

Macedo, D. (1994). *Literacies of Power: What Americans Are Not Allowed to Know.* Boulder, Colo.: Westview Press.

Macedo, D. (2006). *Literacies of Power: What Americans Are Not Allowed to Know.* 2nd ed. Boulder, Colo.: Westview Press.

May, T. (1993). *Between Genealogy and Epistemology: Psychology, Politics, and Knowledge in the Thought of Michel Foucault.* University Park, Penn.: Penn State Press.

Mills, C. (1956). *The Power Elite.* New York: Oxford University Press.

Miner, B. (2004). Why the Right Hates Public Education. *The Progressive.* www.progressive.org/jan04/miner0104.html

Newell, C. (2006). Where the Money Goes (Oil and Gas). *CoffeeCrew Blog.* www.cofee.bc.ca/april

Nicholson, L. and S. Seidman (eds.) (1995). *Social Postmodernism: Beyond Identity Politics.* New York: Cambridge University Press.

Ohanian, S. (1999). *One Size Fits Few: The Folly of Educational Standards.* Portsmouth, N.H.: Heinemann.

Owen, D. and M. Doerr (1999). *None of the Above: The Truth behind the SATs.* Lanham, Md.: Rowman & Littlefield.

Panitch, L. (2004). September 11 and Its Aftermath Through the Lens of Class. In M. Zweig (ed.), *What's Class Got to Do with It? American Society in the Twenty-First Century.* Ithaca, New York: Cornell University Press.

Piven, F. (2004). Neoliberal Social Policy and Labor Market Discipline. In M. Zweig (ed.), *What's Class Got to Do with It? American Society in the Twenty-First Century*. Ithaca, New York: Cornell University Press.

Quan, K. (2004). Global Strategies for Workers: How Class Analysis Clarifies Us and Them and What We Need to Do. In M. Zweig (ed.), *What's Class Got to Do with It? American Society in the Twenty-First Century*. Ithaca, New York: Cornell University Press.

Rodriguez, N. and L. Villaverde (2000). *Dismantling White Privilege*. New York: Peter Lang.

San Francisco Independent Media Center (2006). Riot 2005 in France. http://sf.indymedia.org/news/2006/06/1729703.php

Steinberg, S. (2001). *Multi/intercultural Conversations: A Reader*. New York: Peter Lang.

Steinberg, S. (2003). *Kinderculture: The Corporate Construction of Childhood*. 2nd ed. Boulder, Colo.: Westview.

Tabb, W. (2004). Neoliberalism and Anticorporate Globalization as Class Struggle. In M. Zweig (ed.), *What's Class Got to Do with It? American Society in the Twenty-First Century*. Ithaca, New York: Cornell University Press.

Teitelbaum, K. (2004). Curriculum Theorizing. In J. Kincheloe and D. Weil (eds.) *Critical Thinking and Learning: An Encyclopedia*. Westport, Conn.: Greenwood.

Third Presidential Debate between Al Gore and George W. Bush (2000). www.australianpolitics.com/news/2000/00-10-17.shtml

Zweig, M. (2004). Introduction: The Challenge of Working Class Studies. In M. Zweig (ed.), *What's Class Got to Do with It? American Society in the Twenty-First Century*. Ithaca, New York: Cornell University Press.

CHAPTER 2

Exploring Critical Theory and Critical Ethnography in the Context of the Production and Reproduction of Social Class

Natalie Mixon

The goal of this chapter is to provide a solid foundation for understanding critical theory and critical ethnography as it is applied to the investigation of the role that education systems in capitalist societies have in the production and reproduction of social class. Developing an understanding of critical theory and critical research is important for teachers and teacher educators because it can provide relevant insight concerning how we can improve our education system in order to provide students with equal educational opportunities. Critical theorists are interested in how knowledge is structured to legitimize the position of those in power, and have built their arguments from their "deep concern with power, representation, voice, social justice, diversity, democracy, and equality" (Vinson 1999, 307). Due to the paradigmatic elements and epistemology of critical theory, ethnographic techniques provide a parsimonious approach to researching systems of inequality and constructing knowledge of how the maintenance of social class, or the socially constructed status quo, is perpetuated by institutions of education.

Critical theory presents educators with a framework from which they can understand how institutions of education in capitalist societies impact the structure of society itself. Critical theory applied to education emerged in the wake of the Vietnam War and the civil rights movement when educational scholars began questioning and challenging the inequalities experienced by marginalized students in capitalist economies (Torres 1998). Although until recently, critical theory was not widely applied to the institution of education, it has been valuable in allowing educators and social theorists to see the connection between seemingly commonsense practices in schools and ideologies in the greater society (Beyer 2001). It is my contention that critical forms of educational philosophy should be introduced in teacher-education programs because prospective educators, in order to be successful in teaching marginalized populations, must be able to understand and to develop a critique for the maintenance of the status quo. After all, if we are serious about developing teachers that are capable of critical and reflexive thought, critical inquiry should be included in teacher-education programs (Kincheloe 1995). In order to be effective educators, teachers should be able to comprehend how cultural, social, and political issues are interconnected with classroom dynamics which are, in turn, reproduced in society as our future generations develop.

It is crucial for educators to understand the extent to which the production and reproduction of social class occurs within educational settings as it has important implications to society. Research cited by Fine (1991) indicates that social class is the greatest predictor of who drops out of high school. Unfortunately, among race, class, and gender issues "there is no doubt that class has been the least fashionable . . . despite the fact that all the evidence suggests that class remains the single most powerful determinant of life-chances" (Collini, as quoted in McLaren and Scatamburlo-D'Annibale 2004, 43). As Payne (1996) cogently argues, students from lower social classes are often faced with confounding hindrances to upward intergenerational mobility based on any permutation including a lack of financial, emotional, mental, spiritual, or physical resources, a lack of a nurturing relationship, or an absence of the knowledge of the hidden rules of the middle and upper classes (16–18). Not to mention that, with the deindustrialization of Western society, working-class individuals and their students are presented with a scenario for the future that offers a lackluster job market and a devaluation of the culture that has been formed by their previous experiences.

Since social class encompasses a wide variety of variables that impact educational success, such as ethnicity and gender, social class as a holistic category has become fragmented in recent research by educators who are interested in exploring variables related to equal educational opportunities. Ogbu (1988) notes that characteristics related to social stratification—class, gender, race—have their own educational consequences and that "the academic problems and achievements of each category cannot be completely understood in terms of social class alone" (168). However, when data regarding all categories associated with social class are combined, the importance of social class resounds as a significant variable determining educational achievement. By attacking this social class dilemma holistically and head-on, critical ethnography provides educators and lower-class individuals with an opportunity to understand the mechanisms that work at school (tracking and unequal access to resources) and in the society (gender relations, poverty, and ethnicity) that serve to produce and reproduce the social class stature of the next generation. If structural mechanisms inherent in the institution of education that cause the obstruction of lower classes' intergenerational mobility are understood by educators, a curriculum that combats equality issues related to social power and hegemony in our schools can be developed and pervasively implemented.

Critical theory attacks the "two educational myths of liberalism . . . the notion that education is a neutral activity, and that education is an apolitical activity" (Torres 1998, 1). This theoretical approach to education is unique because it is interested mainly in the daily lives of people and the structures and cultures that shape their life experiences. It is concerned with how "the actual social and economic exchanges and patterns that are created within a society shape the consciousness of people" (Beyer 2001, 5). For marginalized populations, critical theory provides an opportunity for them to have a voice in education. For these groups, the belief that the education system is fair to all "runs against the grain of their neighbors' experiences, their families' experiences, and their own encounters with the labor market" (MacLeod 1995, 71). Despite these voices, teachers are trained to believe that schools are politically neutral, meritocratic institutions separated from social, cultural, political, and economic issues which plague our society (Beyer 2001). It is these experiences that remind us that the institutions of education in our society do not live in a sanitized vacuum, separated from the outside hardships of the real world.

It is important to note that I do not believe the marginalization of lower-class students is deliberate. It is my contention that almost no one sets out to be intentionally unfair to children. However, institutions of education in our society can be seen as a primary instrument allowing for the reproduction of social, racial, and economic class. This is because schools, as institutions *of* the society, are instruments for the reproduction of society as it is (Noddings 2004). "In other words, schooling revolves around the necessity of differentially reproducing a citizenry distinguished by class, race, and gender injustices" (McLaren 1997, 119). The production and reproduction of the status quo occurs in schools because the education system holistically functions in a manner which undermines the ability of lower-class individuals to achieve upward social mobility. The basis of this hegemonic relationship is the speculation that the cultural capital lower-class students bring into the classroom tends not to be valued by the schools themselves (MacLeod 1995).

Upon reflecting on my own classroom practices, I am painfully aware that, as a teacher, I am an agent of social reproduction. It is my own subjectivity and situatedness as a middle-class white female that leads me to construct a classroom structure that has, in effect, devalued lower-class experiences and cultural capital. As a member of the culture of education *and* a member of the dominant culture, I have been doubly encultured to devalue lower-class cultural capital. As a researcher and educator concerned with these sociocultural inequalities inherent in our education, critical ethnography provides me with an opportunity to construct a relevant knowledge that I can use as a catalyst for my own transcendence as an agent of social reproduction.

While analysis of one's privilege has often been minimized by members of the dominant society, several academics have reflected on the privileged experience of the white dominant class as a way to better understand how they benefit from being members of the upper classes of society (e.g. Scheurich 1993; Douglas 2001; McIntosh 1988). For example, in his analysis of racism and upper-class privilege, Scheurich (1993) is able to acknowledge that the middle-class and upper-class culture has been able to set the standard in social "measures of merit, student assessment, predictors of success, correct grammar, appropriate behavior, and so forth" (7). The dominant class has been afforded the luxury of being able to write and dictate the rules of society. These rules, of course, are congruent with the culture of those who have power and authority, and with the dominant groups seemingly ascribed the right to dictate to educators what knowledge is best for our children. According to Mullen (1999) issues of "whiteness," of belonging to a dominant social group, have not been made relevant in teacher-education programs. This lack of understanding prevents future educators from being able to examine the link between their social stature and the power relationships inherent in classroom settings. I would suggest that teacher-education programs encourage students to use ethnographic techniques to take a look into themselves and into their own subjectivity from the critical perspective of scholar-practitioners.

Research questions should guide the selection of the research methods as "certain designs are better suited to address particular kinds of questions under particular conditions than others" (Shavelson and Towne 2002, 98). Methods of inquiry related to institutional mechanisms of hegemony, to how social reproduction occurs, are suitably answered with critical ethnography. Critical ethnography as a method of inquiry guides research in that it acknowledges the particular economies of truth, value, and power in social-class structure that perpetuates the production and reproduction of social class. Furthermore, using critical ethnographic methods can provide researchers with new understandings of social-class reproduction if they are able to situate and analyze field research as a discourse entangled within a larger structure of power and privilege (McLaren 1995). For example, acknowledging that I am an agent of the production and reproduction of social class as a member of the dominant culture enables me to understand how my own enculturation as an educator impacts the marginalized students that I teach. Critical ethnography can be used as a tool to clarify the existence of Eurocentric perspectives. The rationale for using critical ethnography in educational research designs stems from the importance of critical research questions to be answered in the form of a story about a group from that group's perspective (LeCompte and Schensul 1999, 27), and the acknowledgment of the role that point of view has in developing the story itself.

Education researchers, social scientists, and anthropologists frequently use qualitative ethnographic tools to construct and project for their subjects a voice that is often underrepresented in society. Going further than providing or lending a voice to subjugated populations, critical ethnography provides lower-class populations with the opportunity to make their life experiences valid and to construct for themselves an emancipatory and empowering sense that their own experiences in the labor force and school system are true—not devalued and disenfranchised as they often are by the dominant culture. In critical ethnography, "the marginalized have the first right to name reality, to articulate how social reality functions, and to decide how the issues are to be organized and defined" (Mihevc, as quoted in McLaren 1995, 289). McLaren explains this placement of the ethnographer in relation to the subject and as a subject in the research itself. "It is also essential that ethnographic researchers act *with* the oppressed, not *over them* or *on behalf of* them. Critical ethnography must be *organic to* and not *administered upon* the plight of struggling peoples" (291).

In the context of critical ethnographic inquiry and the production and reproduction of social class, it is the lower class's daily experiences and world views that shape our understanding of the mechanisms present in the institutions of education and in the family structures that socialize working-class and lower-class youth to fail to achieve upward social mobility. It is the working-class and lower-class experiences uncovered through critical ethnography that can serve as a starting point for the development of grassroots policies aimed at nurturing the development of community empowerment, social activism, and social reform.

SOCIAL REPRODUCTION

Attributes that parents pass on to their offspring play a significant role in whether or not a student is able to achieve his or her academic potential in the United States. From the beginning of the public education system in the United States, social theorists such as Herbert Spencer (2000) defined the relationship the education system has with the industrialized world:

> you need but to . . . observe social organization in its peculiarities, to see that these are neither supernatural, nor determined by the wills of individual men . . . but are consequent on general natural causes . . . It has not been by the command of any ruler that some men have become manufacturers, while others have remained cultivators of the soil (11).

According to Spencer, some people are inherently better than others, born leaders of the working class and poor. It is innate within our species that there are haves and have-nots. This group of scholars, the Social Darwinists of the early twentieth century, preached that the poor are inherently poor because of their biological composition, using this theory to justify the often harsh class stratification in industrial societies (Gould 1981). The impetus behind reinforcing the Social Darwinists' eugenics movement was the public education system in the United States which, from the beginning of its history, adhered to and based its overarching structure and practices on the eugenics movement's assumptions. However, the Darwinists' assumptions that intelligence determines success and that intelligence is biologically determined are false (Gould 1981).

According to contemporary social reproduction theorist Pierre Bourdieu (1974), institutions of education play a significant role in maintaining the status quo regarding social class structure:

> Education is in fact one of the most effective means of perpetuating the existing social pattern, as it both provides an apparent justification for social inequalities and gives recognition to the cultural heritage, that is, to a social gift treated as a natural one (32).

For Bourdieu, the cultural capital "is what makes the game of society—not least, the economic game—something other than simple games of chance offering at any moment the possibility of a miracle" (1983, 241). Students are stratified based on the extent to which they possess varying social characteristics indicative of the dominant culture. In other words, the elite members of our society have a head start at becoming successful because the curriculum values their knowledge about the world more so than the knowledge about the world that the lower classes possess. For example, an upper-class family who acts and thinks like an upper-class family is likely to raise their offspring in a manner which fosters upper-class actions and an upper-class mentality, which in turn is highly valued by institutions of education in our society. Reproduction of social class becomes cyclical in nature (see figure 2.1) and the cycle is difficult to overcome without the intervention of a curriculum reform that has taken the time to examine closely

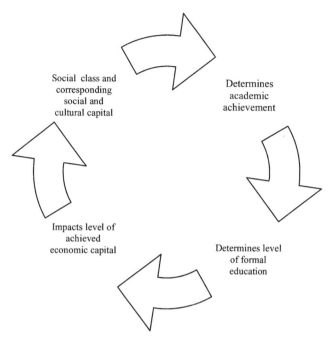

Figure 2.1.   The Reproduction of Social Class

and descriptively the relationships between social class, culture, power, and privilege.

In many Western societies, minority groups are faced with additional challenges to upward intergenerational mobility. Ogbu (1988) explores how involuntary immigrant status, class stratification, and racial stratification contribute to educational inequality and the lack of social mobility for minority groups in the United States. Lower-class African American students, because of their status as an involuntary minority group, experience and respond to academic achievement differently than voluntary immigrant groups often do. Lower-class African American students understand that schooling is important for them in order to escape poverty and its related social problems. However, their behavior in school undermines their ability to be successful students (Ogbu 1988). This may be because of the formation of cultural characteristics of minority youth that are oppositional to the culture of schools.

African Americans are members of what Ogbu refers to as an involuntary minority group, a group that was ascribed into a subordinate social-class position due to their forced historical enslavement. Involuntary minority groups, such as African Americans, often struggle with issues of distrust when interacting with public schools and authority school personnel; this distrust likely stems from their status as a minority group forced to become members of our society (Ogbu 1990, 54). In response to their status as involuntary immigrants, African Americans students have developed coping mechanisms which may or may not contribute to their academic achievement, including weak acceptance of school norms and rules, disillusionment, developing a belief that one can "make it," or "acting white" (Ogbu 1990). Weak acceptance of school norms and disillusionment are forms of a developed oppositional process. It is the "acting white" and the belief that one can make it that either leads to success or back to an oppositional disillusionment due to persistent racial stratification in our society (Ogbu 1990).

African Americans students are aware of and generally associate academic learning with the learning of the culture of power—the culture associated with white America. Therefore in order to succeed many African Americans believe they have to "learn to think and act white" (Ogbu 1988, 177). Despite this, the mentality that African American students need to "act white" in order to achieve academically will not always guarantee success. This may be because African Americans, as well as other involuntary minorities, remain subject to inferior education and therefore fail to qualify for adult careers that require a good education (Ogbu 1990, 50).

The formation of a culture of resistance among minority and lower-class groups in schools impacts their ability to attain the necessary academic qualifications to achieve upward intergenerational mobility. Oppositional coping mechanisms conflict with the culture of education. The oppositional structures that lower-class individuals develop are created based on cultural disparities arising from the placement of these groups in the social hierarchy.

Understanding theories related to social reproduction provides a framework for understanding the variables that make our society an unequal one. Research supporting these theories can give educators the insight necessary to enact effective reform in our educational institutions. In addition, ethnographic research illustrates how particular subcultures are affected by the variables related to social inequality. A wide theoretical background and high quality research can assist educational reformers in the development of curriculum and pedagogical practices that can empower lower-class students.

ETHNOGRAPHIC EVIDENCE

In this section, I will discuss the ethnographies of Michelle Fine, Lois Weis, Paul Willis, and Jay MacLeod and provide a foundation for understanding how critical ethnography can be used to understand and uncover the mechanisms that reproduce social class. These individuals have conducted ethnographies in working-class and lower-class environments in order to develop a richer understanding of the attitudes, perceptions, and life experiences that function as oppositional structures to upward intergenerational mobility. In their studies, qualitative data are supplemented with quantitative data which create a sense of the geosociopolitical setting. However, it is their ethnographic analysis of the subjects that provide the participants with a coherent voice, with a definition of the subjects as humans with real and valid experiences, moving away from the subject in the placement of the all-too-often removed definitions of "otherness." Their conclusions point to a mismatch between the culture of schools and the culture of the lower classes.

Success predicated on hard work is the fundamental principle operating in the public education system's belief that it will be able to "level the playing field" for children from diverse ethnic, social, and economic backgrounds. As Nolan and Anyon (2004) point out, "schools are ideological institutions that serve to justify their own existence through a discourse of social mobility" (143). However, the conviction that upward social mobility in our society is based on a system of meritocracy is erroneous, according to MacLeod's (1995) research in a low-income neighborhood in Chicago. Nevertheless, the school system perpetuates this myth of our society as a meritocracy by using the familiar mantra, "behave yourself, work hard, earn good grades, get a good job, and make lots of money" (97).

MacLeod is able to point out in his ethnographic data that, due to the steadfast belief of the dominant culture that we exist in a meritocracy, this mantra is often pushed aside by the lower classes and replaced with sentiments of personal failure. MacLeod uses the metaphor of running an uphill race when discussing upward social mobility in the eyes of his subjects. One of MacLeod's two distinct subject groups, a Caucasian group known as the Hallway Hangers, has given up because they believe that the odds of winning, or even finishing the race, are against them. Interestingly, most of the Hallway Hangers are confident that they will eventually be killed or end up in jail—this is likely based on the plight of their older siblings. In contrast, the African American group, the Brothers, have higher aspirations—they feel their chances for success are better, partially due to affirmative action policies.

In his research, MacLeod discusses how the Hallway Hangers' racist beliefs are counterproductive to their economic success. "Their identification of class-based barriers to success and their impression that the deck is fairly stacked against them, insights which could catalyze the development of . . . political consciousness . . . is derailed by their racism" (122). Consequently, the Hallway Hangers believe, like most neoconservatives, that affirmative action has taken jobs from whites.

Paul Willis's (1977) ethnographic research in England has similar parallels with MacLeod's subjects. For example, the subjects in both ethnographies exhibit a partial understanding of the social inequalities which serve as barriers to success, and the subjects all experience class-related barriers which produce and reproduce their future as members of the lower classes (MacLeod 1995). According to Willis (1977), working-class or lower-class students believe that conformity to school will not result in future prosperity—this is likely related to attitudes projected by their parents. In Willis's subject group, the Lads, working-class cultural practices that are produced and reproduced at home were perceived as expressions of resistance at school. Concurrently these expressions had the effect of producing for the Lads a space in the working class (McLaren and Scatamburlo-D'Annibale 2004). In this way, lower-class attitudes about school and the institution of school contribute to social reproduction.

Willis's attitude towards the Lads' culture is more accepting and hopeful; it is also more optimistic than MacLeod's, based on the perceived ability of his group to be able to make progressive social change, perhaps due to the more socialist structure of English society.

As MacLeod (1995) notes, "the British working class, with its long history, organized trade unions, and progressive political party, has developed an identity, pride, and class consciousness that are [sic] lacking in the United States" (122). Furthermore, the American working class "has been described as 'fractured,' historically along regional racial and ethnic lines, and more recently by the displacement of industrial workers and the erosion of the labor union as a social and political collectivity" (Stevenson and Ellsworth 1993, 269).

Ethnographic evidence clearly demonstrates that a family's social and economic status reproduces itself in Western societies. Despite the Brothers' attempts, high aspirations, and willingness to "run the race," they were unable to attain their goals because of racial issues and because they did not possess the cultural capital needed to be successful at school and later on in the job market. The Hallway Hangers knew that the odds were against them and did not even bother "running the race." Paul Willis' Lads, due to their own partial understanding of how the society they lived in functioned, rebelled against school and adopted the attitudes and behaviors of their parents which indoctrinated them into the working-class culture. MacLeod's and Willis's ethnographies provide the insight that educators and social theorists can use to identify how various structural inequalities function as agents of social reproduction by exposing the attitudes, values, and life experiences of the lower classes. In these two ethnographies, the subjects' experiences with the middle- and upper-class values of education have alienated them from the possibility of attaining their potential as students.

Weis (1993) conducted her ethnography in a working-class town experiencing economic hardships due to the downward shift in the economic demand for working-class jobs. The white working-class culture Weis studied can be characterized as one which exhibited and expressed anger toward white women and people of color and valued male-dominated homes and masculine expression. Similar to MacLeod's Hallway Hangers, the subjects of Weis's study felt that affirmative action policies had taken jobs from them. A main theme in this ethnography is that the white working-class position of privilege has disappeared with deindustrialization and subsequently, the "new" voice of the white working-class is a direct reflection of their loss of privilege (Weis 1993). Like MacLeod (1995) and Willis (1977), Weis notes that white working-class males desire male-dominated homes and exhibit expressed racism and sexism. The subjects of Weis's ethnography, like MacLeod's Hallway Hangers, have found their attitudes and beliefs effectively couched in the "profamily rhetoric and coded racism of the New Right" (258). The upper classes of our society likely benefit from the lower classes' division by racial issues as is illustrated in the Willis, MacLeod, and Weis ethnographies.

Stevenson and Ellsworth (1993) discuss in their research how the issue of lower-class students dropping out is "rarely addressed in terms of racial and class inequalities in schooling or in the broader society" (261). White and minority students internalize their failure to graduate from school differently. Their findings suggest that white working-class dropouts internalize their academic failure as personal deficiencies. In contrast, as noted by Ogbu (1988), minority dropouts are more critical of the educational system for their failed educational attainment.

The culture that working- and lower-class students bring to the classroom may be incongruent with the culture of education. However, that does not absolve the system of education from forcing lower-class students out of schools. Fine (1991) found that the structure of a comprehensive high school in New York City discharged lower-class students at such a rate that only 20.5 percent of admitted freshman made it to graduation. Students from this school were discharged (no longer in attendance) mostly because of behavior issues, family problems, entering the work force, or seeking alternative schooling.

Behavior problems at school, when comparing the clash between cultures, can be seen as norm violations on behalf of lower-class students in regard to the established academic and behavioral rules, values, and expectations of the culture of schools. The setting of Fine's ethnography (CHS) is known as a relatively safe urban school; despite this, students were frequently suspended or discharged for carrying knives or guns. In an urban setting where adolescents are shot at or stabbed and where violence is a pervasive part of students' life experiences, carrying a weapon is frequently an issue of safety, not a means for perpetuating violence. In many instances related to fighting, weapons charges, or vandalism, the students were not aware of their right to remain in school after their suspension and were frequently coerced by administration, in an effort to flush an overcrowded school of "miscreants," into dropping out. These norm violations, especially the nonviolent ones, do a great injustice to students who come from a culture where the hidden rules of education are not understood.

Poor academic achievement and subsequent grade failure at CHS was associated with negative psychological characteristics such as embarrassment and frustration that led to behavior problems, and perhaps confirmed feelings of inadequacy (Fine 1991, 74). At CHS, of the thirty recent drop-outs interviewed during the course of the ethnography, 80 percent had been retained at least once during their education. The psychological damage done by retaining students leads to behavior problems: adolescents who repeated a grade were more likely to have had school discipline problems and to have been suspended from school (76). Lower-class students whose cultural capital has been devalued academically, leading to retention, creates a psychological state where they are predisposed to engage in norm violation as per the standards set by the institution. Being suspended from school has negative consequences for students who violate social norms; it diminishes the likelihood of graduation and increases the probability of dropping out (242).

Students who left CHS because of family problems did not do so simply because they had more important issues to deal with (i.e. supporting a family and having to work full-time to put food on the table), but because there was no institutional structure for them to continue their education. Lower-class students citing family problems as a reason for being forced out of the education system is primarily an issue related to inflexibility of the school and an unwillingness to deal with lower-class students' family situations—situations that often arise due to low-income individuals' vulnerability to familial health problems that have the power to cripple the economic stability of the family unit. As Fine (1991) found, "in many cases, however, 'family problems' is offered as the reason students drop out of high school precisely because the high school experience has been discouraging, unengaging, and disinviting and because schools have been structured in ways that do not accommodate students experiencing family problems" (77).

Another theme found in Fine's ethnography is the silencing of disempowered voices. "Silencing shapes low-income public schools more intimately than relatively privileged ones. In such contexts there is more to hide and control and indeed a greater discrepancy between pronounced social ideologies and lived experiences" (Fine 1991, 34). The structure of CHS illegitimated the voices of students who felt disengaged and dissociated from the education they received. Their voices were not heard, they were not important, and because of this they were left with a sense that their life experiences were invalid. At CHS, students' life experiences and views were voiced, and then promptly negated when teachers dictated the "truth" which rendered the students' voices irrelevant (45). The attitudes expressed by several students indicate that many of them felt that the teachers believed they had the right to dictate morality, when most of the middle-class faculty had never experienced a life of poverty and hardship to the extent that they had. The mismatch between students and teachers occurred largely because of differences in cultural and ethnic background (151). The effect of this attitude projected by the teachers left the students disinterested and disillusioned with the educational process.

What the students at CHS were learning was not relevant to them and to the world they lived in. Furthermore, the silencing of students' dialogues about their life experiences and daily struggles systematically alienated them and ultimately severed them from becoming engaged in the education they were receiving (Fine 1991, 35). This disengagement has serious consequences for lower- and working-class students' motivation to graduate high school and to therefore obtain a level of employment that can generate intergenerational mobility.

Is it fair to say that if the students in these ethnographies had better experiences with teachers and administrators that their chances for successful completion of school would have increased? Would the chances for improving their social stature have increased? Clearly, the students in these ethnographic studies did not have a head start in the race toward the attainment of upward social mobility. From the moment they entered school, characteristics indicative of the social and cultural capital they brought with them were devalued by an institution that had promised them a fair shot at living the American dream.

MacLeod (1995) alludes to the fact that if these lower-class students struggled through to high school graduation and then on to some form of higher education, our society would still discriminate against them because of their lack of knowledge of the hidden rules of the middle and upper classes, namely of middle- and upper-class cultural capital. In this way, the structure of the school system can be detrimental to lower-class individuals. Fine (1991) notes that psychologically, lower-class high school drop-outs fare much better than their counterparts who decide to stick it out and "play the game." It is truly ironic that, in doing so, we are damaging our lower-class students with the treatment that is supposed to provide them with emancipation from poverty.

CURRICULUM AND SOCIAL REFORM

Antonio Gramsci reminds us that "every relationship of 'hegemony' is necessarily an educational relationship" (Giroux 2000, 112). From this perspective, lower-class students are caught in a power relationship where the forms of power that benefit the dominant class are, in effect, a detriment to the lower class (Díaz-Rico and Weed 2002). Curriculum in our country has participated in the production and reproduction of social class because it is biased toward those who have power in our society. Contemporary curriculum in Western society is based on a cognizant "decision to define some groups' knowledge as the most legitimate, as official knowledge" (Apple 1993, 222). Because the knowledge and culture of school produces and legitimizes a particular way of life through both the overt and hidden curriculum, the hegemonic nature of the institutions of education in Western society are disguised with the false promise of upward social mobility (Giroux 2000).

Fine (1991) points out that "in the United States, public schools, particularly secondary schools, were never designed for low-income students and students of color" (31). Distribution of educational resources mirrors this social attitude. "Middle-class white children are viewed as more valued and deserving of the material resources and cultural goods of the larger society than are poor and nonwhite children" (Giroux 2000, 42). In poorer school districts, students do not have the same resources that students in wealthier districts do. Kozol (1991) notes that "typically, very poor communities place high priority on education, and often they tax themselves at higher rates than do the very affluent communities . . . But, they are likely to end up with far less money for each child in their school" (55). Spring (1996) discusses how property taxes determine how much funding a school district receives. School districts in the United States receive approximately 50 percent of their financial support from local taxes. Students in more affluent areas with higher property taxes receive more funding than students in less affluent areas with lower property taxes. Even grants allocated by state politicians are doled out in lesser amounts to the districts that need financial support the most. For example, in New York City, "the poorest districts in the city get approximately 90 cents per pupil from these legislative grants, while the richest districts have been given $14 for each pupil" (Kozol 1991, 98).

Due to economic inequality, students in less affluent areas suffer from unequal educational access because their districts cannot afford to buy the newest and best material resources. Poorer school districts, often inner city and rural districts, cannot afford to have top-of-the-line technology in classrooms. This further perpetuates a digital divide in our country which severely limits children's access to the technological know-how that is becoming a cornerstone to academic and economic success in the twenty-first century. The lower classes' limited access to resources because of economic inequality reproduces social class in that lower-class students are not given the opportunity to learn and develop skills which are valued in a society that is no longer reliant on industrial skills, and in which information and technology skills are necessary.

The hegemony of the upper classes over the lower classes that is inherent in the education system creates a structure which makes upward social mobility difficult. The language of educators and politicians is frequently structured in a manner which makes culturally relevant pedagogy inaccessible or unavailable to those who are oppressed. According to Paulo Freire (2004), "one cannot expect positive results from an educational or political action program which fails to respect the particular view of the world held by people" (129). Curriculum then takes on a form such that students become mindless depositories of information generated by those in power, all in an effort to support and maintain a situation which is mostly beneficial to society's upper classes (Vinson 1999). Lower-class students are victims of hegemony in an education system that stems from a curriculum that is designed by upper-class individuals for the educational attainment of upper-class offspring. As educators, it should be our responsibility to "rethink the ways in which culture is related to power and how and where it functions both symbolically and institutionally as an educational, political, and economic force" (Giroux 2000, 149).

In a pluralistic society such as ours, critical theory and critical ethnography provide educators with a framework for improving an education system that has failed to provide many lower-class and minority students with an opportunity for upward social mobility. By lending voice to those who have been subjugated by the elite in our society, the institutions of education in the United States can begin to work toward attaining equal educational opportunity for all students. In order to be able to detect forms of educational hegemony on the part of the social elites, Vinson (1999) identifies several questions that should be addressed by curricula developers at both the state and national level:

- Whose interests does the curriculum benefit?
- Who does it not?
- How do they affect the status and evolution of social justice, equity, freedom fairness, and opportunity?

These poignant questions are aimed at exposing the methods of the dominant culture that preserve the existing social structure of our society. These questions also expose whose curriculum is being taught and whose knowledge is the official knowledge of our nation's prized education system (Apple 1993). From a critical perspective, another question that beckons to be posed is: Whose voices have been silenced? Whose voices have been the victims of a historic amnesia, forgetting that equal educational opportunities have never been fully achieved? Fine (1991) expressively writes:

> The silenced voices are disproportionately those who speak neither English nor Standard English, the voices of the critics, and the voices which give away secrets that everyone knows and feverishly denies. Their secrets tell of racism; of an economy that declares itself prosperous while many live in poverty, sickness, and substandard (or no) housing; of an ideology of education as the Great Equalizer when there's little evidence; and of the secrets of sexism that claim the bodies and minds of their mothers, sisters, aunts, and themselves (25).

These voices must no longer be ignored. When they are acknowledged and *listened to* in a humane manner that implores and demands education for social activism by an educational and political system that is not in denial, much needed emancipatory curriculum reform can be recognized and implemented.

If the voices of those overlooked by our institutions of education were actually heard, what would an emancipatory and empowering curriculum look like? Lower-class students need to be taught the necessary skills to succeed in a society and culture that has built a stigma around poverty. In line with Vinson's focus on understanding the hegemonic nature of education, Delpit (1995) has outlined a curricular framework that would serve to provide lower-class students with the tools necessary to achieve upward social mobility. Similar to Payne's (1996) recognition that impoverished students do not always know what the hidden rules of the dominant culture are, Delpit (1995) delineates five aspects of power in schools that educators can use as a guide to address their own subjectivity in the classroom and to develop a culturally relevant and empowering curriculum for their lower-class students:

1. Issues of power are enacted in the classroom.
2. There are codes or rules for participating in power.
3. The rules of the culture of power are a reflection of the rules of the culture of those who have power.
4. If you are not already a participant in the culture of power, being told explicitly the rules of that culture makes acquiring power easier.
5. Those with power are frequently least aware of—or least willing to acknowledge—its existence. Those with less power are often most aware of its existence (24).

This "culture of power" model provides educators with insight regarding how they can share the cultural and social capital that is valued by our education system and the greater society with lower-class students. In order for the "culture of power" to be taught explicitly to lower-class students, they should be taught the codes of the culture of power that are necessary to be able to reach their academic potential in a manner that also validates and is sensitive to their own sociocultural background. Furthermore, students "must also be helped to learn about the arbitrariness of those codes and about the power relationships they represent" (Delpit 1995, 45). If properly implemented, this acknowledgment of the existence of the culture of power and what it signifies for lower-class students could be a curriculum reform that would cut across the hegemonic aspects of the structure of education by confronting issues of social class and power head-on and by forcing teachers to face their own roles as agents of social reproduction.

CONCLUSION

The structure of the public education system in the United States undermines the goal of a fair and balanced curriculum for all students. At the heart of this issue is a significant problem that has been the focus of this article—social reproduction. As I have demonstrated, social reproduction is a real phenomenon in our public school system by which lower-class students are being denied equal educational opportunities. Our public education system, which has accepted the responsibility of helping lower-class students break out of poverty and achieve upward mobility in a capitalist society, has failed us. Its inability to develop curricula and support an institutional structure that recognizes and addresses the role of power and bias has perpetuated social injustice.

As the reader has seen, it is blatantly apparent that not all Americans are able to achieve their academic potential due to factors which are imbedded in our societal fabric and perpetuated through our system of education. We have seen that the American dream, which reinforces the American belief in meritocracy, is an egregious myth—working hard is *not* in direct relation to success and the assumption itself is based on white, upper-middle-class values. Fortunately, there are educators who are aware of the need to reform our educational institutions in a manner which empowers students from diverse backgrounds so that they can transcend the structural inequality that is ubiquitous in our society.

It is vital to incorporate the implications of critical theory and critical ethnography into any initiative aimed at improving the situation of marginalized students in our society. Critical theory and critical ethnography allows educators and researchers alike to experience the daily struggles of lower-class individuals within a system of education and socialization that has failed to provide them with the tools and skills necessary to meet their goals and aspirations. These methods of inquiry sustain the assumption that social reproduction is a real phenomenon and that students in our country do not receive equal educational opportunities; such an epistemology can further inform us of how state and national curriculum may perpetuate an achievement gap that is detrimental for lower-class and minority groups at both the school and classroom level.

REFERENCES

Apple, M. (1993). The Politics of Official Knowledge. *Teachers College Record* 95 (2), 222–41.

Beyer, L. (2001). The Value of Critical Perspectives in Teacher Education. *Journal of Teacher Education* 52 (2), 151–63. Accessed January 20, 2005, from the Academic ASAP database.

Bourdieu, P. (1974). The School as a Conservative Force: Scholastic and Cultural Inequalities. In J. Eggleston (ed.), *Contemporary Research in the Sociology of Education* (32–46). London: Methuen.

Bourdieu, P. (1983). *The Forms of Capital.* www.viet-studies.org/Bourdieu_capital.htm (accessed July 5, 2004).

Delpit, L. (1995). *Other People's Children: Cultural Conflict in the Classroom.* New York: New Press.

Díaz-Rico, L. and Weed, K. (2002). *The Cross-Cultural, Language, and Academic Development Handbook.* Boston: Allyn & Bacon.

Douglas, L. (2001). How I benefit from white privilege. www.raceandhistory.com/historicalviews/privilege.htm (accessed March 24, 2005).

Fine, M. (1991). *Framing Drop-outs: Notes on the Politics of an Urban Public High School.* Albany, N.Y.: State University of New York Press.

Freire, P. (2004). Pedagogy of the Oppressed. In D. Flinders and S. Thornton (eds.), *The Curriculum Studies Reader* (125–33). New York: Routledge-Falmer.

Giroux, H. (2000). *Stealing Innocence: Corporate Culture's War on Children.* New York: Palgrave.

Gould, S. J. (1981). *The Mis-measure of Man.* New York: Norton & Co.

Kincheloe, J. (1995). Meet Me Behind the Curtain: The Struggle for a Critical Postmodern Action Research. In P. McLaren and J. Giarelli (eds.), *Critical Theory and Educational Research* (71–89). Albany, N.Y.: SUNY Press.

Kozol, J. (1991). *Savage Inequalities: Children in America's Schools*. New York: Crown Publishers.

LeCompte, M. and Schensul, J. (1999) *Designing and Conducting Ethnographic Research*. Walnut Creek, Calif.: AltaMira Press.

MacLeod, J. (1995). *Ain't No Makin' It: Aspirations and Attainment in a Low-Income Neighborhood*. Boulder, Colo.: Westview Press.

McIntosh, P. (1990). *White Privilege: Unpacking the Invisible Knapsack.* http://seamonkey.ed.asu.edu/~mcisaac/emc598ge/Unpacking.html (accessed March 24, 2005).

McLaren, P. (1995). Collisions with Otherness: "Traveling" Theory, Postcolonial Criticism, and the Politics of Ethnographic Practice—the Mission of the Wounded Ethnographer. In P. McLaren and J. Giarelli (eds.), *Critical Theory and Educational Research* (271–300). Albany, N.Y.: SUNY Press.

McLaren, P. (1997). Freirian Pedagogy: The Challenge of Postmodernism and the Politics of Race. In P. Freire (ed.), *Mentoring the Mentor: A Critical Dialogue with Paulo Freire* (99–125). New York: Peter Lang.

McLaren, P. and Scatamburlo-D'Annibale, V. (2004). Paul Willis, Class Consciousness, and Critical Pedagogy: Towards a Socialist Future. In N. Dolby and G. Dimitriadis (eds.), *Learning to Labor in New Times* (41–60). New York: RoutledgeFalmer.

Mullen, C. (1999). Whiteness, Cracks, and Ink-Stains: Making Cultural Identity with Euroamerican Preservice Teachers. In C. T. P. Diamond and C. A. Mullen (eds.), *The Postmodern Educator: Arts-Based Inquiries and Teacher Development* (147–90). New York: Peter Lang.

Noddings, N. (2004). The False Promise of Paideia: A Critical Review of the Paideia Proposal. In D. Flinders and S. Thornton (eds.), *The Curriculum Studies Reader* (163–70). New York: RoutledgeFalmer.

Nolan, K. and Anyon, J. (2004). Learning to Do Time: Willis' Model of Cultural Reproduction in an Era of Postindustrialism, Globalization, and Mass Incarceration. In N. Dolby and G. Dimitriadis (eds.), *Learning to Labor in New Times* (133–49). New York: RoutledgeFalmer.

Ogbu, J. (1988). Class Stratification, Racial Stratification, and Schooling. In L. Weis (ed.), *Class, Race, and Gender* (163–82). Albany, N.Y.: SUNY Press.

Ogbu, J. (1990). Minority Education in Comparative Perspective. *The Journal of Negro Education* 59 (1), 45–57.

Payne, R. (1996). *A Framework for Understanding Poverty*. Highlands, TX: AHA! Process, Inc.

Scheurich, J. (1993). Towards a White Discourse on White Racism. *Educational Researcher* 22 (8), 5–10.

Shavelson, R. and Towne, L. (2002). *Scientific Research in Education.* Washington, D. C.: National Academy Press.

Spencer, H. (2000). The Social Organism. In McGee and Warms (eds), *Anthropological Theory: An Introductory History* (11–27). Mountain View, Calif.: Mayfield Publishing Co.

Spring, J. (1996). *American Education.* New York: McGraw-Hill.

Stevenson, R. and Ellsworth, J. (1993). Dropouts and the Silencing of Critical Voices. In Weis and Fine (eds.), *Beyond Silenced Voices: Class, Race, and Gender in United States Schools* (259–71). Albany, N.Y.: State University of New York Press.

Torres, C. A. (1998). Quote retrieved from Web site, Rage and Hope (p. 1). www.perfectfit.org/CT/index2.html (accessed January 20, 2005).

Vinson, K. (1999). National Curriculum Standards and Social Studies Education: Dewey, Freire, Foucault, and the Construction of a Radical Critique. *Theory and Research in Social Education* 27 (3), 296–328.

Weis, L. (1993). White Male Working-class Youth: An Exploration of Relative Privilege and Loss. In Weis and Fine (eds.), *Beyond Silenced Voices: Class, Race, and Gender in United States Schools* (237–58). Albany, N.Y.: State University of New York Press.

Willis, P. (1977). *Learning to Labor: How Working Class Kids get Working Class Jobs.* New York: Columbia Press.

Part II

CORPORATE POWER, CLASS OPPRESSION, AND EDUCATION

CHAPTER 3

Class, Race, Space, and Unequal Educational Outcomes in the United States: Beyond Dichotomies

D. W. Livingstone and Susan L. Stowe

INTRODUCTORY PROFILES

This chapter offers a basic assessment of the current relationships between social class, place of residence, and educational success in the United States. Primary attention is devoted to school completion rates by family class origins and residential area, as well as race and gender, with particular interest in the relatively low completion rates of those from lower-class origins and inner city or rural areas.

Class and *urban* are often treated as basic notions with little definition in both popular thought and much research. The current educational research literature typically refers simply to middle-class and lower-class families or similar dichotomies, and to urban and suburban or rural areas. Things are not really quite so simple. Both social classes and residential areas are dynamic relationships rather than objective categories. Their configurations are continually changing in advanced capitalist societies in response to interfirm competition, negotiations between different social groupings, technological innovations, and a host of other social processes—including, for example, population shifts directly caused by organizational downsizing and enterprise relocation. But both current class and residential profiles can be approximated using somewhat more complex distinctions and should be if we intend to detect adequately their relations with educational chances.

The number of distinct class positions in advanced capitalist societies, their boundaries, and the use of occupational classifications to estimate them are all matters of considerable debate among Marxist class analysts (Livingstone and Mangan 1996; Wright 1980 and 1997). Some only recognize two fundamental classes, capitalist owners of the means of production and the working class or proletariat of hired wage laborers. Some also distinguish the petty bourgeoisie of self-employed who own small enterprises but do not hire anyone else. Many contemporary scholars also identify several other class groupings or fractions that have developed in intermediate locations between these basic classes. These include small employers between corporate capitalists and the self-employed, and other class locations that play mediating authority or technical work design roles between capitalists and the working class. Some also consider a distinction between blue-collar manual workers and white-collar service workers to be significant. The estimated size of these class groupings varies according to the criteria used, including positions in the relations of production per se, skill levels, income levels, etc. The most readily available evidence is population census data on occupational titles, but owners of enterprises need to be distinguished from employees with similar occupations as well as by whether they employ others and to what extent.

For purposes of the current analysis, eight significant class groupings can be distinguished in the United States and other advanced capitalist societies on the basis of production relations (Livingstone 1983). Large employers or corporate capitalists own major enterprises and have overall control of their labor processes. Small employers employ at least some hired workers and usually need to continue to devote their own productive labor to their business. The self-employed work for themselves without employing others. The rest of the labor force does not have real ownership of enterprises. Managers exercise general authority over the rest of hired workers. Professional employees generally design and have autonomy over their own labor. Supervisors and forepersons exercise immediate authority over other hired workers. These other workers have neither real ownership claims nor recognized prerogative over their own labor power; they include service workers who provide various services and industrial workers who produce material goods. At any given time some portion of hired employees, and especially service and industrial workers, are unemployed. Homemakers, students, and retired people are generally attached to these other class groupings in some way. Just about all of us are associated with one or more of these groupings in terms of family origins and stability or mobility from those origins.

There is much public rhetoric about a middle-class society. But as table 3.1 shows, based on the 2000 U.S. General Social Survey (GSS), over half of the current U.S. labor force is made up of service and industrial workers, clearly working class in Marxist terms. Large employers can be seen as the tiny core of the upper or ruling class (less than 1 percent of the labor force). Small employers and the self-employed both vary widely in the assets of their enterprises from very affluent to impoverished, but they remain proprietors and thereby distinct from employees in class terms; together they make up less than 14 percent of the labor force. Managers, professionals, and supervisors are all in intermediate class relations between the owners and those hired workers without recognized prerogatives. They could be considered as middle class. Their numbers are approaching a third of the active labor force in the United States.

Again, these class distinctions remain fluid. People's own subjective class identities may not correspond very closely. An ideology of *middle classness* prevails among both the general public and scholars in the United States, with few of the rich inclined to identify themselves as upper class and few of those at the bottom of the class ladder wishing to celebrate a lower- or working-class status (Kingston 2000). Of course, class existence is not lived simply at the point of economic production, and these relations may be obscured by various factors (Seccombe and

Table 3.1. Occupational Class by Residential Area, U.S.+ Employed Labor Force, 2000

	Inner City (%)	Suburb (%)	Outer Suburb (%)	Rural (%)	Total (%)	N
Large employer	< 1	< 1	< 1	< 1	< 1	(1)
Small employer/Self-employed	13	15	14	15	14	(304)
Manager	18	21	13	10	16	(338)
Supervisors	2	3	4	3	3	(74)
Professional employees	10	12	13	7	11	(246)
Service workers	39	32	29	30	32	(704)
Industrial workers	18	16	28	34	23	(508)
Total	24	25	36	15	100	(2174)

Source: Davis, Allan, Smith, & Marsden (2002)

Livingstone 1999). Household and community relations are important constitutive aspects, and cultural as well as economic relations should be considered in order to begin to understand the learning capacities and cultural capital of different classes, particularly working-class people (Livingstone and Sawchuk 2003). But, as we shall see, economic class origins in the above terms can have very substantial effects on people's educational chances and should not be ignored or grossly simplified. Economic class origin is likely to matter in education, even if many deny it.

Similarly, residential area or spatial location can have important shaping effects on educational chances, but not in a simple linear way. Industrialization drew increasing proportions of the population into urban centers throughout most of the last two centuries. Since World War II, more expansive, cheaper living spaces and lower taxes have attracted growing proportions of inner-city dwellers to the surrounding suburban areas. Large parts of inner cities became run down by the 1960s with the flight of more affluent, and mainly white, classes to the suburbs. Some regentrification of inner cities by affluent suburbanites has occurred since then. But the vast majority of office space built in the 1990s was in suburbia, much of it in office parks along interstate highways. Rapidly growing numbers have moved out to the sprawling "exurbs" beyond the big city suburbs and commute in to suburban jobs (or increasingly telework from) these outer suburb areas (Brooks 2004). Manufacturing industries have also increasingly located in these vast exurban zones and have drawn population from more outlying areas. These more remote rural areas have few population settlement centers and have been increasingly depopulated with the decline of agricultural labor. In sum, the basic tendency has been for the U.S. population to become increasingly concentrated in very large metropolitan zones, including inner cities, suburbs, and outer suburbs or exurbia, with constantly declining rural numbers.

The current populations of these spatial areas can be estimated on the basis of census categories. Inner-city residents live in the central cities of the largest standard metropolitan statistical areas, most of which are over 250,000 people and all of which are over 50,000 people. Suburb dwellers live outside the limits of central cities within these same standard metropolitan areas. The outer suburbs generally surround standard metropolitan zones and include other counties having towns of 10,000 or more. Rural areas typically include counties having no towns of 10,000 or more and are mostly smaller areas with towns under 2,500 or open country. According to the GSS 2000 estimates summarized in table 3.1, inner cities and suburbs each contain about a quarter of the U.S. population, the outer suburbs now make up around 35 percent, and only about 15 percent remain in rural areas.

These four spatial areas tend to have somewhat different demographic makeup in terms of occupational classes, average income, and ethno-racial origin. In terms of class, as shown in table 3.1, the suburbs are the only region in which the working class is a minority (48 percent), and industrial workers (16 percent) make up a smaller number than managers (21 percent). Inner cities are most distinct in having higher proportions of service workers (39 percent) than other areas and much lower proportions of industrial workers (18 percent) than the more rural areas (28 to 34 percent). Rural areas have the smallest proportions of managers (10 percent) and professional employees (7 percent), and the largest proportions of industrial workers (34 percent) and combined industrial and service workers (64 percent). The outer suburb areas have class profiles fairly similar to the inner cities except that they have more industrial workers and fewer service workers. The proprietorial classes (large and small employers and the self-employed) are fairly similar proportions across all areas. These class profiles are not profoundly different between areas but substantial enough that potential interactive effects of class and residential area on educational outcomes should be considered. According to the GSS, Americans living in rural areas have the lowest average annual incomes (about $21,000), followed by those living in inner cities and outer suburbs (both about $23,725). Those living in the suburbs have significantly higher average incomes ($32,500).

Ethno-racial distinctions are also more complex than simple white/black or white/colored dichotomies can reflect. Whites remain dominant in all areas. What counts as white has varied considerably over the past century. At the moment, Hispanics are the fastest growing part of the white population, but in many respects they share the economic disadvantages of the blacks whom they will soon outnumber (Fullerton 1999). Other minorities, including aboriginals, Asians, and

Table 3.2.   Ethno-Racial Origin by Residential Area, U.S. 25+ Population, 2000

	Inner City (%)	Suburb (%)	Outer Suburb (%)	Rural (%)	Total (%)	N
White	62	78	89	90	80	(2030)
Black	32	15	8	8	15	(392)
Other	6	7	3	1	5	(120)
Total	100	100	100	100	100	
N	(614)	(634)	(1023)	(271)	(2542)	

Source: Davis, Smith, and Marsden (2002)

many others, exhibit great variation in economic origins and educational outcomes and should be treated separately in thorough studies (Anyon 1997). In the U.S. GSS, estimates of ethno-racial origin are limited to white, black, and "other." Based on these classifications, we can see in table 3.2 that there is a much higher percentage of blacks in the inner city (32 percent) than in any other area. The further away one is from the inner city, the less the diversity in terms of either blacks or other minorities, with outer suburbs and rural areas containing minorities of around 10 percent. Our further analysis here will focus on white/black differences, but we must recognize the growing significance and diversity of other minorities.

Gender differences should also be understood in social relational terms, including homosexual orientations as well as heterosexual ones. Indeed, those who assume homosexual identities may be more prone to experience both economic and educational discrimination. However, only male/female distinctions are available in the GSS data, which is the most accessible recent data set for this analysis. In terms of participation in the active paid labor force, men still outnumber women, about 53 percent to 47 percent (Fullerton, 1999).

PROFILES OF EDUCATIONAL OUTCOMES BY CLASS, SPACE, RACE, AND GENDER

Few prior national-level survey analyses have examined both class- and residential-area patterns together in much detail in relation to educational outcomes. Prior research focused on socioeconomic status, which roughly approximates social class, has generally found it to be the most significant correlate to student academic achievement (Hough and Sills-Briegel 1997). U.S. studies that have looked at the results of nationwide standardized testing have found that students from economically disadvantaged backgrounds perform poorly (Bussière 2001). The lack of success in grade school and high school carries over to participation in postsecondary education. National Center for Educational Statistics (NCES) findings (Wirt et al. 2003) confirm once more that the higher the family income of high school graduates, the more likely they are to enroll in postsecondary education. In 1998, only 33 percent of low-income students attended postsecondary education compared to 47 percent of middle income and 77 percent of high income (National Center for Education Statistics 1998; Wirt et al. 2003). In spite of recent increases in general participation in post secondary education, rates remain low for lower-income/working-class students from inner-city and minority ethnic groups. These students still do not experience a smooth transition from school to work or from school to further education or training (Archer and Yamashita 2003; Stowe 2001).

Some demographers are beginning to identify more complex population patterns than simple urban/suburb or rural dichotomies in relation to inequitable early schooling conditions (e.g., Hodgkinson 2003). Previous research has found that broadly defined different residential areas tend to provide different resources to schools. Urban *and* rural schools have been more poorly funded than suburban schools. Students in urban and rural areas have faced more barriers in school compared to their counterparts in suburban schools. Overall, students in urban and rural schools have performed consistently worse than students in suburban schools on standardized measures (Thirunarayanan 2004). Urban and rural schools both serve a disproportionately high percentage of students living in poverty (Hatfield 2002; National Center for Education Statistics 1998; Sherman 1992). Distinct barriers faced by rural schools include very small enrollments with limited courses and educational opportunities (Monk and Haller 1993; Archer and Yamashita 2003). Another disadvantage is that there often are multigraded classrooms (Archer and Yamashita 2003; Edington and Koehler 1987; Hudson and Shafter 2002). Many rural students must spend hours every day commuting to school. The commute also limits their extracurricular activities. Other consequences are limited access to community services, other schools, museums, organized sports, recreational facilities, arts and culture events, and "visitors" (Collins, Press, and Galway 2003). But, as documented extensively in other chapters, inner-city schools generally are also much more poorly supported than suburban schools and often suffer from the opposite condition of serious overcrowding (Davidson 2002; Kozol 1992; Valdez 2000; Wrigley 2003). The lowest completion rates for high schools in the United States are in large inner cities such as New York City, where black and Hispanic working-class youths predominate and completion rates are currently under 40 percent (Swanson 2004).

Indeed, the interrelation of space and race in schooling has been widely noted. Discrimination in funding has been found to be based on race as well as the urban, suburban, or rural location of the school (Kozol 1992). In 1990, in the six largest urban centers of the United States (New York City, Chicago, Los Angeles, Atlanta, Detroit, and Miami), over half of students were African American or Latino (Ginzberg 1993). The majority of students who live in these cities are from working-class backgrounds with very low incomes (Anyon 1997). Suburban schools outspend urban schools despite equalization policies (Cuban 2004). A large portion of the funding that urban schools receive is put toward necessary special services including English as Second Language programs (Button 1993; Firestone, Goertz, and Natriello 1994; Kozol 1992).

Virtually all large-scale studies using comparative evidence have confirmed the discrimination against inner-city schools (and less frequently rural schools), black children, and those from lower-class origins, but few have looked at the interactive influence on long-term educational outcomes.

The most straightforward measure of educational success is school completion rate. If there were a condition of equality of result, roughly equal proportions of youths from all social backgrounds would be completing respective levels of schooling. In the United States with universal availability of high schools, the majority of students now finish high school. Recent estimates find that over two-thirds of all students now complete high school roughly with their age cohort, including three-quarters of whites and about 50 percent of blacks, 72 percent of females compared to 64 percent of males, and 76 percent of those in low poverty districts (as indicated by a dichotomized measure of free lunch programs) compared with 57 percent in high poverty districts (Swanson 2004). But postsecondary schooling has become the main level for social selection. The United States leads the world in the proportion of people completing university degrees, a figure that has been continually increasing since WWII (Statistics 2002). About a quarter of the entire adult population over twenty-five now have a university degree. Comparisons of university completion rates by class, residential area, race, and gender should be broadly indicative of the extent of discrimination that persists on these lines.

Our analyses, using the 2000 U.S. GSS, focus on university completion rates for those over twenty-five years of age, cohorts that have had a reasonable time to complete a degree program.

Differences in university completion rates by class of origin are very large. The average university completion rate for the entire over-twenty-five population in 2000 was around 25 percent. There are indications in these GSS data and from other sources that the vast majority of those from the tiny number of corporate capitalist families have completed university (Livingstone and Sawchuk 2003). Small employers and the self-employed cannot be disaggregated in these GSS data but prior studies have shown that children of small employers tend to have completion rates similar to managerial employees, while those from self-employed family backgrounds have completion rates similar to the children of industrial workers (Curtis, Livingstone, and Smaller 1992). The majority of children of managers and professional employees have completed university. About a quarter of the children of supervisory employees complete university, about the same proportion as children of service workers. Among the children of industrial workers, less than 15 percent have completed university. In sum, completion rates by class origin range from nearly universal among corporate capitalists' children to very small minorities among industrial workers' children. Class clearly matters.

Completion rate differences by residential area are less pronounced. Completion rates tend to be somewhat higher than the national average in suburban areas (32 percent) and just below the national average in both inner cities and outer suburbs. The major difference is the much lower completion rates among those in rural areas (13 percent). Children from all metropolitan areas are twice as likely as those from rural families to complete university.

Completion rates are greater for whites than for blacks. The national average for whites is about 27 percent, for blacks around 14 percent, a ratio of about 2:1. Gender differences in university completion rates in favor of males have narrowed in recent decades, but among the entire over-twenty-five population males are still somewhat more likely (28 percent) than females (23 percent).

For further analyses of class differences in relation to race and space, we will compare professional and managerial employees, sometimes termed the *professional-managerial class* (PMC), with service and industrial workers, often considered the core of the working class. Overall, as table 3.3 summarizes, about 55 percent of those from professional-managerial-class families have completed a university degree, compared to only 17 percent from working-class households. The average formal educational attainment of the U.S. population has increased very significantly in the post-WWII era, but the ratio of university completion for those from PMC and working-class origins has remained fairly constant at more than 3:1 (Livingstone 1999). It should be stressed here that the differences between those with capitalist-class origins and more marginalized or underclass members of the working class are much greater.

The ratio differences in completion rates by class origin are fairly constant across residential areas. While the majority of those from PMC families in all metropolitan areas have completed university, only a third of those in rural areas have done so. Nevertheless, the ratio of PMC completion compared to those from workers' families remains about 3:1 even in rural areas, because the completion rate for working-class children is even lower there (11 percent). About 20 percent of working-class kids in urban and suburban areas complete university, but this is significantly lower than the one-third of PMC kids who complete university even in the most rural areas. Class effects are considerably stronger than residential effects.

We should also note here that the ratio of white to black completion rates varies substantially across residential areas. The ratio is higher in inner cities (2.5:1) than suburbs (2:1) and outer suburbs (1.3:1), but highest in rural areas (4:1), which have much lower general completion rates and the lowest proportion of blacks and other minorities.

Table 3.3. University Completion Rates by Father's Occupational Class and Residential Area, U.S. 25+ Employed Labor Force, 2000

	Professional/Managerial					Industrial and Service Workers				
	Inner City	Suburb	Outer Suburb	Rural	Total	Inner City	Suburb	Outer Suburb	Rural	Total
N	53% (64)	58% (88)	59% (112)	32% (28)	55% (292)	21% (221)	19% (237)	16% (357)	11% (139)	17% (954)

Source: Davis, Smith, and Marsden (2002)

In examining class and race patterns of completion rates across spatial areas, as table 3.4 shows, we find that class and race effects are generally strong and mutually reinforcing. Whites in all classes and areas appear to have significantly higher university completion rates than blacks in the same class and area. The most extreme difference is between whites from suburban and exurban PMC families who have completion rates over 60 percent and blacks from rural working-class families who appear to have very little chance to complete university at all. Within urban areas, 53 percent of all of those from PMC families complete university degrees compared with 21 percent of those from workers' families. Race accentuates these class differences. From white PMC families, 57 percent obtain degrees, compared with 33 percent from black PMC families, 27 percent from white working-class families and 11 percent from black working-class families.

These national level statistics for university completion correspond quite closely with the most recent studies of the association of class and race with indicators of dropout rates at lower levels of schooling. Class and race both matter but class effects on educational outcomes are somewhat stronger when both are considered together (Rothstein 2004).

When gender effects are added, the extremes in university completion rates are somewhat greater. White suburban males from PMC origins have completion rates of 68 percent while black inner-city females from working-class origins have rates of 8 percent. Again, black rural working-class kids, especially girls, have virtually no chance to complete a degree.

In sum, the available recent national survey statistics find very large differences in educational outcomes by class origins that are accentuated by race and less so by gender. Those from rural areas are consistently disadvantaged whatever their class origins, race, and gender. Within urban areas, white PMC kids are nearly five times as likely as black working-class kids (56 percent vs. 12 percent) to complete university. These findings suggest that there are still many discriminatory conditions and barriers that need to be better documented and overcome in order to approach any sort of educational equality both within urban areas and more generally.

Table 3.4. University Completion Rate by Father's Class, Race, and Residential Area, U.S. 25+ Employed Labor Force, 2000

| | Professional/Managerial | | | | Industrial and Service Workers | | | |
	Inner City	Suburb	Outer Suburb	Rural	Total	Inner City	Suburb	Outer Suburb	Rural	Total
Whites	56%	62%	61%	33%	57%	27%	21%	16%	11%	18%
Blacks	38%	25%	50%	*%	33%	12%	11%	15%	0%	11%
Total	53%	58%	59%	32%	100%	21%	19%	16%	11%	100%
N					(152)					(156)

Source: Davis, Smith, and Marsden (2002)
*N too small for reliable estimate

CASE STUDIES OF BARRIERS TO EDUCATIONAL EQUALITY

Many researchers have attempted to examine some of these profiled differences in more depth, although typically using simpler class and space distinctions. We offer a brief review of these studies here with particular reference to those which have attended to class differences.

Class and Curriculum

Numerous studies have documented the "hidden curriculum," showing how teachers tend to treat students from different socioeconomic backgrounds differently and tacitly discriminate against working-class children (Rosenthal 1968). More rarely, some researchers have conducted comparative case studies of how the curriculum is delivered in schools with clearly different social class compositions.

The most relevant of these is probably the ethnography of grade five classrooms in urban and suburban New Jersey communities of contrasting social class composition in 1980 by Jean Anyon. Anyon did a detailed observation of the curricular, pedagogical, and pupil evaluation practices in these schools. The schools included an executive elite school and an affluent professional school in suburban areas and working-class schools in urban areas; that is, these schools were in communities where corporate capitalists, top managers and professionals, and workers, respectively tended to predominate. There were striking differences between these classrooms.

Students in the executive elite school were being trained to develop their analytical skills by reasoning through problems independently. They were given a great deal of autonomy and responsibility in both assignments and movement about the school. Teachers were generally available before and after school to provide extra help if needed. This is an extremely exceptional public school, both because of the very tiny numbers of capitalist-class families and because most of their children probably attend private schools. The school was also all white.

In the affluent professional school, student work was generally creative activity carried out independently and often led to a strong sense of project ownership. The teacher constantly negotiated with the class rather than giving direct orders. But there were some explicit restrictions on student movement.

In the working-class schools, students were expected to follow orders and procedures in a mechanical form with very little opportunity to make decisions. Students were not told why the work was being assigned or the idea behind the work, and they needed permission to leave the classroom at all.

Other studies have also illustrated that the curriculum being taught in schools differs based on the predominant social class of the students in schools (Hallinger and Murphy 1986). Clearly, students in these schools were being groomed for future higher levels of schooling or work based on their social class. Admittedly, in many communities the class composition is much more mixed and the classroom practices will probably be as well. On the other hand, in the inner cities of large metropolitan areas, such as New York and Cleveland, the concentration of working-class kids of minority backgrounds may be even greater and the curricular practices may be even more biased against their success.

"High Poverty" Schools

Low-income students usually attend impoverished schools whether they are located in urban or rural areas (Stephens and Jenkins 1994). The following description of a low-income school gives a good example of the type of environment students encounter. These conditions play a significant role in the ability to succeed in school.

The principal at Locke High School in Los Angeles, California, describes the low SES school: "Three thousand students attend the school, which has an average class size of 37 students. More than half of the school's 120 teachers have fewer than two years teaching experience. The 9th grade class of 1,200 students shrinks to approximately 250 students by senior year. Textbooks for specific classes are apt to be unavailable." This school's setting—characterized by unwieldy class sizes, inexperienced teachers, large numbers of at-risk students, low expectations for its student body, and lack of resources—differs enormously from the settings of more-affluent schools: "A few miles away in Beverly Hills and Santa Monica, where the high school principals don't have to worry about textbook availability, large class size, poorly trained teachers, or students who won't make it to college" (Winerup 2003).

In addition, inner city schools in the United States are now generally old buildings that have not been well maintained; they are dirty and are not well equipped with supplies (New Jersey State Department of Education 1994).

Teachers and Teacher Expectations

Students in both urban and rural schools are faced with greater teacher shortages than the suburbs. In both areas, students have teachers with the lowest qualifications (Monk and Haller 1993; Wirt et al. 2003). Teachers at urban or rural high school levels are more likely to be teaching out of their areas of study; students are more likely to be faced with teachers with less than three years' experience or who were hired based on "emergency" credentials, and teachers who are long-term substitutes (Sparks 2000). Teachers in urban schools are paid less than those from suburban schools and they are more likely to suffer from burnout if they have been teaching in the urban system for a long period of time (Andrews and Morefield 1991; Miron and St. John 2003). Rural schools are faced with the difficulty of luring teachers to remote areas with low salaries (Collins et al. 2003).

The more impoverished the students are in both urban and rural communities, the lower the expectations held by their teachers (Capper 1990; MacCleod 1995). The expectations teachers have for the success of their students has been shown to have direct and indirect impacts on the educational experience of students in both urban and rural schools (Edington and Koehler 1987; Kozol 1992). Furthermore, students in both areas perceive that teachers do not normally expect high achievements (Brown, Anfara Jr., and Roney 2004; Neito 2003).

The following quotes drawn from Anyon's (1997) more recent observations in urban New Jersey working-class classrooms illustrate the persistence of low expectations among at least some teachers in these setting:

"Shut up and push those pencils. Push those pencils—you borderline people!" (Black teacher to his class of Black and Hispanic sixth graders)" (29)

"If I had a gun I'd kill you. You're all hoodlums." (White fifth grade teacher)" (29)

"Don't you have *any* attention span? You have the attention span of cherries!" (White principal trying to quiet a class of Black and Hispanic fourth graders)" (30).

Parental School Involvement

Students from poor families have been found to own on average fewer books; to be read to much less often; be less likely to be taken to museums, public libraries, a play, or to participate in dance, art, music, or craft classes; to spend more hours watching television; be more likely to have only one parent; and to move their residence more often (Lee and Burkam 2002; Rothestein 2004). All of these differences aid students from more privileged backgrounds to be more successful in the conventional "middle class" school curriculum. Students from low-income families are also less likely to participate in after-school activities that boost confidence and allow parents to discuss their children's schooling (Lareau 2000; Rothstein 2004). Students from rural areas are further disadvantaged by the distance to many of these activities and the lack of accessibility for their parents.

Parent involvement in the management of schools has been shown to have a positive impact on the effectiveness of the school for their children (Leithwood and Montgomery 1986; Long 1986). Parents of working-class children are less likely to get involved (Rothstein 2004). Rural lower-class parents are even less likely to participate due to additional distance barriers.

Student Voices

In light of the many barriers faced by working-class students, especially black working-class students, in inner city (as well as rural) settings, it is hardly surprising that ethnographic studies that have listened to these kids' own voices have frequently heard very pessimistic stories. For example, among the elementary students from urban working-class homes in Anyon's (1997) more recent study, the following are representative:

> A thirteen-year-old white girl was asked by the interviewer why some kids don't do well. Her response: "Kids don't want to learn. They be playin' in the halls. They don't study." The interviewer asked, "Why not?" "It's boring and they get mad at teachers." Interviewer: "How do you think the teachers feel about that?" "They don't care. [Pause] If we don't learn, they teachers still gets their paycheck" (32).

> A ten-year-old African American boy describes his teachers:
> "Most teachers here don't teach us." "Why not?" "Because of the kids. They runs the halls and makes the teachers upset." "Why do they do that?" "Um, they think [teachers] just doin' the job for the money, they don't care" (32).

> A nine-year-old African American boy talks about his teacher:
> "He says we're animals. Hooligans. He said we should be in a zoo. I feel bad when he say that. I get kinda sad" (32).

Older urban working-class kids often recount stories about the process of being selected out of any prospect of postsecondary education. For example, in Jay MacLeod's (1995) study of Oakland high school students, a white working-class boy talks about how he ended up getting streamed into a vocational stream at school:

> "You start school as a freshman and you start cutting one class, right, and when that teacher starts giving you a hard time—this is how it started with me: I wasn't good in history and spelling and shit—and he wouldn't ever have got me a tutor or nothing. So then I said, "Fuck it." He wasn't passing me so then I stopped going to his class. Then he would spread the word around to the other teachers, and they would give me a hard time, and I'd stop going to their classes" (94).

These voices may or may not be representative of urban working-class children's general experiences in U.S. schools. But, at minimum, they express deep-seated systemic barriers overcome only by exceptional perseverance.

CONCLUSION

The research reported here indicates a massive amount of wasted talent among the U.S. working class, especially those living in inner-city areas as well as remote rural areas. Race discrimination certainly accentuates the waste of talent in all classes but particularly in the large working class. Gender discrimination also persists, although not as pronounced a current factor in educational outcomes. This talent use gap is hardly unique to the United States (Livingstone 1999; Livingstone and Sawchuk 2003). But the increasingly high general level of formal educational attainment makes the inequality of educational outcomes appear most evident here. On the other hand, the extensive development of institutions at all levels of formal schooling does provide *relatively* straightforward opportunities for educational reforms within existing institutions to begin to address these inequities.

Among the most immediately feasible reform steps are the following (Hodgkinson 2003; Johnson, Boyden, and Pittz 2001):

- Fully implement a Head Start program to assist working-class children to begin school on a fairer footing
- Provide decently funded early child-care programs to assist working-class parents to more effectively balance employment and nurturing duties
- Reform existing schools in urban areas by breaking them into smaller schools often within the same building (e.g., Julia Richman model in New York City), and in rural areas by using more mobile pools of teachers to ensure less commute time for students. In both cases, closer relations of teachers and working-class parents could be nurtured.
- Create some small demonstration schools in each area designed to operate with a deep commitment to principles and practices of class, race, space, and gender equity and fuller awareness of the systemic and interactive biases documented by the research discussed here.

As we argued in a prior book about the history of working-class streaming and designs for more equitable school systems (Curtis et al.

1992), dominant (capitalist and PMC) class politics have continually aided and abetted the construction of harsh and destructive streaming practices on all of the above criteria. Some form of more democratic class and race alliances probably will be needed to move toward seriously challenging the discriminatory exclusion, especially in inner city and rural areas, of working-class children.

REFERENCES

Andrews, R. L., and Morefield, J. (1991). Effective Leadership for Effective Urban Schools. *Education and Urban Society* 23 (3), 270–78.

Anyon, J. (1980). Social Class and the Hidden Curriculum of Work. In W. Pinar (ed.), *Curriculum and Instruction*. Berkeley, Calif.: McCutchan Publishing Corporation.

Anyon, J. (1997). *Ghetto Schooling: A Political Economy of Urban Educational Reform*. New York: Teachers College Press.

Archer, L., and Yamashita, H. (2003). 'Knowing Their Limits'? Identities, Inequalities and Inner City School Leavers Post-16 Aspirations. *Journal of Education Policy* 18 (1), 53–69.

Brooks, D. Take a Ride to Exurbia. *New York Times*. November 9, 2004.

Brown, K. M., Anfara Jr., V. A., and Roney, K. (2004). Student Achievement in High Performing, Suburban Middle Schools and Low Performing Urban Middle Schools. *Education and Urban Society* 36 (4), 428–56.

Bussière, P. (2001). *Measuring Up: The Performance of Canada's Youth in Reading, Mathematics and Science : OECD PISA Study: First Result for Canadians Aged 15*. Ottawa: Statistics Canada.

Button, H. W. (1993). City Schools and School Systems: Sources of Centralization and Bureacracy. In S. W. Rothstein (ed.), *Handbook of Schooling in Urban America*. Westport, Conn.: Greenwood Press.

Capper, C. A. (1990). Students with Low-Incidence Disabilities in Disadvantaged, rural settings. *Exceptional Children* 56 (4), 338–44.

Collins, A., Press, H., and Galway, G. (2003). Maintaining Quality Programming in Rural Newfoundland and Labrador: A Case Study in Policy and Structural Change. *Education Canada* 43 (3), 20–23, 38–39.

Cuban, L. (2004). Meeting Challenges in Urban Schools. *Educational Leadership* (April 2004), 64–69.

Curtis, B., Livingstone, D. W., and Smaller, H. (1992). *Stacking the Deck: The Streaming of Working-Class Kids in Ontario Schools*. Toronto: Our Schools/Our Selves Education Foundation.

Davidson, J. (2002). Oakland's Community Propels Change for Equity: The Small Schools Initiative's History and Challenges. *Horace* 18 (4).

Davis, J., Allan, T., Smith, W., and Marsden, P. V. (2002). *General Social Surveys, 1972–2002: [CUMULATIVE FILE][Computer File]*

Edington, E. D., and Koehler, L. (1987). *Rural Student Achievement: Elements for Consideration.* http://newfirstsearch.oclc.org (accessed September 25, 2004).

Firestone, W., Goertz, M., and Natriello, G. (1994). The Myth of Bottomless Pits and Crumbling Lighthouses: Two Years of New Jersey's Quality Education. In J. Anyon (ed.), *Ghetto Schooling: A Political Economy of Urban Educational Reform.* New York: Teachers College Press.

Fullerton, H. (1999). Labor force projections to 2008: steady growth and changing composition. *Monthly Labor Review*, 19–32.

Ginzberg, E. (1993). The Changing Urban Scene: 1900–1960 and Beyond. In H. G. Cisneros (ed.), *Interwoven Destinies: Cities and the Nation.* New York: W.W. Norton.

Hallinger, P., and Murphy, J. F. (1986). What's Effective for Whom? School Context and Student Achievement. *Planning and Changing* 16 (3), 152–60.

Hatfield, L. L. (2002). *"Up the Back Holler, Down the Dusty Road, Cross the Windy Prairie": Issues, Perspectives, and Strategies for Research in the Crisis of Improving Mathematical Education of Rural Youth.* Athens: Ohio University.

Hodgkinson, H. L. (2003). Leaving Too Many Children Behind: A Demographer's View on the Neglect of America's Youngest Children. *Source* (April 2003), 25.

Hough, D., and Sills-Briegel, T. (1997). Student Achievement and Middle Level Programs, Policies, and Practices in Rural America: The Case of Community-Based Versus Consolidated Organizations. *Journal of Research in Rural Education* 13 (1), 64–70.

Hudson, L., and Shafter, L. *Vocational Education Offerings in Rural High Schools.* (Fall 2002). http://nces.ed.gov/pubs2002/2002120.pdf (accessed September 20, 2004).

Johnson, T., Boyden, J. E., and Pittz, W. J. (2001). *Racial Profiling and Punishment in U.S. Public Schools: How Zero Tolerance Policies and High Stakes Testing Subvert Academic Excellence and Racial Equity. Research Report [and] Executive Summary.*

Kingston, P. (2000). *The Classless Society.* Stanford: Stanford University Press.

Kozol, J. (1992). *Savage Inequalities: Children in America's Schools.* New York: Harper Perennial.

Lareau, A. (2000). *Home Advantage: Social Class and Parental Intervention in Elementary Education,* 2nd ed. Lanham, Md.: Rowman & Littlefield Publishers.

Lee, V., and Burkam, D. (2002). *Inequality at the Starting Gate.* Washington, D.C.: Economic Policy Institute.

Leithwood, R., and Montgomery, D. (1986). *The Principal Profile.* Toronto: OISE Press.

Livingstone, D. W. (1983). *Class, Ideologies and Educational Futures.* London & Philadelphia: Falmer Press.

Livingstone, D. W. (1999). *The Education Jobs Gap: Underemployment or Economic Democracy.* Toronto: Garamond Press.

Livingstone, D. W., and Mangan, J. M. (1996). *Recast Dreams: Class and Gender Consciousness in Steeltown.* Toronto: Garamond Press.

Livingstone, D. W., and Sawchuk, P. (2003). *Hidden Knowledge: Organized Labour in the Information Age.* Toronto: Garamond Press.

Long, R. (1986). *Developing Parental Involvement in Primary Schools.* London: MacMillan Education.

MacCleod, J. (1995). *Ain't No Makin' It.* Boulder, Colo.: Westview Press.

Miron, L. F. E., and St. John, E. P. E. (2003). *Reinterpreting Urban School Reform: Have Urban Schools Failed, or Has the Reform Movement Failed Urban Schools?* Albany, N.Y.: State University of New York Press.

Monk, D. H., and Haller, E. J. (1993). Predictions of High School Academic Course Offerings: The Role of School Size. *American Educational Research Journal* 30 (1), 3–21.

National Center for Education Statistics. (1998). *The Condition of Education 1998.* Washington, D.C.: U.S. Department of Education, National Center Education Statistics.

Neito, S. (2003). School Reform and Student Learning: A Multicultural Perspective. In J. A. Banks and C. A. McGee Banks (eds.), *Multicultural Education: Issues and Perspectives*, 4th ed. New York: John Wiley & Sons.

New Jersey State Department of Education. (1994). *Comprehensive Compliance Investigation of the Newark Public Schools.* Trenton: Author.

Rosenthal, R. (1968). *Pygmalion in the Classroom; Teacher Expectation and Pupils' Intellectual Development.* New York: Holt, Rinehart & Winston.

Rothstein, R. (2004). *Class and Schools: Using Social, Economic, and Educational Reform to Close the Black-White Achievement Gap.* Washington, D.C.: Teachers College, Columbia University.

Seccombe, W., and Livingstone, D. W. (1999). *"Down-to-Earth People": Beyond Class Reductionism and Postmodernity.* Toronto: Garamond Press.

Sherman, A. (1992). Children's Defense Fund Reports on Children in Rural America. *Family Resource Coalition* 11 (1), 12–13.

Sparks, D. (2000). High-powered Professional Development for High Poverty Schools. *Principal Leadership* 1 (4), 26–29.

Statistics, NCFE (2002). *The Conditions of Education 2002, NCES 2002–2005*. Washington, D.C.: U.S. Government Printing Office, 2002. National Center for Education Statistics.

Stephens, J. C., and Jenkins, S. J. (1994). Affective Middle Grade Program Elements and Criterion Based Achievement in Georgia Schools. *Reading Improvement* 31 (2), 66–71.

Stowe, S. L. (2001). *Mind the Gap: Accessibility to Canadian Universities*. Unpublished manuscript. University of Toronto, OISE, Toronto.

Swanson, C. B. (2004). *The Real Truth about Low Graduation Rates, An Evidence-Based Commentary*. San Francisco: Education Policy Center, Urban Institute.

Thirunarayanan, M. O. (2004). The "Significantly Worse" Phenomenon. A Study of Student Achievement in Different Content Areas by School Location. *Education and Urban Society* 36 (4), 467–81.

Valdez, V. (2000). *An Evaluation of the Chicago Public Schools' Efforts to Relieve Student Overcrowding at Elementary Schools. Progress Report*. Chicago, Ill.: Joyce Foundation.

Winerup, M. A Test for Schwarzenegger: Adding Muscle to Bare Bone. *New York Times*. November 5, 2003. A-21.

Wirt, J., Choy, S., Gerald, D., Provasnik, S., Rooney, P., Watanabe, S., et al. (2003). *The Condition of Education 2002*. Washington, D.C.: National Center for Education Statistics; U.S. Department of Education.

Wright, E. O. (1980). Class and Occupation. *Theory and Society* 9, 177–214.

Wright, E. O. (1997). *Class Counts: Comparative Studies in Class Analysis*. Cambridge: Cambridge University Press.

Wrigley, J. (2003). Centralization Versus Fragmentation: The Public School Systems of New York and Los Angeles. In D. Halle (ed.), *New York and Los Angeles: Politics, Society, and Culture: A Comparative View* (225–50). Chicago: University of Chicago Press.

CHAPTER 4

Corporate Consciousness and the Failure of Higher Education

Phil Graham, Carmen Luke, and Allan Luke

INTRODUCTION

Academics who worked through the 1960s' critical reinvention of the university could be excused for indulging in a bit of historical romanticism, nostalgia for a golden age of academic freedom where the pursuit of knowledge was valued in and of itself. Of course, there are those of our senior colleagues who lost their tenure and jobs during the McCarthy era who would tell us a different story. And there are many of our colleagues who continue to work in universities throughout the world where government maintains strict surveillance and censorship of academic work. Universities in the political economies of the North/West today are caught in a pincer move of ideologically, though not systematically, related forces. This entails, on the one hand, an ongoing surveillance and attack from neoconservatives and the Christian right on what they perceive as an ongoing left turn in the humanities and social sciences. This is illustrated by the recent call from conservative student groups at UCLA to report lecturing staff who veer too far off the current "PC neo-con" stance. Yet it dovetails from another movement that runs to the heart of university governance, the management of everyday life, and the reemphasis on the political-economic significance of universities: the explicit reframing of universities as businesses, adjuncts and extensions of multinational corporate structure, governance and market ideology.

This entails an ideological shift toward the values of the corporatist state, a revaluing of knowledge and power in the university that impacts both hierarchy and stratification of knowledge, fields and staffing of *Homo academicus* transformed into *Homo economicus*. This has very real consequences in everyday life for the academy: from changing modalities of instruction, shifting syllabus content, prioritization of grants and consultancies according to corporatist agendas, and the emergence of technical grids of specification for micronizing, quantifying and monitoring almost all aspects of academic endeavor: teaching and learning, research and scholarship, student practice, and the structure and availability of intellectual and textual archives. Faced with these trends, a bit of utopianism and romanticism among academics—whose self-objectification in discourse is their very stock and trade (Bourdieu 1990)—might very well be in order. But this must be tempered by a healthy skepticism toward the very idea of an academy uncontaminated by dominant political-economic trends and forces. This chapter provides a history of the present, the presence of corporate consciousness in the postmodern Western university, and failure of the higher education systems' custodians to critically address the more pernicious impacts of corporatism upon the future of human understanding.

A BRIEF HISTORICAL PASTICHE OF ACADEMIC SUBSERVIENCE

Since the blueprint for the western university was created under Charlemagne in the ninth century, higher education has been subservient to external political aims and interests. After the collapse of Roman influence in Western Europe, learning and literacy went into severe decline (Thurow 1996, 281–88). Charlemagne issued his *admonitio generalis*, a significant part of which was to establish "schools near the cathedrals or in the monasteries" (Ganshof 1949, 522). The main purpose of this part of his constitutional edict (the other concerned with establishing a system of law for his new empire) was to provide intellectual labor for the careful transcription and correction of "biblical and liturgical texts," and to ensure at least minimal literacy standards among clergy (1949, 522). Charlemagne's edict simultaneously provided the founding model of the contemporary higher education university system and the modern legal system.

By the thirteenth century, the higher education system in Western Europe had developed into a flourishing, formalized system of knowledge production designed to produce ecclesiastical, bureaucratic, and professional elites for the organization of new political and ideological systems, and which spanned increasingly larger areas (Haskins 1904; Strayer 1970):

> In the intellectual life of the middle ages the University of Paris occupies a place of preëminent importance. "The Italians have the Papacy, the Germans have the Empire, and the French have Learning," ran the old saying; and the chosen abode of Learning was Paris. The University of Paris was generally recognized as "the parent of the sciences" and the first school of the church, and its supremacy was manifest not only in its position as the centre of scholasticism and the bulwark of orthodoxy, but also in the large number and wide distribution of its students, in its influence upon the establishment and the constitutions of other universities, and in its large share in the political and ecclesiastical movements of the later middle ages (Haskins 1904, 1).

In his investigation of the sermon form in the higher education system that emanated from Paris, Haskins notes that, like contemporary government policies, "sermons are not historical but hortatory" (1904, 2). That is, their primary purpose was "to get people to do things," just as contemporary government policy aims to do (Muntigl 2001, 147).

It can be argued that Charlemagne's higher education system was the basis of modern mass media systems insofar as its pedagogical forms and functions were deployed to produce sufficiently uniform attitudes, perceptions, and regulatory effects across large cultural and geographical spaces to shore up centralized political power. In its more mature incarnations, clear similarities can be seen between the systems of pedagogical dissemination used by the Paris university system and those developed for contemporary mass media. These include the development and formalization of generic forms of expression (genres), a concomitant development of public boredom with these increasingly predictable and formulaic modes of expression, and an incipient "attention economy" (Goldhaber 1999) that took hold within the populations exposed to official genres of the day (Graham and Hearn 2000). A case in point is the spread of the sermon form for populist, political, and ecclesiastical purposes. It led to a proliferation of exempla, the stories "with which the sermons are embellished" to demonstrate the recurring pedagocial *thema* (themes) of thirteenth-century dogma and *doxa* (Haskins 1904, 3). Like contemporary mass media, these stories "came from all kinds of sources—fables and folk-lore, bestiaries, lives of saints, historical manuals, and personal experiences" (1904, 3). From "reality" TV, to the beatification of media and political personalities, to the Grimm Brothers folk fantasies remediated by Disney, the generic appropriations of contemporary mass media remain the same in essence, purpose, and degree of formalization as those of the thirteenth-century university system in western Europe: attention, agenda-setting, the exercise of power in the fullest sense through generic identification with instructions given in sermon form.

Similar effects of ritualizing public discourse (which is what the sermon form was in the thirteenth century) can also be seen during this period. Just as "the battle for attention" has become a key focus of strategic communication in the current environment (Goldhaber 1999), the popular preacher in the thirteenth century had to work very hard to get attention once the sermon had become the means of communication for all kinds of public discourse:

> In order to hold the attention of the people the preachers found it necessary to be entertaining, as well as simple and direct, and to make abundant use of marvels, anecdotes, and pointed illustrations from everyday life. If his audience showed signs of nodding, the speaker would begin, "There was once a king named Arthur," or shout suddenly, "That fellow asleep will not give away my secrets" (Haskins 1904, 3).

This is a description of "edutainment" by any other name. Haskins comments on Abelard, a popular twelfth-century professor, who was "a classroom entertainer, bold, original, lucid, sharply polemical, always fresh and stimulating and withal able to move to laughter the minds of serious men" (1957, 40). University chancellors of the day "were themselves masters and generally distinguished preachers as well" (Haskins 1904, 8). Given the power of both clergy and aristocracy at the time, it is not surprising that knowledge first begins to get confused with power. This illusion persists. It has become an uncritical, mantric assertion since Francis Bacon that "knowledge is power" (KIPP 2005).

Knowledge and power are not isomorphic—knowledge is not power. Power is enacted in one's ability to directly convert and mobilize one's words into the actions of others; hence the etymologies of "dictator" and "authoritarian," the political categories of orally and scribally enacted political coercion. Rather than demonstrating that "knowledge is power," the history of higher education is better summarized in the words of an early twentieth-century "business man": namely, that "brains are cheap" (Perry 1916, 443).

By way of explanation he went on to say that any one could hire a college professor for $5,000 a year. Many would doubtless detect a non sequitur in this reasoning; but it is clear that in self-defense a college professor is bound to insist that being expensive is not the only way of being valuable. He may be driven to retort that the cheapest things in the world, things that are given and free, such as the grace of God, are often the most esteemed (1916, 443).

Perry's assertion emphasizes that institutions of higher education have continued to function largely as organs of contemporary political power, whatever the basis, orientation, and legitimating principles of that power. The alleged "academic freedom" inscribed in so many contemporary university constitutions is a double-edged sword. While the ideal has existed for centuries, the reality remains that academic freedoms exist only insofar as dominant political forces permit. John Wilson is worth citing at length on this point:

> The "war on terror" provides justification for many of the worst infringements of academic freedom, but beneath the veneer of "patriotic correctness" a deeper assault on academic values was accelerating: the corporatization of higher education. During a time of budget cuts at campuses across the country, whether caused by state deficits or stock market woes, academic freedom sometimes is sacrificed for the bottom line (2005).

The corporate influence on academia is often direct, via corporate sponsorships of athletic programs, buildings, probusiness departments, and scientific research. But the corporate model is equally damaging, imposing a cult of efficiency and authoritarianism upon the collegial ideal of higher education. According to the corporate model, profit making trumps liberty, and appeasing the most powerful economic interests is the duty of every administrator. Following corporate America's embrace of temp workers, today 43 percent of college faculty are adjuncts or part-timers, more than double the level two decades ago. Under the corporate model, liberal education is secondary to money-making training (Wilson 2005).

Yet the phenomenon of education "appeasing the most powerful economic interests" is neither new nor confined to the United States. As with the current trend to turn the organs of higher education into a massified corporatist credentialing system in which preparation for employment and other forms of wealth generation have become fundamental institutional motivators, the sixteenth-century English higher education responded to demands by the new "propertied classes"—a historically new class created by enclosures and Puritan "leveller" movements—to produce a higher education "boom" of quite dramatic dimensions (Stone 1964). The boom was in large part a response to demands "for vocational training by sons of bourgeoisie, professional classes and clergy" (Stone 1964, 41).

> What seems to have been happening is this: in the middle years of the sixteenth century the propertied classes began demanding University education for their children, and seized upon the college system for this purpose . . . The result was a flow of charitable gifts to increase the capital assets and buildings of the Colleges and a sharp rise in the emoluments of dons, who now made a comfortable living by the supervision of these well-heeled pupils (1964, 67).

Consider a similar scenario today: the MBA and corporate benefice. Every working person is either a manager, aspires to be one, or is strongly encouraged to be the very model of one (cf. Fairclough 2000). The Macquarie Graduate School of Management (Australia) identifies the significance of an MBA in the current climate:

> The MGSM MBA is designed for individuals already in positions of responsibility who have been identified as possessing higher management and leadership potential, or those who aspire to a position of general management. The MBA is a generalist degree designed to give students a solid grounding in the core aspects of general management. It aims to provide a strategic business perspective, focusing on the competitive advantage of the enterprise. The MBA teaches students how to manage

functional areas and understand the language they use, not how to perform the functions with technical expertise (MGSM 2006).

According to the above, the Macquarie MBA is not a technical degree. It is a philosophical enterprise: functional, linguistically based, applied, and entirely corporatist. It is designed to appeal to "leaders" only, or to those who have the aspiration and financial capability to become one. The University of Queensland Business School (Australia) is quite explicit in its claim that competitive advantage in assessing MBAs lies in the degree to which corporate representatives underwrite and endorse the degree program:

> . . . every course in the MBA ensures strong practical links with industry through the involvement of practicing managers as guest presenters. We enjoy supportive relationships with some of Australia's leading organisations, including ACCC, Accenture, ANZ Bank, Austrade, Boral Group, Boston Consulting Group, Brisbane City Council, Building Services Authority, Colmar Brunton, Commonwealth Bank, David Jones, DBM Australia, Deloitte Touché Tohmatsu, Endeavour Foundation, Flight Centre, Golden Casket, GRM International, JP Morgan, KPMG, Macquarie Bank, PricewaterhouseCoopers, Queensland State Development, Queensland Transport, Queensland Treasury, Queensland Public Works, Robert Walters/Dunhill Management Services, Suncorp, Telstra, Tanner Menzies and TMP Worldwide.
>
> And what enthusiastic aspirant to upper management could resist such a lineup of prospective contacts, employment and networking opportunities? These groups and their representatives are the most powerful elites in the state, many representing powerful National and International interests. For public universities, with state funding levels falling at accelerating rates, the imperative (or excuse, depending on one's point of view) is clear: corporates are "the only game in town" as funding sources; industry patronage is essential to financial survival; aspiration to the higher echelons of the corporate world is a primary motivational source for student enrollment; MBA students pay full fees and can be lucrative sources of significant philanthropy. Funding policy also feeds into the imperative to align educational with corporate interests. "Linkage" funding (so called in Australia but common almost everywhere under one name or another) requires that university researchers have a corporate partner to be eligible for federal or "matching" funding.

Universities throughout the western world are being urged to "commercialize" research and the number of patents, journals, and academic papers are booming as national funding agencies increasingly tie "national research priorities" to corporatist, "outcomes-based" research (e.g., Australian Research Council [ARC] 2006; Social Sciences and Humanities Research Council [SSHRC] 2006).

This trend is similar to the many changes in educational orientation since early modernists conceived of nationhood, industrialization, and their attendant implications and imperatives in regard to pedagogies those enterprises required (Strayer 1970). The imperatives of modernism's projects extend to the most quotidian and personal aspects of existence and consciousness, including and especially language:

> The official language is bound up with the state, both in its genesis and in its social uses. It is in the process of state formation that the conditions are created for the constitution of a unified linguistic market, dominated by the official language. Obligatory on official occasions and in official places (schools, public administrations, political institutions, etc.), this state language becomes the theoretical norm against which all linguistic practices are objectively measured (Bourdieu 1991, 45).

The development of the industrialized state follows the same logic as the nation-state:

> . . . in order to unify the whole system, the characteristic limitations of the House of Terror[1] were introduced as far as possible into the school: silence, absence of motion, complete passivity, response only upon the application of an outer stimulus, rote learning, verbal parroting, piecework acquisition of knowledge—these gave the school the happy attributes of jail and factory combined (Mumford 1934/1963, 176).

And, just as mid-twentieth-century education was oriented toward producing citizens for "New Deal" nation-states in the process of renewal and rebuilding, Dewey (1928), Taylor (1911/1997), and Wilson (1887) heralded the early-twentieth century move to political economic and education systems based on scientific method. They were the "fathers" of, respectively, scientific education, scientific management, and scientific public administration. The orientation aspects of education systems historically coincide with the orientation forces of political-economic context more generally. The systemic and structural aspects of technologized societies had been developing for centuries, all the while responding to the demands of dominant political economic forces. Bacon's "statists" (Ranney 1976, 143) are the progenitors of modern technocracy, and education systems are the media through which their ends have been achieved over the centuries. Education—particularly higher education—is the most powerful mass medium of the modern and premodern eras. All children must pass through institutionalized schooling and credentialing and all professional and industrial-business elites are processed and "certified" through higher education. In an age of corporatism, it should come as no surprise that higher education has become oriented toward producing elites for the corporate world and that the mark of university "excellence" in an era of corporatism is the ability to attract corporate investment.

But while there is a historical regularity in the coincidence of corporatized university with corporatist states, there is at the same time a unique difference in kind for higher education that springs from the character and ethos of global corporatism. Early medieval "higher education" systems were geographically and discursively situated in and around monasteries, churches, and royal palaces: the education system was auspiced by, and located within, ruling aristocratic and religious institutions. Similarly, during modern nation-state development, schools, colleges, and universities were primarily organs of the state. Even in the United States where industrialists such as Ezra Cornell, John Rockefeller, Leland Stanford, and other "robber barons" founded U.S. Ivy League higher-education institutions, the need to produce persons who would fit the ideal model for citizenship in industrialized states was paramount in the establishment of these ostensibly philanthropic endeavors. Leland Stanford echoes the political-economic spirit of his day, providing an endowment for an institution that would

> qualify students for personal success and direct usefulness in life; and to promote the public welfare by exercising an influence on behalf of humanity and civilization, teaching the blessings of liberty regulated by law, and inculcating love and reverence for the great principles of government as derived from the inalienable rights of man to life, liberty, and the pursuit of happiness (Stanford University 2005).

Stanford dictated a charter with the explicit aims of

> creating a great university, one that, from the outset, was untraditional: coeducational, in a time when most were all-male; nondenominational, when most were associated with a religious organization; avowedly practical, producing "cultured and useful citizens" . . . (Stanford 2005).

In short, just as the medieval higher education system was firmly situated inside the sociopolitical structures of the church and aristocracy and designed to produce personnel for the maintenance of the system, Stanford's charter, like those of his contemporaries, reflects the spirit of the day: a nationalistic, technologically oriented, secular higher education institution designed to produce people who would become model leaders of secular, postenlightenment capitalist states.

HISTORICAL NOVELTY AND THE CHARACTER OF CORPORATE CONSCIOUSNESS

Three differences distinguish corporatist higher education. First, the most influential corporatist universities are rarely genuine corporate entities or offshoots. That is, they exist largely outside formal corporate structures. Exceptions such as the McDonald's Corporation "Hamburger University" usually focus on narrow training purposes: "exclusively to instruct personnel employed by McDonald's Corporation or employed by McDonald's Independent Franchisees in the various aspects of the business" (McDonald's 2005). The current trend is toward the creation of many more corporate universities, a profitable move not only for generating tax deductions, but also for providing corporation-specific "human capital" (albeit at taxpayers' expense) because corporately nonsponsored universities are inherently unprofitable as "businesses," if only because the continued search for "pure" or "basic" knowledge is such a long-term proposition.

Global Learning Resources Inc. (2005), a corporation specializing in setting up universities for other corporations, ascribes the impetus for corporately owned institutions to a decreasing workforce comprised increasingly of low-skilled workers:

An early response to these pressures was to increase the amount of training available to all employees, and to focus extra effort on executive development. We saw a plethora of management offsite, strategic development seminars, and executive MBAs. General Electric's John F. Welch Leadership Center at Crotonville, New York became a model for other firms to emulate. Jack Welch became the model CEO, leading the training sessions and becoming the champion of continuous development (Global Learning Resources 2005).

Whether or not these kinds of corporate universities proliferate to any substantial extent and become intellectually and politically influential remains to be seen. The Association to Advance Collegiate Schools of Business (AACSB), an influential business school accreditation body, noted that 1,600 corporations were operating their own universities, "including 40 percent of Fortune 500 companies," predicting that "the number of corporate universities will exceed the number of traditional universities by the year 2010, if not sooner" (AACSB 1999). Whether or not this happens will be symptomatic of corporatist assessments of highly specialized education. The main implication of this first characteristic of the corporatized university is that the most influential exist outside the formal structures of corporatism. And yet they increasingly depend on corporate benefice and, importantly, corporatist consciousness shapes the most influential higher education institutions. This leads to the second historical difference: corporatist modes of coercion.

Marx and Engels made the fairly noncontentious statement that the "ideas of the ruling class are, in every age, the ruling ideas; the class which is the dominant material force in society is at the same time its dominant intellectual force" (1846/1972, 118). The capitalist propertied class had as its primary means of coercion the constant threat of starvation among the working classes. Today, the ruling class is the corporate "executive" class. Corporatist relations are essentially feudal (Graham and Luke 2005) and have unique modes of coercion based on systematic, personal indebtedness. Today's benefices granted to corporate vassals are contingent upon loyalty to one or more corporate "lieges." As far as the bulk of students are concerned, indebtedness begins from the moment they enter the higher education system: those not fortunate enough to have the benefit of parental patronage must incur a massive debt in the form of a student loan. It is usually the first of many loans that the educated, "aspirational" citizen of the present will incur: loans for vehicles, goods and chattels, and houses typically follow. A general credit system is a means of coercion that mitigates against unionism and labor strikes, turnover of personnel, single-income families, labor mobility, and many other characteristics of the fading "New Deal": capitalism of the mid- to late-twentieth century. Debts must be serviced, and that service structures the life pathways of most individuals and families.

The credit system is coercive at the most basic levels of human existence. As Marx puts it,

> Credit is the economic judgement on the morality of a man. In the credit system man replaces metal or paper as the mediator of exchange. However, he does this not as a man but as the incarnation of capital and interest . . . Human individuality, human morality, have become both articles of commerce and the material which money inhabits. The substance, the body clothing the spirit of money is not money, paper, but instead it is my personal existence, my flesh and blood, my social worth and status. Credit no longer actualizes money-values in actual money but in human flesh and in human hearts (Marx 1844 [1975], 264).

This is an important point at present, when individual, national, and global debt is larger and more common than at any time in history. The progress of money-as-medium—as a media system through which goods and services flow through people's labor and consumerism—has turned upon humanity, making persons the media through which money moves (Graham 2006). A general credit system generates a systematic claim over massive amounts of future (as-yet-unlived) human life. Extended to the national level, as expressed in the term "national debt," and personally mediated through national- and state-tax systems, the degree to which persons are individually indebted has become literally incalculable. In fact, the degree to which current practices are indebting unborn generations is also incalculable, if only because interest rates are inherently unpredictable. The implications of credit become even more bizarre with the emergence of supranational credit systems, such as those having their origin in the Bretton-Woods agreement (World Bank, IMF, etc.). A direct consequence of these institutions is that even the abstraction we call "the nation" state is now judged in terms of its moral, intellectual, and monetary worth—as if it were also a personal embodiment of the general credit system, like the indebted individual (cf. Pilger 2001). One clear consequence of such a system is that the ideal contemporary nation-state is now required to masquerade as a corporation: that is, a person at law (Nace 2004). Public administration and political systems thus become systems of financial and commercial management, with all the imperatives that entails: history, culture, human life, and governance are assessed in terms of productivity and efficiency, measured by monetary values alone.

The levels of personal debt are historically high in every industrialized nation (see, for example, Kane 2006). Yet, because they are tied to the lives of individual, mortal persons, the interest from personal debt is insignificant in comparison to that of national and supranational entities (Rozenberg 2005). Such entities extend through time for decades and sometimes centuries and can therefore place a mortgage upon many generations to come. And so the seemingly simple concept of "consumer credit" now extends to encompass the indebtedness of generations, with countries like Italy, Greece, and Belgium having "national debt levels roughly equivalent to 100 per cent of GDP" (Rozenberg 2005). Relatedly, the "developing world" is indebted in perpetuity to a new class of corporate colonizers who dole out corporate benefice in the form of "aid" through the World Bank, WHO, Asia Development Bank, and other supranational "benefactors" via IMF directives. Such debts are typically held by transglobal corporate entities and therefore translate into national policies of "belt tightening" designed to ensure that nations can "service the debt," just as personal actions, habits, and attitudes become oriented toward servicing personal debts. Debt teaches. Similarly, systems of higher education are increasingly indebted to corporate benefice, and coerced—directly and indirectly—to behave in ways that ingratiate them to actual and potential corporate "benefactors."

The third and perhaps most salient characteristic that differentiates the corporatist period from others in the history of the university is its impersonality. While much has been written about corporate "personhood" stemming from apocryphal interpretations of the "Santa Clara" ruling (see, for example, Nace 2004), very little has been said about the impersonal qualities of corporate entities. The most powerful corporations exist beyond the lifespan of most human beings. Their constitution constantly changes, as evidenced by the many takeovers, mergers, acquisitions, de-mergers, and so forth over the last two decades. Many might be surprised to find that General Electric (GE) is the world's largest financier. Marshall McLuhan (1964) would not: GE began amassing its fortune by selling light bulbs. That is to say, it by selling information commodities. In many senses, money is pure information: it is an almost perfect fusion of information, mediation, and power. Its general meaning is now manipulated globally through the credit system controlled by the largest corporate entities.

The historical fact that GE has moved from a company that traded information in the form of electric light to one that moves information in the form of money is a move made by many of the largest corporations: General Motors, IBM, and Reuters are just three examples of major corporations that now make the bulk of their income trading in forms of debt. Similarly, universities have "diversified" into property, IT services, on and offshore holdings and services, research companies, etc. These trends in corporate functional and organizational vagueness involve enormous efforts in human resources, acquisition, policy manipulation, political coercion, legal costs, and the endless costs of expanding in all directions at once. One consequence of this systematic vagueness is that the contemporary corporation cannot be defined in functional or organizational terms. Nor can it be defined in terms of the people who comprise them: the corporation will most likely "outlive" them. The impersonal character of corporate entities is most publicly revealed in every major corporate "failure" (e.g., Enron), usually involving the loss of many millions or billions, often (if not definitively) representing the savings of many thousands or millions of people. Typically, at least as far as onlookers or victims are concerned, nobody appears to be responsible. In the failure of Enron, for example, blame was publicly shifted from executives, to auditors, to energy traders, to banks, to organizational "culture" in what Associated Press (2003) calls "a circle of blame." After no initial allegations were laid against Ken Lay, Enron's chairman, after a $100 million investigation, public discourse on the matter became more and more confusing:

"I am highly encouraged," said Michael Ramsey, one of Lay's attorneys. "There is no allegation of crime, no claim of intentional wrongdoing, and no assertion of fraud on the part of Ken Lay. After a nearly $100 million investigation, the bankruptcy examiner suggests only negligence, which we strongly deny" (AP 2003).

The chair of the Enron enquiry attributed criminal actions to another vague and amorphous agent: "Enron's *culture* drove officers to manipulate finances to pump up the stock price and ensure fat bonuses for meeting earnings targets—but they had lots of help" (Batson, as cited in AP 2003, our emphasis). Enron's accountants, Arthur Andersen LLP, allegedly "helped design accounting techniques to beautify Enron's books and failed to closely examine some deals" (AP 2003). But against such allegations, an Andersen spokesman claimed that "Enron often hid crucial facts that would have prompted the firm to block some deals, such as secret side agreements to buy back assets ostensibly 'sold' to third parties." Enron lawyers also joined the circle: "Vinson & Elkins and others approved questionable deals that Enron used to book earnings or hide debt" (AP 2003). Enter the banks: they "reaped millions in fees by participating in shady deals even when they knew the accounting was suspect" (AP 2003).

This is just one example of the convoluted, impersonal "personhood" of the corporate complex as expressed in a single news article. The impersonal character of corporate persons is expressed repeatedly in an almost complete lack of personal responsibility. And this is the very essence of the corporation: its original function was to limit liability (Nace 2004). The core of corporate organization is essentially feudal: it is committee based, a term stemming from *comitatus*, a group of warriors whose political organization was based on personal loyalties to a chief or king (Koehl 1960; Stephenson 1941 and 1943, 245). The feudal comitatus "was essentially a public relationship: the followers swore fealty to their leader, gave him warlike service, and were subject to his judicial control" (Stephenson 1941, 792). The corporation is a public company, held in common by shareholders. The comitatus was also "fundamentally aristocratic," comprised of free men "who considered the bearing of arms a distinction and companionship with a famous warrior a source of honor" (1941, 796). Any doubts about the explicit and conscious identity between business and war can be dispelled by a quick scan of management literature. White House chief of staff Andrew Card explains on air why the U.S. administration took until September 2002 "to make its case against Iraq": "From a marketing point of view, you don't introduce new products in August" (Schneider 2002). In corporate consciousness, business is war and war is business. In fact war is the most profitable of all manufacturing enterprises (Saul 1997). The global system of warfare we have called elsewhere "neofeudal corporatism'" (Graham and Luke 2003, 2005) now defines the policy directions of major countries throughout the world. In his most recent budget, President George W. Bush proposed cuts to every major welfare program in order to channel money into a war that appears to have no end. Higher education has a key role to play in this war according to the United States Department of Defence (DOD).

IMPLICATIONS OF GLOBAL CORPORATISM FOR HIGHER EDUCATION

> Finding new ways to harness strategic communication to the flexibility and creative imagination of the private sector will be central to successful strategic communication in the twenty-first century. The commercial sector has a dominant competitive edge in multi-media production, opinion and media surveys, information technologies, program evaluation, and measuring the influence of communications. Academic and research communities offer vast untapped resources for education, training, area and language expertise, planning and consultative services (DOD 2004).

The ethereal globalization movements of the 1990s, championed and implemented by global corporations faced with a new global media space to conquer, has materialized into its fully concrete form: globally dispersed warfare with no specific enemy, no territorial boundaries, and no time limits; just a promise that the war will "be fought in dozens of countries and for decades to come" (Tisdall and MacAskill 2006). In an age of corporate-sponsored warfare, higher education is expected to join the amorphous, impersonal, and bloody fray. Curriculum development is one key area of academic participation identified by the U.S. Department of State (DOS) (2005):

In an exciting new outreach initiative, the Bureau of Public Affairs produced a high-quality historical video and curriculum package on terrorism for use in high school classrooms around the country. *A War Without Borders* was designed to give students a brief overview of the history and impact of terrorism and help them understand its relationship to their own lives. Distributed to nearly 13,000 social studies teachers, *A War Without Borders* reached more American students than any other post-9/11 curriculum package, according to an independent university study. Feedback has been overwhelmingly positive, and many teachers have decided to reuse the package annually. The video is the first in a series created especially for students to help them understand both the complexities and opportunities of the world in the twenty-first century (DOS 2005).

In this passage, an apparently decades-long, multitrillion dollar, highly controversial campaign being waged by "the coalition of the willing" throughout the Middle East and elsewhere, involving torture, corruption, public deception, no-bid contracts for billions (e.g., Halliburton), and unprecedented levels of public surveillance in the United States and everywhere else, is being sold as if it were a new kid's toy, brand of soap, or novelty ice-cream. The examples we have noted here indicate strange new convergences, all of which implicate the tentacled and influential organs of higher education. The increased emphasis on the importance of "information warfare" in the military "mix"; the deployment of managerial and marketing discourse; psychological warfare potentials amplified and streamed en masse through new global media channels; the decline of political legitimacy in the developed world—all these phenomena implicate higher education. It is the systems of higher education that provide research, teaching, and training for managers, psychologists, IT professionals, marketers, lawyers, and politicians. Deep corporate impressions are already evident in the simulated replication of corporate structures and functions in universities; in the making of the debt-ridden, aspiring student-consumer-executives; and in the emergent, corporately mediated knowledge economies that were once merely the talk of 1990s intellectual and policy circles throughout the world (Graham 2006). That is to say, the reconstruction of academic research as corporately funded knowledge commodities, which, at the same time, has shifted the ground from public access to "public (knowledge) goods" to a user-pays logic. Who benefits? Not the researcher or the public. Not the university or its students. Corporatized mega-merged behemoths of the publishing industry such as Elsevier, Thomson, and the Taylor & Francis Group reap immediate rewards on a day-to-day basis (cf. Luke 2005). Further afield, but still directly along the corporate "value chain," biotechnology, pharmaceutical, and mining companies, along with the political parties who mediate and legitimate corporate power, all reap long-term benefits from university research and technological developments, discovering ways to conquer nations and governments without firing a shot; to buy intellectual property rights over genetic pools of whole states and countries in perpetuity; to enclose forms of human knowing, meaning, and relating: words, slogans, signs, and songs; principles, techniques, and conceptions are the higher education system's raw materials and the raw materials of the so-called knowledge economy. Regardless, or perhaps because of, their amorphous and impersonal character, corporations "just do it." Contemplative thought is anathema. And the state's withdrawal of funding for higher education has left the system both vulnerable and amenable to corporate values, structures, and behaviors (e.g., quality audits, performance reviews, marketing, branding, etc.) by commercializing the supply of credentialed "student goods" and hyping demand for user-pays customers. Such trends powerfully illustrate the collusion between governments, market forces, and industry in shaping the political economy of higher education in an emergent age of neofeudal corporatism.

And though the historical pattern of higher education reveals itself to be one of adaptive subservience to political-economic powers du jour, the higher education system infused with corporate consciousness is already showing itself to be entirely new in kind for the reasons we have noted above. Most of all it is the impersonal aspect of corporate consciousness that undermines the civilizing potentials of universities that has been demonstrated throughout the last millennium. Ostensibely, the primary role of universities in the West, at least since the thirteenth century and probably well before, has been to generate, retain, and disseminate understandings about the world we inhabit for the betterment of civilization. In other words: a view of higher education as a public good has predominated. When dominated by the impersonal character of the corporation, with its sole reason for existing being to maximize profit, the dominant view of knowledge becomes one based purely on its ability to "privatize" and lock down knowledge in the name of profit. Progress toward deep understanding—by which we mean constantly new and better ways of comprehending the worlds we inhabit—has and always will be a function of interpersonal related-ness. That is merely to say that new knowledge cannot be created by individuals in isolation. Nor can it be created by mere "transmission" through media such as infoscreens, books, and the like. Human under-standings of the world are social, embodied, interpersonal, and cultur-ally bound phenomena. The fully corporatized consciousness does not recognize cultural, legal, geographic, social, or personal bonds as any-thing other than barriers to growth and profit. Hence corporate con-sciousness is antithetical to the very conditions that make knowledge possible. Perhaps unfortunately, the university is a historical precursor to the corporation and therefore is perfectly suited to a partnership with global corporatism. Higher education gained its force and influence by systematizing and propagating ways of seeing and knowing across vast geographical and cultural spaces. Its original purpose was to propagate and maintain Christian doxa, thus accruing political economic profits for the church by means of a transcultural, globally oriented, future ori-ented theology.

Like the doctrine of debt, Christian theology demanded daily sacri-fice for rewards in some imagined future. It was mediated by a com-mon language, and through a knowledge monopoly of the written word, its essential materials, and the means of producing those materi-als. At its foundation, though, was a conception of public good. The failure of a higher education system confronted with corporate con-sciousness, and the reason the system has never realized the aims ex-pressed in the creeds of Dewey and other such influential figures who saw that education for its own sake was the highest public good, is firstly that custodians of the system have almost unerringly failed to seize the opportunities to define the purpose of the system as an end in itself: a public good, a public service, and an essential part of civiliza-tion as most would wish it to be. The custodians of public knowledge have given themselves over to a system that conditions its constituents to see themselves as part of a complex of profit centers; as workers in giant knowledge factories oriented to turning out "commercially" viable research; as an intellectually legitimating arm of corporate-funded political parties and their governments; and, most important, as vendors in a mass credentialing system for aspirational consumers (formerly students) who can only, as consumers of knowledge and "clients" of a university, be in an adversarial relationship based on the distrustful retail principle: manufacturers and sellers must strive to reduce costs and maximize profit at the consumer's expense; the consumer must strive to reduce the price, time, and effort required to purchase an "end product" to which there is—ideally—no end.

NOTE

1. The House of Terror is explained by Mumford as follows: "At the opening of this [paleotechnic PG] period, in 1770, a writer had projected a new scheme for providing for paupers. He called it a House of Terror: it would be a place where paupers would be confined to work for fourteen hours a day and kept in hand by a starvation diet."

REFERENCES

Association to Advance Collegiate Schools of Business. (Fall 1999). Corporate Universities Emerge as Pioneers in Market-Driven Education. AACSB Newsline. www.aacsb.edu/publications/printnewsline/NL1999/spcorporat.asp

Australian Research Council. (2006). Linkage-Projects. Canberra: Government of Australia. www.arc.gov.au/grant_programs/linkage_projects.htm (accessed February 2006).

Bourdieu, P. (1991). Language and Symbolic Power, Trans. G. Raymond and M. Adamson. London: Polity.

Dewey, J. (1928). Progressive Education and the Science of Education. *Progressive Education* 5, 1928: 197–204.

Ganshof, F. L. (1949). Charlemagne. *Speculum* 24, (4): 520–28

Global Learning Resources. (2005). Brief History of the Corporate University. www.glresources.com/ls_cu_xhist.php (accessed January 20, 2006).

Goldhaber, M. (1997). The attention economy and the net. *First Monday* 2, (4). www.firstmonday.dk/issues/issue2_4/goldhaber/ (accessed April 2001).

Graham, P. (2006). *Hypercapitalism: Language, New Media, and Social Perceptions of Value*. New York: Lang.

Graham, P. and Hearn, G. (2000). The Digital Dark Ages: A Retro-Speculative History of Possible Futures. Internet Research 1.0: The State of the Interdiscipline. Paper for the First Conference of the Association of Internet Researchers. September 14–17, 2000. University of Kansas.

Graham, P. and Luke, A. (2003). Militarizing the Body Politic: New Media as Weapons of Mass Instruction. *Body & Society* 9, (4): 149–68.

Graham, P. and Luke, A. (2005). Militarizing the Body Politic: Feudal Influences in the Language of Bush, Blair, and Howard. *Language & Politics* 4 (1): 11–39

Haskins, C. H. (1904). The University of Paris in the Sermons of the Thirteenth Century. *The American Historical Review* 10, (1): 1–27.

———. (1957/1923). *The Rise of Universities*. Ithaca, N.Y.: Cornell University Press.

Kane, F. (January 1, 2006). Time to Pay the Bill. *Guardian*. http://money .guardian.co.uk/creditanddebt/debt/story/0,1456,1676193,00.html. (accessed February 20, 2006).

Knowledge is Power Program (2005). KIPP. www.kipp.org/ (accessed November 22, 2005).

Koehl, R. (1960). Feudal Aspects of National Socialism. *American Political Science Review* 54 (4): 921–33.

Luke, C. (2005). Capital and Knowledge Flows: Global Higher Education Markets. *Asia Pacific Journal of Education* 25 (2): 159–74.

Marx, K. (1844 [1975]). Excerpts from James Mill's Elements of Political Economy. In Marx, K. (1975). *Early Writings*. Trans. R. Livingstone and G. Benton. London: Penguin: 259–78.

Marx, K. and Engels, F. (1846/1972). The German Ideology. In R. C. Tucker (ed.), The Marx-Engels Reader. New York: W. W. Norton, 110–66.

McDonalds. (2005). Hamburger University. www.mcdonalds.com/corp/ career/hamburger_university.html (accessed January 21, 2006).

Mumford, L. (1934/1963). *Technics and Civilization*. New York: Harcourt Brace.

Muntigl, P. (2000). Dilemmas of Individualism and Social Necessity. In P. Muntigl, G. Weiss, and R. Wodak (eds.). *European Union Discourses on Unemployment: An Interdisciplinary Approach to Employment Policy-Making and Organizational Change*. London: Benjamins. 145–84.

Nace, T. (2004). *Gangs of America: The Rise of Corporate Power and the Disabling of Democracy*. San Francisco: Berrett-Koehler.

Perry, R. B. (1916). Economic Value and Moral Value. *Quarterly Journal of Economics* 30, (3): 443–85.

Pilger, J. (July 14, 2001). Spoils of a Massacre. *Guardian Weekly*: 18–29.

Ranney, A. (1976). "The Divine Science": Political Engineering in American Culture. *American Political Science Review* 70, (1): 140–48.

Rozenberg, G. (2005). EU Warned over Debt and Pensions. Times Online. http://business.timesonline.co.uk/article/0,,13130-1456619,00.html (accessed February 16, 2006).

Saul, J. R. (1997). *The Unconcious Civilization*. Penguin: Australia.

Schneider, W. (September 12, 2002). Marketing Iraq: Why now? Cable News Network. http://archives.cnn.com/2002/ALLPOLITICS/09/12/schneider .iraq/ (accessed July 2005).

Social Sciences and Humanities Research Council (SSHRC). (2006). Strategic Research Clusters Development Grants. Ottawa, ON: Canadian Federal Government. www.sshrc.ca/web/apply/program_descriptions/cluster_development_e.asp (accessed February 2006).

Stanford University. (2005). History. www.stanford.edu/home/stanford/history/begin.html (accessed January 21, 2006).

Stephenson, C. (1941). The Origin and Significance of Feudalism. *American Historical Review* 46 (4): 245–65.

———. (1943). Feudalism and its Antecedents in England. *American Historical Review* 48 (2): 245–65.

Stone, L. (1964). The Educational Revolution in England, 1560–1640. *Past and Present* 28: 41–80.

Strayer, J. R. (1970). *On the Medieval Origins of the Modern State*. Princeton, N.J.: Princeton University Press.

Taylor, F.W. (1911/1998). The Principles of Scientific Management. Harper: New York.

Thurow, L. C. (1996). *The Future of Capitalism: How Today's Economic Forces Will Shape Tomorrow's World*. St. Leonards, Australia: Allen & Unwin.

Tisdall, S. and MacAskill, E. (February 15, 2006). America's Long War. *Guardian*. www.guardian.co.uk/usa/story/0,,1710062,00.html (accessed February 15, 2006).

U.S. Department of Defense. (2004). *Report of the Defense Science Board Task Force on Strategic Communication*. Washington, D.C.: Office of the Under Secretary of Defense.

U.S. Department of State. (2004). Strategic Goal 11: Public Diplomacy and Public Affairs: Increase Understanding for American Values, Policies, and

Initiatives to Create a Receptive International Environment. In Financial Year Department Summary. Washington, D.C. www.state.gov/s/d/rm/rls/perfplan/2005/html/29276.htm (accessed July 2005).

Wilson, J. K. (2005). Academic Freedom Under Fire. www.collegefreedom .org/03.htm

Wilson, W. (1887). The Study of Administration. *Political Science Quarterly* 2, (2): 197–222.

Part III

CLASS, CURRICULUM, AND EVERYDAY LIFE IN SCHOOLS

CHAPTER 5

Social Class and Curriculum: Theoretical-Political Possibilities and Practical Matters

Philip M. Anderson

It has become seemingly commonplace in recent years to admit that there is a relationship between social class and curriculum in schools, but to say very little about it. For decades, U.S. education has been resistant to social-class discussions, preferring to focus on race. In recent years, in response to the insights of feminist pedagogy, gender has achieved almost equal status to race in discussions of schooling. But in general, discussion of class appears to be treated as almost "un-American," as in the tendency of neoconservatives to dismiss social-class discussions, particularly critiques of inequality, as "foreign" ideology. Somewhat ironically, the neo-con revolution of the past twenty-five years began with a forceful claim that liberal-progressive ideas of schooling were class-biased because of the prevalence of ability tracking. That assertion became a key argument for the common core curriculum now being promoted in U.S. schools. As we shall see below, one of the first steps in assessing school curriculum is sorting out the contradictory policies and practices.

The substitution of *race* for *class* in U.S. policy discussions complicates matters, because there are certain correlations between class and race in our society. As Michael Harrington reported in *The Other America* (1962), the book that helped spark the 1960s War on Poverty, higher percentages of people of color live in poverty than the general population. He also reported that, based on population statistics, the largest numbers of citizens living in poverty are white. Sometimes we say "class" when we mean "race," and sometimes it is the other way around because of the elision of the terms. In what follows, I will undoubtedly also mix race and class in ways that are problematic. But one only need recall the exclusionary practices of golf and country clubs to recognize that class is not just about socioeconomic status, and that it is confounded with race and ethnicity within all parts of society.

One key reason for the avoidance of social-class debate in American educational thinking centers on the idealized meritocratic assumption that schooling eliminates class distinctions—Horace Mann first articulated the great advantage of education as an "equalizer" in a democratic society in 1840s. And, most popular education discourse in the meantime has uncritically adopted that equalizing function. Education, and the spread of education, is seen as inherently democratic. While the question of social class does appear in the writings of influential scholars writing about education, most of the social-class arguments about schools appear to come from postwar sociology (Aronowitz 1993, Bourdieu 1993, e.g.). or economics (Bowles and Gintis 1976).

The better-known education scholars who focus on social class, Apple (2004), Giroux (2001), and Kincheloe (2005) being examples, tend to write about knowledge and power rather than curriculum, and work under the banner of cultural studies rather than curriculum theory. The critical pedagogy model is a very powerful analytic tool, though, and much of what I will do in this chapter is indebted to its insights. I suppose it would be foolish to try to add anything philosophically significant to what Joe Kincheloe (2005) recently articulated and synthesized in *Critical Pedagogy*, but I want to take aim at the "practical" elements of curriculum.

The critical pedagogy emphasis on power and political process, with the concept of hegemonic ideology at its heart, appears too deterministic for curriculum-in-action in individual classrooms. Many policy decisions are made out of fear and ignorance (e.g., current government decisions concerning privacy), and most public policy is deeply contradictory and/or confused. School practice, despite the current emphasis on federal and state accountability, is rarely controllable, and much of the oppressive practice in schools has as much to do with parental pressure on administrators and school boards (and the local Fox network affiliate) than oppressive elected officials. Further, studies of "top-down" policies made at the state level usually reveal that those policies are modified to meet local conditions—*modified* here means *subverted* (Loveless 1999).

I also perceive that there has been a removal of class and curriculum discussion on the Left because discussions of pedagogy and curriculum are misconstrued as "traditional" discussions of planning and
technique. The critical pedagogy movement in the United States has
been notorious for avoiding classroom-based curricular discussions,
focusing instead on institutional and cultural analysis, cultural capital
reproduction and distribution within the culture, and educational pol-
icy/law. All the time spent on analyzing cultural context rarely leaves
time for looking at school curriculum. On the other hand, Apple's
analysis of the science and social studies curriculum in *Ideology and
Curriculum*, especially the "hidden curriculum" of social values and
norms, is a necessary baseline for any attempt to unpack curriculum
and practice (2004).

But, here's the point: the time for analysis is over. We live in times
when people want answers, as in the federal government's push to publish guidelines on "What Works" in teaching and the new Department
of Education declarations that we know "what works" based on "scientific" research (see U.S. Department of Education What Works
Clearinghouse Web site 2006). On the other side, the critical pedagogy
traditions rarely provide "answers" (constructed as oppositional, they
are focused on critique rather than construction). As a result, the "practical" minded tend to have inordinate influence on new curriculum.
One only need look at the success of E. D. Hirsch Jr. (1987) promoting
"cultural literacy" as philosophy, psychology, pedagogy, and product to
see the advantage of practicality. In uncertain times, the functionalist
agenda will take precedence.

There have been some singular efforts addressing social class in
classroom settings, namely Paul Willis's *Learning to Labor* (1981, set
in England, of course), or, for that matter, Cameron Crowe's *Fast
Times at Ridgemont High* (1981), but even those are much less interested in actual curriculum and classroom practice than the social construct called "schooling." Basil Bernstein's work on social-class dialect in Great Britain in the 1960s is a good example of curriculum
specific, social-class critique in its time (Bernstein 1971). But, in an
apt illustration of my previous point about race and class, all of the
subsequent discussion of sociolinguistic differences in social class di-
alects in the United States became an obsession with "Black English."

That discussion continues to this day with the not-so-long-ago cause célèbre surrounding "ebonics" in Oakland, California.

Basil Bernstein places the class divisions squarely within the sociolinguistic demarcations undergirding communication (1971). In Bernstein's analysis, even the linguistic codes discriminate, an argument picked up later by Lisa Delpit to argue against progressive (in this case, "naturalistic") language practices used by white teachers in schools populated by low Supplemental Educational Services (SES) African American kids (Delpit 1988). The irony in Delpit's position, at least to me, is her contention that allowing low SES kids to employ their own language is a form of class discrimination in teaching. Neo-cons call anything that accounts for racial difference the "soft bigotry of low expectations" (Bush 2004). Both Bernstein's "class, codes, and control" argument and the debate over Black English explicitly argue class-based rationales for a single, common curriculum, though one that eliminates the "lower class" dialect of the low SES students.

I know that some readers are now saying, probably out loud, that I am being foolish here. Surely most American scholars concerned with pedagogy are interested in social-class differences. I would reply that most studies of class, such as Jonathan Kozol's books, are merely a list of deficits that afflict poor children. There have been some interesting writings on class and curriculum in U.S. schools, but little "practical discussion." Recent interest appears as an argument over whether the class bias exists, since "class bias" tends to disappear and reemerge as "ability tracking." Nowadays, the standard neo-con response to assertions of class bias by any thinker is that the "liberals" are trying to promote "class warfare" and that kids really need direct instruction to make up for their cultural deficits. Coupled with the neo-con assertion that tracking is a liberal-progressive legacy, the liberal policy maker finds it as difficult to argue for a class-free curriculum as to label oneself as a "liberal."

What I would also argue here is that the *we* and *they* in the class debate have been confused. Ever since the Heritage Foundation and the other conservative think tanks were founded after the humiliating defeat of Barry Goldwater and right-wing ideals in 1964, the Right has been turning liberal and even radical discourse on its head. The Right has made liberal discourse the enemy, but then uses liberal arguments to accuse liberal progressive teachers of racism, sexism, and elitism. Lisa Delpit, interestingly, was the first to score big in the Orwellian arena when she attacked the liberal notions ascribed to whole language as "racist." E. D. Hirsch Jr., of course, was the most successful of all the conservative Orwellians with his coining of "cultural literacy." And, in higher education, who can forget Allan Bloom's diatribe against liberal thinking, *The Closing of the American Mind* (1988); even the title is beautifully Orwellian, suggesting that liberal thinking has "closed" the mind.

What I want to look at here is not the neo-con "solutions" to the "elitist" curriculum promoted by liberal progressive thinking over the past century: the exceptionally "practical" curriculum solutions provided by Hirsch (1987), Ravitch with Finn (1988), and Bloom (1988) have been disseminated and discussed. They have also been implemented through NCLB and other initiatives at the state and local levels. Instead, I want to take a look at the "practical" solutions to class-biased curriculum from both the liberal and leftist positions. I want to reference representatives from those two positions to show how the "solutions," if there are any, to class-based curriculum in schools (and among schools) are just as problematic as the neo-con cultural literacy model. The positions of the Left tend to be deterministic and the positions of the liberals tend toward the essentialist, neither of which addresses the problem of class-biased curriculum in the long run.

Folks on the left/liberal side of the scale as ideologically disparate as Jean Anyon and Theodore Sizer have written, famously, about class differences in schooling and have made specific suggestions for fixing the problem (Anyon 1980; Sizer 1984). The general argument goes like this: Schools are tracked by "ability grouping." Ability grouping correlates with class (i.e., SES or socioeconomic status, in sociological terms). Ergo, goes the argument, American schools are segregated by class. (You can see where the neo-cons got the argument in the first place.) The alleged meritocracy of ability testing merely recapitulates the class-biased strata of society outside of school (Lemann 1999). Some critics have even argued that the class struggle goes on within even the wealthiest and most elite schools themselves (Mathews 1998). In any case, goes the argument, different social classes (different SES groups) receive different treatment in school programs, classroom conditions, curricular choices and opportunities, and career counseling. Anyon and Sizer are both grounded and "practical" in their approaches—each has a plan.

Anyon's and Sizer's arguments, respectively, are particularly telling, since both have become popular constructions of the class bias argument as it relates to classroom practice and curriculum transformation. Anyon argues that the different academic tracks represent different approaches to student learning and career expectations (see Anyon 1980, for the oft-reprinted article). The upper tracks receive information that the lower tracks do not, and more important, are treated differently. The upper-track—and, therefore, upper-class—kids are asked to engage in critical thinking and encouraged to express their ideas. Lower-track— that is lower–class—kids are taught to repeat information they have been asked to "learn" and are rarely asked about their thoughts on a subject. The origin of this system, and its maintenance, is conscious and unconscious elitism based on differential expectations for these students in society.

Anyon's solution to class-divided schools is a Marxist utopian endgame, articulating the social justice argument that schools will never be equal until society is equal (see *Radical Possibilities*, 2005). The fatal problem with this argument is ignoring the curriculum as not important, or at least not of interest, until the necessary changes in the system bring about social justice. In the end, even a society that is "just" does not automatically enact a curriculum that is common to all and fair to each one, or even meritocratic for that matter. Michael D. Young's *The Rise of the Meritocracy* (1994) provides a very clever, and chilling, illustration of what might happen in a society built around social justice, and how inequality (and privilege) will always be a problem in any utopian scheme. Kurt Vonnegut's short story "Harrison Bergeron" (1968) also skewers the assumptions of "equality" in a utopian future in which the "Handicapper General" limits the abilities of "gifted" citizens to make them equal with the less able. The deterministic argument assumes a one-way assertion of power over the curriculum rather than a reciprocal relationship between school and society (and certainly not the radical progressive notion of curriculum as culturally transformative).

This "put the curriculum off until we fix society" approach is done at a peril, since it assumes that change in the school curriculum, or maintenance of the class-divided curriculum, does not contribute directly to the societal problem. The first thing the Reaganista neo-con revolution attacked was the school curriculum, arguing that it was a "cafeteria" or a "shopping mall" style hodgepodge of electives, and asking that it be controlled, reduced, authorized, and sanitized for your protection. The culture wars are fought at the school level for most citizens, not in the editorial pages of elite magazines and newspapers. The debate over creationism in science class cannot wait for a just society.

The shopping mall image comes from a "Study of American High Schools," the most famous volume of which was Theodore Sizer's *Horace's Compromise* (1984). (Another volume, by Arthur Powell and others, from that study was titled *The Shopping Mall High School*). Sizer's argument represents the neoliberal argument with a sort of nostalgia for Horace Mann's academies. Sizer's practical project is called the "Coalition of Essential Schools" for the type of curriculum the schools meant to offer (Coalition of Essential Schools National Web site 2006). The essential school curriculum is the "less is more" model, reducing the school curriculum to its basic academic elements. Schools are stripped of sports and band and all the other accoutrements of the modern suburban high school. But, also, the curriculum is "less" and the study is "more." Sizer's vision of the "essential curriculum" as a curriculum for all addresses his complaints about the class divisions in American high schools.

Sizer's solution is what I would term the "shining city on a hill" (Matt. 5:14–16, a central Reagan metaphor even referenced at his funeral), or "New Jerusalem" (the Puritan version of Utopia) argument, in which all class differences are eroded by returning to a simple Puritan existence. In the Puritan utopia, drawing on Thomas More's original vision of utopia, the object of life is shunning pride. In Sizer's school model, the leveling argument is expressed as the essential curriculum. Despite its old-time liberal origins, Sizer's curricular vision is what the neo-cons have lighted on to produce the No Child Left Behind (NCLB) act. The George W. Bush administration's rewrite of Title I into NCLB represents itself as a classless document—it argues for a common, limited, testable curriculum for all classes.

The religious connotations of the essential curriculum, as Puritan culture, do echo throughout the Bush administration's vision of education, since much of the discussion appears to be about behavior and character. I remember President Bush talking about rewards and consequences during much of the speechifying concerning NCLB (The National Forum 2000). Certainly, "rewards and consequences" is Orwellian Newspeak for "rewards and punishments," since both are *consequences*. Indeed, much of the rhetoric around NCLB responses by state and local authorities has been focused on controlling the curriculum as a means of controlling the teachers and the kids. The control of character, based on assumptions of the traditional Protestant work ethic, is part and parcel of the puritan essentialist curriculum. Liberals (and Leftists) who objected to the removal of curricular complexity were tagged, in an Orwellian twist, "elitists," but you can see how the religious metaphors also question the "character" of those who objected. The basic anti-intellectualism of the neo-con essentialist agenda has its roots in religion as well, especially evangelical Christianity, but more about anti-intellectualism later.

While many liberals and Leftists see NCLB as a plan for the systematic destruction of the public school system, the neo-con rhetoric has been to present NCLB as a democratic and leveling instrument of salvation. NCLB is the logical extension of the Reaganista de-funding of vocational education in high schools in the early 1980s (even before *A Nation at Risk*), on the basis of the argument that the vocational track amounted to class-based discrimination in the curriculum. The vocational track was originally established in 1918 by the Smith-Hughes Act that created the comprehensive high school, which also led to expectations for universal K–12 schooling. Good conservatives have always fought the comprehensive elements (vocational tracks, health, counseling, anything outside the basic academic curriculum) as unnecessary expense. (In the 1994 Texas gubernatorial debates, George W. Bush argued for reducing the curriculum to the four academic subjects based on an *economic* argument.) The Reaganistas shifted vocational and technical training to postsecondary proprietary institutions; of course, the first results of that policy shift were the student loan scandals of the 1980s. What the neo-cons have done, in applying the common, controlled curriculum to schools, is erase the comprehensive high school and replace six to eight years of basic schooling with twelve years of basic schooling. The high school exit examinations now in place all over the country, required by NCLB, guarantee it.

Given the various correlations between poverty and ethnicity in the United States, it is also interesting to view some of the other assumptions of the democratizing influences embodied in NCLB with its emphasis on standardized testing, especially as it relates to college admissions. First, I might mention a key moment in the "Texas School Miracle" of the 1990s, the main source of the federal NCLB legislation. The Texas courts ruled that affirmative action was not beneficial to the citizens of Texas, so affirmative action by race was replaced by a class-based system. The court ruled that since Texas schools remained de facto segregated fifty years after Brown v. Board of Education, the "fair" thing to do was admit the top 10 percent of students graduating from any high school in Texas to the University of Texas system (Horn and Flores 2003). The confusion of "access" with "opportunity" should be clear to anyone with any reasoning skills, but the fact remains that this is a class-based affirmative action model. Replacing race with class, while simultaneously making class a marker of race (given the de facto segregation of the schools), strikes me as pretzel logic.

I certainly do not want to single out the southern states for intractable racism and elitism. There used to be an old school joke about Long Island, the mostly segregated suburban paradise east of New York City: On Long Island, it is said, SAT scores are correlated with distance from the water. The connection between SES (and housing) and standardized test performance is well documented. Real estate agents may be responsible for most of the class-based problems in the United States, but they are only meeting the expectations of their clients. If one reads the real estate listings in the Long Island newspapers, one sees coding related to school districts. In listings for towns where a majority of the local schools' population is minority (and that is a small number of towns) there is an indication if the particular house's neighborhood is zoned for an adjoining (meaning acceptable, i.e., nonminority) school district. I am sure that is the case in many other communities across the United States.

That standardized testing correlates with class is a bit obvious anyway. One could easily argue that if the bias in favor of the higher SES groups did not appear in the scores of the students that the tests would be abandoned. Why would the ruling classes use a test that did not provide a justification for their advantages? Enforcing federally mandated fair housing laws has been subverted at every turn, why shouldn't the meritocratic elements in standardized testing also be subverted? The truly elite universities argue that they go well beyond the SAT in admissions decisions. But what is that but another way of discriminating against those who score well on the tests but do not have the leisure or the income to engage in significant charitable or community pursuits or interesting hobbies. I cannot help but point out the decline in the influence of SAT scores in elite college admissions now that Asian students have become a "problem"; in other words, "too many" Asians with high SAT scores are applying to a select number of universities (Mathews 2005). Since a quota system like the one used against Jewish students in the 1930s is now out of the question, the elite schools now argue they need a diverse student body (meaning not too many Asians, apparently). To this day, legacies, the children of alumni, are generally three times as likely to be admitted to Ivy League schools as other applicants. Some have called this affirmative action for the rich.

TEACHERS AND CURRICULUM

Most discussions of the curriculum leave out the teacher's influence. The curriculum is not just its content. The operationalized curriculum includes the teacher, the ideas and concepts taught by the teacher, and the teacher's stance relative to the students. The argument about African American and Latino teachers as role models for African American and Latino students is rarely applied to the class divisions between teachers and students in predominantly white schools. Though, interestingly, much of the recent agitation to "improve" teaching has implicitly argued a set of assumptions regarding the class of origin of public school teachers. The common belief is that teachers traditionally exhibit blue-collar origins. In any case, teachers are from the "lower classes" in most discussions of recruiting and educating teachers and in discussing the failings of schools.

Here is another conundrum for us to sort out. The traditional "blue collar" origin of many teaching professionals has been constructed as a "problem" by the Reaganistas, to be solved by replacing them with temporary craftspeople from the middle and upper classes recruited through "alternate route" certification programs. Sympathy for working-class and poor children is certainly more likely to be promoted by liberal progressive thinking implicit in the professional model (and those who have experienced social mobility themselves), than a group of dilettantes from the privileged classes who see the kids in static, class-biased terms and do not see the schools as place for social mobility. It is interesting how those who appear to promote the notion of teachers as nonprofessionals tend toward conservative views of the school's social and political function (see Chester Finn's Fordham Foundation as the best example).

If one reads a classic like Pamela Grossman's *The Making of a Teacher* (1990) through that lens, one can see that the differences between traditional professional training and the new alternative routes are a conflict between class-based ideologies. Wendy Kopp, founder of Teach for America (based on her undergraduate thesis [!] at Princeton; so much for the value of experience), certainly embodies the Reaganista notion of "trickle down" in her basic argument for "new" people in teaching and a "mission" for the elite college graduates before they go off to professional school (Kopp 2003). She argues that teaching cannot be taught (think about the logical problem in that reasoning), and so one can only assume teaching is a matter of inherent class and character (both essentials of our neo-con world). Elite curriculum, as I will discuss below, is always "different" from what the regular folks get, so it essential to the recruitment of "better class" people into teaching that the certificate route be an "alternate."

Teaching has been constructed as lower class (or low SES, as in "You can't make any money in teaching.") when it applies to professionals certified by state authorities and professional standards. If the job is constructed as a temporary position that needs little preparation other than a basic liberal arts degree, then it is considered something worthy of doing for the elite classes. In fact, the current rhetoric seems to suggest that noblesse oblige, or a missionary model to mix in with our religious metaphor, is a major factor in saving our society from the excesses of the hippie liberals who have destroyed our schools by promoting freedom and choice (consult any neo-con report or pop culture document on schooling in the past twenty-five years for the reference here). The missionary model is a neocolonialist view of low SES kids, a colonialist view more obvious when accounting for the number of new immigrants in those poor schools. Harvard Professor and *Clash of Civilizations* author Samuel Huntington's recent book, *Who We Are: The Challenges to America's National Identity* (2004) makes the argument directly: Americans need to colonize the new immigrants within our borders or risk losing "American" values which explicitly includes "Protestant" Christianity.

SCHOOLS AND CURRICULUM

Reform in schooling has traditionally only affected the working class and poor. Curriculum has not really changed for the upper classes — it is just remains different from what the other kids get. Mostly, elite curriculum reinforces a familiarity with European culture of the past. Here in New York City, we have been undergoing our own special form of school reform in response to NCLB (tagged something ironic like "Children First") and wrestling with the new political leadership model that brings in lawyers and other nonprofessionals to run the school system. In keeping with the mandates of NCLB, Chancellor Klein (under the mayor's "leadership") has instituted a common curriculum for all schools in New York City. He simultaneously released the top-performing 200 schools from the curriculum mandates. They could do whatever they wanted, since they were "successful." The majority of the schools on the list (a very carefully selected list, politically) were traditionally "elite" schools in the system, either by testing (the famous all-borough high schools like Bronx High School of Science) or, de facto, by politically powerful neighborhoods.

One could certainly argue class bias in this scheme. Students in all but the most elite settings are subjected to a reduced and common curriculum, to be reinforced by tests that would punish as well as promote. But what is most puzzling is the set of assumptions that would ignore the top-performing schools as curriculum models for the rest of the system. The only reason for that assumption would be a class-biased assumption that the high-performing schools were not just "better" than the rest but "different." Illogically as well, at least based on the common culture argument of the neo-cons, was the idea that not everyone got the same curriculum, even though they all took the same tests. Wasn't the new argument, that tests should test specific information taught by teachers in lock-step sequence, the rationale for using a common curriculum in the first place? And here we have school officials saying that the top-performing schools can teach anything they like as long as the kids score well on the tests. Maybe there are several twists in that logic beyond my comprehension, but it all looks like privilege to me.

But here we have the class issue exposed for all of its pernicious effect. What one actually finds in the elite schools is not just a special curriculum (though it doesn't matter which, since its only distinguishing factor is that it is "different"), but extensive "extracurricular" activities denied the poorer schools (conflating all meanings of "poor"). If that is not enough, in the Reaganista fee-based society, many of those extras need to be paid for by the parents who wish their children to participate. Even the desire for extracurricular activity is undermined by the fiscal reality for poor children and poor schools. The attitudes that rationalize this situation are truly shocking to me, a beneficiary of baby boom school-funding policies. Most shocking was the public pronouncement of a colleague of mine at my public university that has traditionally served the poor: "If these kids want counseling, guidance, and advising, they should go to a private university and pay for it." I think he was a war baby, and not a boomer. I believe most U.S. politicians think in similar terms, at least judging by all recent federal and state reductions in funding for public education.

And so here's the point, the essential curriculum is class-biased curriculum because it provides limited curricular and extracurricular choices to those who cannot afford in both time and money to seek them outside of schools. The kids whose parents cannot afford to provide them with an enriched curriculum outside of school (or in some districts get together with the other parents to buy time and circumstance) are stuck with the basic curriculum. For the Leftists who think the curriculum does not matter until the revolution happens, we are currently teaching a basic curriculum to a new generation of students who will not be able to grasp the "emancipatory moment" when it arrives, because they will not have the political imagination to envision a different world of possibility and equality. Further, while the content of the curriculum may now be controlled through testing, the form still isn't. Scripted lessons, the latest educational "innovation," are the next step in that process. The glimmer of hope here is that scripts are always meant to "played," not merely followed, but that will depend on the teacher assessment schema and its "consequences."

As I write this, the federal government has proposed a new student-aid plan that rewards low-income students who have completed "a rigorous secondary school program of study," with the definition of "rigorous" left up to the Secretary of Education, herself famously a non-professional (Dillon 2006). "Larger amounts" will also be available to "college juniors and seniors majoring in math, science, and other critical fields." My guess is that "rigorous" curriculum for low-income students is not the same as the curriculum needed for the math and science students. The low-income students will also be less likely to attend schools that provide the science and math courses needed to qualify for this student aid. "Rigor" has a moral and disciplinary quality to it, and suggests a de facto reduction in aid for low-income students unless they shape up and behave themselves. Many of the low-income students never get to be juniors and seniors in college anyway. Will the low-income students have access to a full college preparatory curriculum in their underfunded schools that will allow them to take advantage of the science and math awards? Class-biased school planning would suggest it is a waste of time to spend the money.

I would also like to leave a footnote on the relationship between immigration and class, recognizing that most immigrants suffer various forms of class-biased curriculum and schooling in the United States. For example, foreign language knowledge is deemed a "good" among the upper classes. But, when the multilanguage marker is applied to lower-status—and lower-class—immigrants, multiple languages are considered a barrier to learning and, more important, a threat to society. The difference: the political ideology of the ruling classes and the conservative influence of those classes. The foreign language scholar Terry Osborn has asked the important question regarding foreign language in a period of significant immigration: what exactly is "foreign" in foreign language study in the United States today (2000)? The answer, of course, rests in who you are and what you have to gain or lose in the definition. Poor immigrants are "handicapped" by their bilingualism, say the authorities, and they are treated for their deficits. Conversely, even in these patriotic times, an elite student who has not studied a foreign language is considered poorly educated.

CULTURAL CHANGE AND CURRICULUM CHANGE

The problem with most theories of class and curriculum is that they are static rather than dynamic. Here is the reason we do not want to buy into the essentialist curriculum argument or the deterministic political argument: both are based on assumptions about the nature of culture and cultural change that are too simplistic. For example, the Left determinist view holds that there is a neoconservative dominant culture that can be replaced with a culture dominated by social justice—the notion is that there are two cultural positions at war with one another (the Hegel-Marx dialectic). One criticism of deterministic theory is the demonstrated tendency for the power structure of elitism to reassert itself after a revolution, so a "just" society like the Communist revolution–inspired Soviet Russia will always re-create an elite class and attendant educational structure. The liberal essentialist view holds that most of popular culture—that is, everyday experience—is irrelevant or merely distracting from true knowledge—the notion being that there is a real culture hidden underneath all the distractions and false knowledge. You can see how the conflict metaphor basic to one and the religious metaphor basic to the other as they play out in those positions.

But, at any given point in time there is no single culture but a multitude of cultures. Schools, especially in the curriculum, normally represent only the official culture. Major parts of culture are not represented in school curriculum, the best current example being all forms of popular new media. One assumes that that the official curriculum ignores popular culture as a means for de legitimizing it. Yet, all efforts to standardize, homogenize, and eliminate popular culture have failed.

Raymond Williams has speculated on cultural development and argued that at any given time a culture includes a dominant culture, but also an emergent culture, reflecting new movements and developments, for example, avant-garde art or new technologies, and a residual culture reflecting deliberately maintained traditions of obsolete culture, for example, opera or horseback riding (Williams 1975, 2003). Residual culture tends to be identified with upper-class conservatism, but also would include religious culture that rejects modern culture, the Mennonites being one extreme. Using this residual-dominant-emergent heuristic for framing curriculum development, one could say that the dominant culture is the official curriculum and is the basis for common school curriculum. The residual culture forms the additional curriculum for the elite classes, especially connected to European sources. Emergent culture is rarely reflected in the official school curriculum—even in progressive college curricula emergent cultural studies tend to be interdisciplinary, or outside the traditional disciplines.

I might add here, referencing my point about common culture curriculum under the Reaganistas, that the current dominant culture is anti-intellectual. The neo-con public relations vision of the ideal American is based on a portrayal of commonsense and action dictated by "confident" leadership. (*Confident* is President Bush's favorite word when asked to provide a rationale for a policy or decision: he says he is confident or he has confidence in the decision. One dictionary definition of "confidence" is "the state of feeling certain about the truth of something.") The president's stance, identical to Ronald Reagan's, is to pose as a cowboy, an outdoorsman of few words and decisive action, the objective correlative and central metaphor of which appears to be brush cutting. One could certainly argue that U.S. culture has never been an intellectual culture (see Hofstadter, *Anti-Intellectualism in American Life*, 1966), but it appears that we are now doing our best to ignore the important changes in the culture and/or resist them (the stem cell debate, censorship of public airwaves, Darwin and "intelligent design," and many other examples reported daily).

Some of the anti-intellectualism is a reaction against the creative and revolutionary elements of the 1960s. The initial attacks on the school curriculum in the neo-con revolution were the attacks on the elective system—the smorgasbord curriculum—that had cropped up in high schools mimicking the elective system in the colleges. Sizer's "less is more" approach fits right into the anti-intellectual model, though he would not agree with the fundamental anti-intellectualism. In the official *Guide to NYC Small High Schools* available to parents, we find this bold heading: "You will learn fewer subjects well" (*New York Post* 2004). The short text following says that students will be "expected to meet state graduation requirements" and that the small schools "will not have hundreds of different classes to choose from" (How is that for policy by negation?). One of the assumptions of this sort of controlled curriculum is that school authorities know what is best for students. It is especially interesting to note that 100 years after the invention of film and fifty after television transformed our culture—not to mention the computer—there is still no form of media study in the official curriculum. Raymond Williams might provide some insight into why this is, in his historical study of British schools, that in a time of tremendous cultural change the curriculum would be restricted:

> It is interesting that at the beginning of the industrial revolution in Britain, when education had to be reorganized, the ruling class decided to teach working people to read but not to write. If they could read, they could understand new kinds of instructions and, moreover, they could read the Bible for their moral improvement. They did not need writing, however, since they would have no orders or instructions or lessons to communicate. . . . The full range of writing came later, with further development of the society and the economy (Williams 1974, 131).

Literacy for the masses cannot be the same as literacy for the gentleperson classes, says the school authority, because the lower classes cannot be trusted to use their new knowledge for the betterment of society. On the other hand, this is a Pandora's box situation, as Williams points out, because, "There was no way to teach a man to read the Bible which did not also enable him to read the radical press. A controlled intention became an uncontrolled effect." Some thinkers such as Williams see the increasing democratization of literacy as an unstoppable force in overall democratization. The recent attempts to reduce the curriculum could be seen as an attempt to stop the democratization of knowledge, or at least control it into meaninglessness.

Now, of course, one might argue that I am overblowing the situation here—I sound like one of those conspiracy theorists. Have the "powers that be" really been trying to keep the children of working-class parents illiterate? Didn't I just say that Raymond Williams showed a historical progression toward more available literacy? I didn't say that Williams said it was an easy process, nor a guaranteed one. Like any good neo-Marxist scholar, he sees the increase in freedom and the growth of literacy as reciprocal. On the other hand, there are all sorts of precedents to show the attempts to keep literacy from the people. In medieval Germany, rulers went so far as to invent a sign system for their illiterate peasants, rather than teach them "real" German. One also needs to be reminded that every first translator of the Bible into the vernacular language, one that could be read by those who were literate but not in Latin, was burned at the stake by the authorities. Even the vernacularly literate were to be kept illiterate when it came to the language of the law and the church, since that remained in Latin for centuries. Upper-class education in Great Britain was conducted in Latin and Greek until the twentieth century, as were the professional discourses. Though the case is not as extreme in the United States, Latin was not dropped as a requirement for college admission until 1912, about the same time British universities moved toward English studies as the dominant discourse.

In the end, the current U.S. policy demanding "rigorous" curriculum probably means teaching simple textual literacy in a world where literacy is complex and multimedia. The Reaganista movement toward standardizing the curriculum is an attempt to stop cultural movement, or return the culture to pre-1932. Neo-cons are not elitists in the old sense, like liberals, but ideologues (some would say fascists) who want to stop time, and then turn back the clock to a time before the liberal transformation of society represented first by Roosevelt's New Deal and enhanced by Johnson's Great Society. This form of elitism is anti-intellectual in nature. It pretends to care about education while providing nothing more than basic knowledge that is then legitimated as real knowledge by a standardized test. Everyone is officially stupid under the neo-con educational model, almost as if Orwell's *1984* had been the blueprint.

But students need diversity and complexity in the curricular options. Much of the rhetoric of the small school movement has been built around educational options, even though the curriculum is standardized and reduced. One of the fears of social thinkers is that the new small schools will become new bastions of elitism. Indeed, along with the small school movement one finds a push for the development of honors colleges within large public universities. This development is also part of the new stratification. The "smart" kids are funneled into special, and small, classes with full-time professors while the "regular" kids continue to attend huge lectures and be taught by adjunct instructors or graduate students. The "smart" kids also tend to get free tuition and other perks such as free laptop computers, while the "regular" students are on their own—sink or swim. One could see the relationship of the new small schools to the rest of the kids in the traditional schools as a similar structural arrangement.

CURRICULUM FOR THE TWENTY-FIRST CENTURY

I would like to suggest several starting points as necessary for redefining curriculum in our time to reduce the overall bias against all citizens outside the ruling classes. First, the obvious anti-intellectualism needs to be accounted for, along with the limitations of subject matter. Reduce tracking, yes, but that doesn't seem too likely, given parental demands. Instead, why not rethink the source of the curriculum and put some faith back in the teaching professionals, if there are any left after the current frenzy for alternatively certified teachers.

First, teachers who want to make a difference should focus on the emergent culture, in relation to the dominant, for the poor and working class. The poor and working-class students rarely receive any exposure to residual culture, except to point out they lack any knowledge of it. Deemphasizing residual culture does not mean removing history—we just need to stop living in the past. Anyway, cultural literacy as defined by Hirsch and others (a mix of dominant and residual) is not dedicated to the transformation of the culture in any case. Develop the emergent culture curriculum, essentially popular culture, around student experience and interest (a variation on Dewey). Certainly the new emphasis on testing is designed to stop us from doing this, but the core of the testable dominant curriculum is so small in the current anti-intellectual less-is-more format that there is plenty of time for study of emerging cultural movements. Schema theory would suggest that connections between a student's mental schema and the school curriculum are essential to meaningful learning in any case. In other words, the students' experience must jibe in some fashion with what you are trying to teach them for any meaningful learning to take place.

Speaking of modern learning theories, situated cognition is also necessary to moving beyond the calcified strata of class-based school curriculum (see Lave and Wenger 1991). The neo-con cultural literacy idea is based on a faulty translation, or misappropriation, of schema theory in which the brain is compared to a computer hard drive with stored data to be accessed at will (Hirsch 1987). Situated cognition returns the temporal and the situational to the engagement and exhibition of knowledge, and returns the prior knowledge teaching strategy to its problem-solving origin as a condition for thinking, rather than a test of trivia and mark of "quality" and "rigor." Situated cognitive experience (versus a recall of information model) changes the class structure of schooling by eliminating the "deficit" rationalization from school tracking assignments. Situated cognition also deflates instructional strategies that assume kids cannot learn because they lack prior knowledge that some teacher in an earlier grade should have taught them. What is prior knowledge for the twenty-first century, anyway, that isn't more about the *now* of dominant and emergent culture than the *then* of residual culture? On the other side of that argument, we have a U.S. president appointing Supreme Court judges who believe in strict constructionism, an approach that says we must look to the original intentions, through literal textual interpretation, of the eighteenth-century authors of that document for the rule of law in the centuries following. How much more important could focusing education on the future be in that scenario?

Having said all of this, I would also argue that the culture is too rich for a school system to remain oppressive or limited for long. School becomes completely irrelevant when it is too controlled. The small schools movement, contradictory to its less-is-more arguments, will develop communities of learners who will begin to define their knowledge differently from state expectations. The college honors students will be the first to rebel against the standard curriculum of the college once they begin to interact with the "regular" students. Differentiated curriculum promotes diversity after all, and diversity introduces complexity back into the argument. We need to promote difference that is not a status difference—though status is a slippery thing to pin down in the world increasingly defined by raw capitalist power and Re-Gilded Age celebrities such as Donald Trump. The small schools movement promotes communities of learners who will assume their own status markers. Recent studies of student use of information technology outside of the official curriculum seem to suggest they are also redefining cultural categories and crossing racial and class lines—the current dominance of hip hop culture should be sufficient evidence for anyone.

I do not doubt that inequality of some sort is likely to continue, but it is impossible to define what the status cultural capital will be in the near future. Who would have thought übernerds such as Bill Gates would have so much power and cultural influence when we were in school during the 1960s? It is always difficult to predict relevance. After failing to make the transition to the Renaissance way of thinking, medieval monasteries were simply shut down by Henry VIII in the sixteenth century. A school system that tries to maintain its connection with the past is doomed to the same fate. That could be what the Reaganistas are up to, returning us to a time in the past when America was for Americans and everyone knew their place in the scheme of things. Others would argue that the Reaganistas are transforming the schools for the brave new world of service workers who need little complex knowledge and very little special training (see Aronwitz 2004). In either case, the result is the same, and the diagnosis, as well as the practical "solution," remains either essentialist or deterministic.

Finally, there is a confusion of the mandated curriculum with the teacher-generated curriculum in most of the arguments about curriculum. The mandated curriculum is always a political wish list and not an operationalized curriculum. When one considers the teacher's role in curriculum development and implementation, one begins to see how the deterministic approach either allows teachers to pass the buck ("I am required to teach only the state-mandated curriculum.") or excuse oneself from participation in the kids' education ("What can one teacher do?"). The essentialist position becomes an excuse for not engaging the world fully; essentialism allows the teacher to aim low and close the door to the classroom. In the worst-case scenarios, the determinist view of school becomes meaningless; the essentialist view reduces the curriculum to "preparatory" study.

The school curriculum needs to be changed primarily to make the lives of children and adolescents better. Right here. Right now. As Dewey said, "Education is not preparation for life. It is life." The curriculum is a major part of that process, and the individual teacher has the key role to play in the classroom experience. The great social forces of popular dissent or a revolution in the street are not necessary to make that change. The teaching professional is necessary though, if nothing else, to allow the kids to explore their world outside the limiting official curriculum. But teachers need to do more that just get out of the way of student learning, and that requires some understanding of how kids learn. It also requires a connection to popular culture, children's and adolescent versions as well as adult versions. Central to that connection with the world outside of school is a movement toward multimedia knowing and representing.

What also appear to be needed are some complexity and a tiny bit of chaos. The new school leadership models, based on hiring nonprofessionals with leadership qualities, are part of the same neo-con movement, an attempt to limit and control intellectual freedom in American education. It is up to the teacher, the individual teacher working with colleagues, including enlightened teaching professionals serving as administrators, who have the same respect for children and education, to subvert the limitations of the official curriculum. This process is not too different from the old question-authority model of teaching, but it allows for a new construction of authority. Barring a fascist roundup of the teachers (I know, it has happened before), the current limited, anti-intellectual system may fail in any case under the weigh of its own absurdity. As Mark Twain opined, "Against the assault of laughter, nothing can stand." If it doesn't, then the armed revolution may be necessary. But we might in the meantime simply engage the world and resist the attempts of others to limit and control our thinking. And then the revolution will come.

REFERENCES

Anyon, Jean. (1980). Social Class and the Hidden Curriculum of Work. *Journal of Education* 162 (1): 67–92.
——. (2005). *Radical Possibilities: Public Policy, Urban Education, and a New Social Movement.* New York: Routledge.
Apple, Michael. (2004). *Ideology and Curriculum.* 3rd ed. New York: Taylor & Francis.
Aronowitz, Stanley. (2004). *How Class Works.* New Haven, Conn.: Yale University Press.

Aronowitz, Stanley, and Giroux, Henry. (1993). *Education Still Under Siege*. 2nd ed. Waterbury, Conn.: Bergin & Garvey.

Bernstein, Basil. (1971). *Class, Codes, and Control: Theoretical Studies Towards a Sociology of Language*. London: Paladin.

Bloom, Allan. (1988). *The Closing of the American Mind*. New York: Simon & Schuster.

Bourdieu, Pierre. (1993). *The Field of Cultural Production*. New York: Columbia University Press.

Bowles, Samuel, and Gintis, Herbert. (1976). *Schooling in Capitalist America*. New York: Routledge.

Bush, George W. (January 8, 2004) Presidential speech. Palm Gardens, Fla. www.newsmax.com/archives/articles/2004/1/9/110923.shtml

Coalition of Essential Schools National Web Site. www.essentialschools.org/

Crowe, Cameron. (1981) *Fast Times at Ridgemont High*. New York: Fireside.

Delpit, Lisa (1988). The Silenced Dialogue: Power and Pedagogy in Educating Other People's Children. *Harvard Educational Review*. 58 (3): 280–98.

Dewey, John. My Pedagogic Creed. *The School Journal* 54, (3) (January 16, 1897): 77–80.

Dillon, Sam. College Aid Plan Widens U.S. Role in High Schools. *New York Times* January 22, 2006. 1 (Late Edition).

Giroux, Henry (2001). *Theory and Resistance in Education: Towards a Pedagogy for the Opposition*. Rev. and exp. ed. Waterbury, Conn.: Bergin & Garvey.

Grossman, Pamela. (1990). *The Making of a Teacher: Teacher Knowledge & Teacher Education*. Professional Development and Practice Series. New York: Teachers College Press.

Guide to NYC Small High Schools. *New York Post*. Supplement. November 11, 2004.

Harrington, Michael. (1962). *The Other America: Poverty in the United States*. Repr. 1997 . New York: Scribner.

Hirsch, E. D. (1987). *Cultural Literacy: What Every American Needs to Know*. Boston: Houghton Mifflin.

Hofstadter, Richard. (1966). *Anti-Intellectualism in American Life*. New York: Vintage.

Horn, Catherine, and Flores, Stella. (2003). Percent Plans in College Admissions: A Comparative Analysis of Three States' Experiences. The Civil Rights Project, Harvard University. www.civilrightsproject.harvard.edu/research/affirmativeaction/tristate.php

Huntington, Samuel. (2004). *Who We Are: The Challenges to America's National Identity*. New York: Simon & Schuster.

Kincheloe, Joe. (2005). *Critical Pedagogy*. A Peter Lang Primer. New York: Peter Lang.

Kopp, Wendy. (2003). *One Day, All Children: The Unlikely Triumph of Teach for America and What I Learned Along the Way*. New York: Public Affairs.

Lave, Jean, and Wenger, Etienne. (1991). "Situated Learning: Legitimate Peripheral Participation." *Learning in Doing: Social, Cognitive & Computational Perspectives*. Cambridge: Cambridge University Press.

Lemann, Nicholas. (1999). *The Big Test: The Secret History of the American Meritocracy*. New York: Farrar, Straus and Giroux.

Loveless, Tom. (1999). *The Tracking Wars: State Reform Meets School Policy*. Washington, D.C.: Brookings Institution Press.

Mathews, Jay. (1998). *Class Struggle: What's Wrong (and Right) with America's Best Public Schools*. New York: Crown.

———. Learning to Stand Out Among the Standouts: Some Asian Americans Say Colleges Expect More From Them. *Washington Post*. March 22, 2005. A10.

The National Forum. (2000). *Responses from Bush-Cheney 2000*. www.mgforum.org/News/forumnews/bush.asp

Osborn, Terry A. (2000). *Critical Reflection and the Foreign Language Classroom*. Waterbury, Conn.: Bergin & Garvey.

Ravitch, Diane, and Finn, Chester. (1988). *What Do Our 17-Year Olds Know?: A Report on the First National Assessment of History and Literature*. New York: HarperCollins.

Sizer, Theodore. (1984). *Horace's Compromise: The Dilemma of the American High School*. Boston: Houghton Mifflin.

U.S. Department of Education. What Works Clearinghouse. www.whatworks.ed.gov

Vonnegut, Kurt. (1968). Harrison Bergeron. In *Welcome to the Monkey House*. New York: Delta.

Williams, Raymond. (2003). *Television: Technology and Cultural Form*. London: Fontana.

——— (1975). *The Long Revolution*. New York: Greenwood Press Reprint.

Willis, Paul. (1981). *Learning to Labor*. New York: Columbia University Press.

Young, Michael D. (1994). *The Rise of the Meritocracy*. London: Transaction Publications.

CHAPTER 6

Issues of Class in Urban Science Education
Kenneth Tobin

whats up doc? since school i havent been able to get 2 a computer and probably wont get to use one for another week or so, but i do have a question. i want to get a new job, but not just any job, a good job. i also want to get away from home, but am afraid to go to the service. unfortunitly my grades in school havent been consistant and college is pretty much out of the question. i dont know what to do. can you help?

My worst nightmare was unfolding. Shakeem, an African American male, was someone I'd worked with since he came into grade nine. Our research team, including teachers from his school, identified Shakeem as a student who was at high risk of dropping out of school. Accordingly, we recruited him as a student researcher and over a six-year period learned to marvel at his quick wit, active mind, and poetic sense of being. Shakeem was playful, very social, and projected self-assurance, and his participation in a summer physics course led me to predict that he would one day graduate with a Ph.D. in physics. I told him of my prediction regularly, as a metaphor for how talented I regarded him. Yet, Shakeem was always on the cusp of trouble with those in authority and routinely violated rules, in and out of school.

As he progressed through high school Shakeem passed some courses and failed others, gradually falling behind his cohort. Yet in any class his talent level always seemed to me to be a step above most others. His record of disrupting class was not good and frequently he was thrown out, leading to numerous suspensions. Accordingly, more than once I had to intervene on his behalf with the school principal, an African American woman, to have him reinstated from suspension. My argument was that it was in nobody's interest for Shakeem to be pushed out of school. The principal accepted this perspective and allowed him to come to school, acknowledging his struggles with poverty, race, and gender. In a school in which most students had limited economic resources, more than 90 percent from households with incomes below the poverty line, Shakeem's peers considered him poor and his clothes, shoes, and hairstyle were signs of poverty and low status—resources for the disrespect of his peers. So, for Shakeem, school was a challenging field academically and socially, exacerbated by the fact that City High, a comprehensive inner-city school, was not his neighborhood school.

CAPITAL PRODUCTION AND SOCIAL CLASS

When we began to work with Shakeem he had lived in Philadelphia for two and a half years having come from housing projects in Atlantic City. Shakeem lived with an adult, his mother and/or his grandmother, learning from them how to do the things he needed to do in the home and outside of it. As he interacted with others in the home, he did so with the purpose of meeting his own goals and helping them to attain their goals. Within this context, Shakeem developed language skills, created values, and built knowledge about many things, including basic literacy and numeracy, social sciences, the arts, religion, health and nutrition, and sports. However, the events that fashioned his learning were not necessarily pleasant. According to Shakeem, his social life was aggravated by his mother's dependencies on drugs, reliance on welfare, and movements from one home to another, and hence from one neighborhood to another.

For the first several years of our research Shakeem lived mainly with his grandmother, in a racially segregated part of the city (97 percent black). Shakeem explained that many of the people in this area are retired and very few of the youth have legal employment; many of the males aged between eighteen and twenty are drug dealers (Seiler 2002). Prior to this stint of residing with his grandmother, Shakeem lived with his mother in a neighborhood in which crime and drug use were pervasive and many buildings were abandoned, some being used as crack houses. However, because his mother was unable to pay the rent, Shakeem moved back to his grandmother's home, where he and his mother had lived when they first moved from Atlantic City. Moving in and out of neighborhoods created difficulties for Shakeem and his campaign for the respect of peers.

In all the neighborhoods in which he lived Shakeem interacted with people of the same race and with a similar degree of poverty. Through play and life activities Shakeem developed forms of capital to allow him to succeed—notably, he learned ways of speaking, forms of physical activity, and how to create and use social networks. In each new neighborhood Shakeem had to earn the respect of the neighborhood youth, initially through basketball where his efforts to participate were rebuffed. Persistent efforts, talent, and a willingness to fight when necessary eventually allowed him to get involved, earn respect, and gain status in a particular neighborhood.

Although Shakeem regarded his grandmother as a pain because she wanted him to remain active and help with the household chores, it is apparent that he loved and respected her. Similarly he showed affection for his younger brother and knew exactly what his brother needed to do if he were to make a success of his life. Shakeem was willing to act as a role model for his brother, to give him advice on what and what not to do. Shakeem was not conscious of, some aspects of being a role model for his brother, who shared many of his attributes, including oral fluency, and an ability to think on his feet and interact quickly with witty and caustic comments. Like Shakeem, his brother also used rhythm and rap and was often poetic.

Shakeem participated in many fields, initially as a peripheral participant and, as he accrued the necessary capital, his roles became more central. For example, the church, the basketball court, and the streets, including stairwells leading down to the entrances of apartments, were salient fields. Not only were these places for Shakeem to go and hang out, but also fields in which he could learn, meet people, and establish his identity. In the process Shakeem built reservoirs of capital that could be enacted to meet individual and collective goals. The capital he built was a primary part of his agency, positioning him in social space with others having similar capital.

One way to think about social class is in terms of economic, cultural, social, and symbolic capital. As capital increases, agency (that is, the capacity to act) expands, and there is a possibility of attaining more goals and improving the quality of social life. Different forms of capital are more useful than others in a given field. For example, in Shakeem's lifeworld he created the capital needed to succeed in his home and neighborhood. However, the capital needed for success in the streets differed significantly from the capital needed to meet his goals when he was at church. Similarly, Shakeem's capital did not equip him well for success in school.

Life in the Neighborhood

Shakeem projects an image of trusting few people, self-reliance, sensitivity to the needs of others, loyalty, and dependability. He explains that at age fifteen, since he was 260 pounds and 6 foot 1 inch tall, he is one of the bigger kids in his neighborhood. He describes how he is respected for what he can do and focuses on his athletic agility, despite his size.

In an interview with Shakeem, a striking factor is how he represents his neighborhood as dangerous for outsiders and his home circumstances as poor. While depicting his neighborhood as dangerous, Shakeem identifies getting shot as a possibility of coming to visit him and warns a white female interviewer to "be sure yo' tires have air and that there is gas in the tank." He explains that there are no taxis in the 'hood and no public transportation either. The implication is that cabs will not come to this neighborhood, even when called. Shakeem suggests that people in the neighborhood like to keep to themselves and are unlikely to help if a stranger gets into trouble.

There is no doubt that Shakeem's neighborhood can be dangerous and that his descriptions are accurate. However, in focusing on violence Shakeem appears to be playing with his female interviewer, presenting images to show how his neighborhood differs from where she lives. A more balanced picture of the neighborhood is obtained from the two video ethnographies Shakeem produced in his role as a student researcher involved in collaborative research on teaching and learning science in urban high schools (Tobin, Elmesky, and Seiler 2005).

Two features emerge from an analysis of the video ethnographies: oral fluency and pervasive use of profanity. Shakeem is very fluent in his oral exchanges, self-assured in his neighborhood, and interacts successfully across age ranges from very young to quite elderly. The video depicts Shakeem involved in friendly and tender interactions with babies, mothers, relatives, young children, and adults ranging in age from the early twenties to mid seventies. The video also shows gardens, parks, verandahs, pavements bustling with people, the living room of his grandmother's home, the ball court at 2:30 A.M. and in the daylight, and various staging grounds where Shakeem and other youth gather in the streets. Despite his description of the neighborhood as dangerous, Shakeem does not regard it through deficit lenses and enjoys living there. He points out that the 'hood is a place in which he has his family and friends and he only goes outside to attend school and visit his mother, who had moved back to New Jersey. Otherwise, almost all of what Shakeem does out of school is accomplished in the neighborhood.

With peers Shakeem speaks fluently, talks trash to them, and uses profanity prolifically. Rap is part of his everyday life as he interacts with peers in the streets and in the stairwells outside their homes. There is often a free flow of talk that begins as prose and ends up being poetic, often expressed as rap. The coordinated movement of the body as peers interact is rhythmical and attuned to the oral commentary.

Within his neighborhood it is evident that Shakeem has effective communication skills that allow him to interact successfully across boundaries of age, gender, and family. He has a strong sense of belonging that transcends family lines. For example, he refers affectionately in his video ethnography to his young son[1], Lil' Steve, a child for whom Shakeem is a role model. Shakeem beams with pride when Lil' Steve performs a rap that, like Shakeem's raps, are laced with violence and profanity. Later, inside his grandmother's house he introduces a set of peers, including "Young Bol, my alibi," a friend for almost a decade. His sense of belonging to his neighborhood, his solidarity with it, is evident in the network of people with whom he interacts successfully, and the places that symbolize to him the essence of social life in his neighborhood. Although Shakeem's family has little income to support it, and most of the neighborhood lives in similar economic conditions, Shakeem knows how to live a comfortable and happy life in his neighborhood and he uses his agency to choose certain pathways and avoid others.

Drugs, guns, and violence are part of the neighborhood and Shakeem has experienced each at a young age—has taken and dealt drugs, has owned a gun, and has been involved in physical violence. Yet he has turned his back on these and other negative aspects of his neighborhood, dreaming of leaving, earning some money, and taking his family and friends with him from poverty toward a life in which more material goods are a reality. Like so many African American males, he sees his hope in sports—the National Football League because he is big and the National Basketball Association because he is tall. Initially Shakeem made some choices based on his goal of creating a better life through sports. He chose to come to City High because the school had a stronger reputation as a football school than some of the others he may have attended. However, as it became clear to Shakeem that he would not make the high school sports teams he changed his goals, always declaring that a college education was a necessary minimum for obtaining a good job.

OVERVIEW

In this chapter I explore the relationships between Shakeem's social class and possible reasons for his failure to succeed in high school—managing to graduate several years after most of his cohort. Shakeem's graduation was cause for me to celebrate, although I had grave doubts that his success would produce prospects for a better social life. Before addressing Shakeem's participation in high school science and his work with me as a student researcher I explore some aspects of school life for Tyrone and Nicole, two students who share some of the same characteristics of race and social class as Shakeem.

YOU CALL THIS AN OPPORTUNITY?

I have been nagged by the thought that a diploma from an urban high school is analogous to counterfeit currency. I am sure many have used the term *opportunity*, but it struck a chord with me when Gale Seiler used it in relation to students who were doing research with us. These students were in a special small learning community[2] created for those who need a fresh start to high school. Ironically the small learning community was termed *Opportunity*—some might argue a last opportunity or perhaps no opportunity. The reasons for students being assigned to Opportunity include one or more of the following: failure to settle down in school, unacceptable performance, high frequencies of suspension, sporadic attendance at school, and extended absence for reasons such as having a child or being incarcerated.

In many respects an assignment to Opportunity was a sentence to the worst that urban schools can offer. For example, Opportunity had only one science teacher who had to teach all four required science courses and electives. He was a new teacher who was young, sincere, hardworking, and liked by most of his students. Though he was certified to teach biology his background in that subject was minimal and his academic record showed no breadth in his studies of science. We observed many contradictions. For example, students in Opportunity were enrolled for a physical science course, but were taught biology. Students were thereby shortchanged because physical science showed on their transcripts yet they did not have opportunities to learn the content others might assume they knew. The teacher justified this approach with an argument that it was better for students to be taught something he knew about rather than something he was learning the night before teaching it. Similarly, school administrators placed students into classes to earn credit for courses that differed from what was taught. This was especially the case in mathematics where many students in Opportunity participated in basic math courses and received credit for Pre-Algebra, and Algebra 1. Getting the credits was seen as an end in itself, a way to get students through high school, and it is not surprising that many students were angered by the curriculum's lack of demand. Contradictions like these were primary reasons for our research team's concern that the diploma students earned would not be negotiable in terms of gaining further education in a university, proceeding to study advanced courses later in high school, or getting a good job. The diploma carried little status and was a symbol of success in graduating high school and little else.

Trouble[3]

Tyrone is an African American male of about sixteen years of age who presents himself as a street kid. His dreadlocks are arranged asymmetrically, his demeanor is gruff, and frequently his dress is unkempt. His teacher, who knew Tyrone well, explained to me that he is a good kid who looks like a thug and interacts with others according to the code of the street (Anderson 1999). Accordingly, Tyrone is often in trouble with other teachers and nonteaching assistants[4] whose job it is to maintain order in the school. Also, his explosive temper often lands him in trouble and leads to his suspension from school. Tyrone is cognizant of his appearance causing problems in the school. He commented:

> Lot of people tell me it's my hair. But I'm not cutting it for no one. I don't understand it. I should be able to wear my hair, or dress whatever how I want. As long as I got my mind, right? It should be cool. It's like people just look at me automatically they just start stereotyping me. You gotta stay on him. He ain't going to do what he got to do. Stay with him. That sometimes really make me mad. It's like I'll be trying my hardest, and people just still down on me.

Tyrone comes to school when it is convenient. He walks to City High and prefers not to do so in inclement weather. He does not like detention, and so, if there's a chance he'll be late and thereby risk detention he does not leave home, or he does not attempt to enter the school building. Also, since his mother sleeps during the day and his father neither speaks to Tyrone nor cares whether or not he attends school, Tyrone just goes back to sleep if he wakes up feeling tired or in a bad mood. Some days he just decides to hang out with friends from his neighborhood. On such occasions he may roam the streets in the northern part of the city, closer to his home than the school. Also, for a variety of reasons, Tyrone gets suspended for five days at a time and,

---

Textbox 6.1
Voice over: Although the description seems apt from the perspective of my social class, the loss of temper implies a loss of control. When he experienced frustration, Tyrone raised the intensity and the frequency of his voice and usually spoke over those with whom he was interacting. I interpret this as enacting practices in school that Tyrone learned and used successfully to resolve conflict in his neighborhood.

because his mother must accompany him to get re-admitted, he often remains away for several days after completing his suspension. Not surprisingly, Tyrone's sporadic attendance at school has consequences for his participation and performance.

When Tyrone is at school he prefers to work alone and sits off to the side so that he is not distracted by others or drawn into trouble by students who are off-task or disruptive. However, because of his poor record of attendance Tyrone needs to be updated by his teachers and he expects them to provide the necessary assistance on demand. If teachers do not make every effort to teach him and assign work that he has missed, Tyrone becomes disgruntled and his impatience often catalyzes confrontations with them. Being respected is critical to Tyrone and he regards the failure of teachers to provide him with the assistance he needs as disrespectful. Also, teachers' efforts to assert control over students are perceived as disrespectful along with myriad practices that we observed as an everyday part of teaching, especially in Opportunity.

> Tyrone: It's all in the teacher's attitude. 'Cause some teachers just see it like this. I'm the teacher. I got the authority. You gonna listen to what I say. Students, they don't like that no more. It not like it was back in the day when you would spank a student for not doing what they supposed to be doin'. Nowadays you gotta treat a student just like you wanna be treated with a little respect. If not then that student ain't gonna give you no respect. I know like me. The way I see it—I respect all teachers if they respect me. You don't respect me why should I respect you? Respect is a two-way street from what I learned.
>
> Certain students, if they don't like a certain teacher then they won't do the teacher's work. They won't listen to the teacher. They'll ignore the teacher and there's nothin' the teacher can do about it. So . . . like . . . the more they try to teach them . . . the more they try to teach that . . . they really don't care for what the teachers talkin' about—even if they're interested in what the teachers talkin' about they don't like that teacher.

Tyrone is intelligent, articulate, and logical in the way he describes his goals and the raw deal he has been dealt at City High. Tyrone's perceptions of his schooling at City High are encapsulated in the following excerpt from an interview with him.

I don't like it because for the simple fact that what they teaching me is too easy. It's not the teachers there, or the students, or how it is. It's the work. 'Cause it's like, they give me some work to do. I'm finished in about twenty minutes. Each period is an hour and fifteen minutes long. So now I'm sitting there for about forty-five minutes doing nothing . . . The work they give me is too just too easy.

Despite the clarity of Tyrone's claim and its centrality in his descriptions of school life, there is a contradiction to be addressed. Tyrone's understanding of science is not strong and yet his claim that the work is easy is typical of those made by his peers. For example, when Tyrone undertook an investigation in which he immersed a penny into a solution of zinc ions he expected the coin to "turn to silver" and, based on a science activity from the previous year, he predicted that it would "turn to gold" if he heated the silver coin in a Bunsen flame. Tyrone participated enthusiastically in the lab and when he confirmed his predictions he announced that when he came back the next day the coins would have reverted to their former state. His explanation was that the color would just rub off. A few days later when Tyrone came to school I handed him the coins. He looked delighted and asked to keep them. When I asked him about the color not rubbing off he looked perplexed and carefully observed the coins, explaining that the colors had rubbed off last year. From his perspective, Tyrone understood what happened, could describe what he had done and how the coins changed, and he was done with this activity (again). However, he did not have the concepts to explain the science of what happened, and he was not interested in knowing more. I wonder if this is because a lab such as this has little relevance to his life and has only curiosity value. If he had been exploring the chemistry of hair treatments the situation might have been different since he spent many hours each week having his hair stylized.

Perhaps the best example of a lack of autonomy given the students in Opportunity is that they have no choice about the electives they take. Within a small learning community the science teacher decides on the electives to be offered and then a school-level roster person assigns students to classes based on filling classes to capacity and what students need to complete the requirements for graduation. Tyrone had virtually no understanding of these requirements or a specific sense of what he had completed, beyond an awareness that, after two years of high school, he was still a freshman. Tyrone's sporadic attendance leads directly to his failure in many courses and also makes it difficult for him to understand subjects like chemistry and gain a passing grade in any of his subjects. The consequences are that he needs to repeat many of his classes, leading to boredom, and a sense that the teachers are wasting his time. In terms of science, Tyrone had taken physical science three times, and biology and chemistry once each for a total of 1.5 credits. I was astonished by the primary contradiction that he was so smart while being a chronic failure at high school. In two years of schooling he had accumulated only 9 credits, leaving 12.5 required to graduate. As I talked to Tyrone about his program of study it was clear that a schedule was something done to him, not an opportunity to study courses of interest or to pursue vocational preferences.

After three years in grade nine Tyrone simply gave up on high school. As soon as he was old enough, Tyrone stopped attending regular school and participated in Twilight, a late-afternoon alternative program for students with serious personal and academic problems. Tyrone never adjusted to being told what to do. He liked to make decisions for himself and then to accept the consequences. The school's emphasis on controlling students from the moment they entered the building was at odds with Tyrone's lifeworld where he had to watch his own back and accept full responsibility for his actions. Hence, it was no surprise that Tyrone soon quit Twilight and became an official school drop-out. After a period of living at home without employment Tyrone enrolled in a charter school that prepared students for the Graduate Education Diploma (GED) while teaching them a building trade. Tyrone liked to use his hands, found the program relevant to his needs, and passed the GED.

Getting Students Through

Many of the students in Opportunity were frustrated by the rhetoric of being given an opportunity to succeed and were highly cynical about their educational opportunities. For example, the following dialogue emerged in an interview with Tyrone and Nicole, a fellow student from Opportunity. Nicole lost her single mother at the tender age of three years and soon after her grandmother also died. Her guardian was her cousin, who declared her uncontrollable. Hence, Nicole had little encouragement to excel at school.

Tyrone: How you feel about this school?

Nicole: I don't like it.

Tyrone: Why is that?

Nicole: Because I don't like the charter[5] I'm in. And I don't like Miss Friar and I don't like some of these teachers in here. They try to discipline you for dumb stuff. Like if I do something wrong I get suspended for five days. What is, I mean, that's not helping me out. That's not helping me get my school together or my behavior together. I mean, I don't like that. I don't like this school, period. I'd like like a different charter, whatever like that. But Opportunity and the people that run it? No. I really dislike them.

Tyrone: So what would you change about Opportunity?

Nicole: I would make Miss Friar and all these NTAs and them leave. I would it make it so that these kids in here can get a opportunity to get better grades. Everybody here in Opportunity is failing. How, how this helping them out? Come on now.

Tyrone: Why you think they're failing?

Nicole: Because they be giving us, I can't curse, right? (Laugh) They giving us dumb work, you know. Work that's not even, you know, challenging to us or nothing. That work is like when I was in like eighth grade. Come on now. Please. I can do that just in a heartbeat. They be callin this *Opportunity*. They supposed to give you the opportunity to do real work. What have I actually learned in Opportunity? Nothing. I had Chemistry, English, and Conflict. What have I actually learned from any of them classes? Nothing. I can sit here and tell you, honestly. Nothing. And this is what charter? *Opportunity* right? It ain't *Opportunity*. It's just a regular dumb charter.

Tyrone: You think the teachers teach the work 'cause they feel as though the students are stupid or can't learn?

Nicole: Yeah. Because they're Opportunity and they feel as though they're not up to standard and they have to give them dumb work to do. Now that's what I think. Come on now. Be for real. This stuff is not even worth me wasting my time. That's why I didn't even want to be in Opportunity. They don't got nothin' in here for me. It ain't helping me. They give me half a credit. I need whole credits to get to the twelfth grade. Now I'm going to be behind because they failed me.

Tyrone: Do you feel as though the tests are not challenging in this charter either?

Nicole: No. Because you can cheat, it be a group test, they give the answers the day before. They don't give you no challenge. All right, I'm gonna give you the answers for the test. You all can study tomorrow for the test. You give me the answers. What's the whole point of me going through my notes and studying? You gave me the answers and if I don't pass, I'm stupid because you gave me the answers. That's just dumb. You're not giving me no type of *Opportunity*.

Tyrone: What's your highest goal in life?

Nicole: It's to not let myself, it's to not let myself, you know, to get, you know down, where everybody else is like on drugs, wind up with disease, or nothing like that, or be a bum, or somebody on the street.

Tyrone: I was told that you got a lot of smarts but you don't want to do the work. You wanna slack back. Why is that?

Nicole: When I do care, I put my all into it. When I feel as though I'm ready to do that, I mean, then I'll change. But until then I'm gonna be me a smart-ass mouth little girl. And I'm not gonna stop. That's who I am. The authority can't do nothin about it. What they gonna do, lock me up, or suspend me? That ain't helping me, not at all. That's making me, . . . alright I don't care, suspend me, whatever. That ain't nothin, a couple days out. They ain't helping the student. . . . They be callin this *Opportunity*. They supposed to give you the opportunity to do real work. They suspend you for five days. That's the whole week. They ain't helping nobody. They just make the kids feel less about themselves.

Nicole might have participated in a more challenging curriculum — she certainly had the tools to succeed. Her interview with Tyrone and numerous verbal exchanges with me underscored her dissatisfaction with the disrespect she felt by being assigned to a small learning community with a curriculum that was too easy. Above all, she did not want to be controlled and it is apparent that any learning environment that would support Nicole's learning would have to allow her to exercise more autonomy. In essence, she was dissatisfied with most of the rules of the small learning community and the classroom. It is possible that Nicole's identities in fields outside of the school were so different that she was unwilling to limit her agency to the extent implied by the rules.

Expanding Students' Agency

As a teacher researcher I never figured out how to teach Nicole, who was feisty and irrepressible (Tobin 2005a). As a Muslim, she wore a colorful hijab and, like so many of the youth in her class, Nicole was orally expressive, fluent, and rhythmical. She showed a preference to move around the class, not to stay seated for too long, and to exhibit high levels of verve in her interactions with others. She gestured, raised her voice, and was very playful, especially in her uses of ritual insults. Just as I did not know how to successfully interact with Nicole, she did not know how, or appear to want, to interact successfully with me. She did not show any overt signs of respect for me, did not regard me as her teacher, and saw me as an authority figure that was part of the problem rather than a resource to improve the quality of her life.

Tyrone, in his role as teacher educator, often informed me to "teach those who want to be taught. They'll come to you when they ready. Don't be no ho." I understood his words but never got the full gist of the power of what he was suggesting. Instead I walked about the classroom, monitored participation of all students, and attempted to redirect students like Nicole when they were not involved in the ways I ex-

---

Textbox 6.2
Voice over: My way of teaching was too confrontational. I wanted Nicole to conform to my image of appropriate student. I expected her to be seated, take her turn at talk in an orderly way, and be respectful to others in the class and me. I wanted to be in control of the class and this was at odds with what was possible. Simply put, I did not understand the culture of Nicole's social class.

pected of them. It never occurred to me that monitoring would be perceived as me not trusting them to work independently and hence a sign of disrespect. My practices were sources of negative emotional energy and created structures that Nicole responded to asynchronously, breaching my teaching and the learning of others. Ironically, if I had followed Tyrone's suggestion of leaving her "to do what she felt she had to do," she may have felt respected and I would not have provided her the structures to disrupt the class. Also, she may have done the work, which was challenging, on her own terms. In other words, my efforts to control her did not allow Nicole to create her own structures to expand her agency and participation.

I created structures with the purpose of inviting Nicole to participate. For example, I included her in a panel of students from Opportunity who were teacher educators for a class of graduate students seeking certification in science. The high school students met with the prospective teachers in small groups, with the prospective teacher groups rotating to have time with each high school student. The class sessions were structured to allow the prospective teachers to acknowledge the expertise of the high school students on "how to better teach kids like me." As were all the students from Opportunity, Nicole was articulate and fluent in her responses to questions. She never hesitated to critique what the prospective teachers said to her and to offer alternatives. The high school students also convened as a panel and took questions from the whole class—that included queries about participation in activities in and out of school. The involvement of high school students in these ways, on several occasions in the semester, were acknowledged as highly influential in shaping how the prospective teachers went about teaching in urban high school classes during their one-year field experience. The high school students also enjoyed getting involved in these ways and the impact on their identities seemed to be significant and positive. Teachers and administrators from the school recognized and acknowledged their valuable contributions, which were therefore status symbols.

Twice a week, as part of an elective Nicole and Tyrone were enrolled in, they taught science to middle school youth at a nearby school. They planned together for three days a week and taught on Tuesdays and Thursdays. I felt this was a wonderful way for the high school students to learn science in detail and then give tutoring assistance to middle school youth. The group of high school peer tutors consisted of ten students, of whom six to eight were present on any given day. I arranged for them to teach in pairs to about six middle school students. However, I underestimated the difficulty of this activity. The middle school students were extremely rambunctious. Their classroom teacher struggled mightily to keep them under control and when the high school students came to teach them they often felt disrespected when they did not do as they were asked. Then, without the patience to deal with disruptive students, they often invoked "street code."

Nicole was quite successful in teaching her students and the biggest challenge she encountered was in being adequately prepared to teach them. The approach to science emphasized inquiry and the use of materials and served the purpose of expanding the agency of the high school youth, providing them with opportunities to participate, build interest, experience success, and consider careers in teaching and in science. However, my lack of understanding of urban youth culture led me to place the high school youth in situations that were socially difficult for them whenever the middle school youth were not compliant.

Learned Lessons

My experiences with urban youth were of great benefit to my own learning and, to my deep regret, of less use to the urban youth. Despite my good intentions I was learning about my own shortcomings and especially how to identify the capital that urban youth have in abundance and in some preliminary ways, how to provide structures for them to succeed in learning science and participate in a wider array of education-oriented activities. My assumption is that the education program Nicole and Tyrone experienced with me, and its associated opportunities, were insufficient to be catalytic. Perhaps I persevered with my approach when a different game plan was needed. Had I understood the centrality of showing and earning respect and the critical importance of interactions with students being successful I would have focused on structuring experiences to yield successful interactions and positive emotional energy. I would have minimized interactions that failed and I would have avoided at all costs creating learning environments in which negative emotions occur and accumulate to create asynchronies and destroy solidarity. As for earning respect, I would interact with those who wanted to learn and provide students with greater autonomy about getting involved and sustaining their participation. Above all, I would minimize the opportunities for students to disrespect me in front of their peers.

In a nutshell, what I appear to have begun to learn is how to interact successfully across a boundary that is largely defined by social class. The dysfunction of Opportunity, as experienced by Nicole and Tyrone, also reflects an inability of teachers and students to interact successfully across class boundaries. At the root of the challenge is the agency-structure dialectic (Sewell 1992; Tobin 2005b). Because structures are dynamic and incorporate the culture enacted by the collective, a central issue in any field, is whether the continuously changing structures are appropriated in ways that are relevant, timely, and anticipated—hence synchronous and adding to fluent and successful interactions. This is not easy to do, and certainly it is not done consciously. However, unless students and teachers produce cultural resources to interact successfully with one another, learning environments that characterize educational settings like Opportunity will continue to produce failure, and evoke negative emotions such as frustration, dissatisfaction, and anger.

MAKING IT THROUGH HIGH SCHOOL

To further explore the ways in which social class is an affordance in an urban high school, I now return to the case study of Shakeem, first focusing on his participation in science education and then exploring some of the contradictions between social life in his neighborhoods and the extent to which his school experiences allow him to build learning around what he knows and can do.

Creating Failure

Shakeem was playful and, as a ninth grade science student, he would mimic my Australian accent and spar with me, barraging me with a flurry of punches that fell just short of my nose and chin. He teased me about being like a punching bag ("you outta shape doc") and with his friends he acknowledged my presence in ways that did not assign me high status. My role was co-teacher and researcher in his biology class in a small learning community referred to as Science, Education and Technology (SET)[6]. Shakeem was very disruptive in class. One day I decided to act and, as I spoke to him sternly, he turned his back and walked out of the classroom. I followed after him and warned that if he left the classroom I would take him directly to the principal's office and he would certainly be suspended. To my amazement he stopped in his tracks. Shakeem apologized and agreed to return to the classroom and do his work. I accepted his apology and shook his hand. From that moment onward Shakeem was friendly, respectful, and taught me aspects of youth culture, such as handshakes and "ghetto analogies." I was not an easy person to teach these things and Shakeem enjoyed me getting it wrong and having to be retaught repeatedly.

Shakeem recognized the centrality of creating social networks at school and tirelessly "worked the halls" shaking hands with peers and talking with numerous students. He was conscious of the need to create effective communication among a wide variety of peers and adults. As I mentioned previously, some students back off when they see Shakeem coming toward them. They might do this because he is a big black male and they are afraid of what he might do to them; or they (especially females) may turn away as a sign of disrespect, based on the darkness of his skin, the clothes he wears, and other embodied signs of poverty. Shakeem regards skin color and poverty as strikes against him, encouraging him not to have too many friends and for conversations to arise, focusing on him being dirty, wearing old jeans and sneakers, and needing a hair stylist. He finds such talk painful and usually ignores it, but occasionally has to "pop someone." Instances of disrespect are reminders to Shakeem of the importance of creating effective social networks.

Shakeem was not challenged by his studies at City High and in class he was highly interactive with the teacher, answering questions and showing no fear of being wrong in front of the teacher and his peers. However, because of the lack of challenge Shakeem appeared to have difficulty in retaining his focus and he drifted in and out of "legitimate" participation, often getting involved in humorous and playful activities that were distracting to the teacher and peers. At other times he simply shut down, placed his hood over his head, and seemingly went to sleep.

We experienced many contradictions in our work with Shakeem—a very intelligent, at times brilliant, student who was lovable, intimidating, and frequently irritating to those in authority. Shakeem's erratic patterns of participation were sources of irritation to many of his teachers and it was just a matter of time before two of the teacher researchers requested that he be removed from the research group because of his attitude in class and at school. Shakeem's relationship with his science teacher was friendly in the research group and in fields outside of the classroom. However, the relationship soured when Shakeem did not perform to his teacher's expectations in a chemistry class and the teacher attributed the poor performance to his participation in the research. The teacher characterized Shakeem as "full of himself." Possibly this comment is a reflection of Shakeem's efforts to make his interactions with this teacher symmetrical with respect to power whereas the teacher expected forms of deference, especially in regard to turns at talk and establishing foci for interaction.

The teacher's claims about his researcher role detracting from his schoolwork were reinforced when Shakeem skipped class one day and turned up instead with a peer to show him our research lab. To me it appeared as if the status of being employed at the university was salient among Shakeem's peers and earned him more respect than another day in class. However, when the teachers cried "Enough!" we reluctantly agreed to establish a three-strikes-and-you-are-out rule. The writing was on the wall. It was only a matter of a short time before Shakeem was off the research team and on a pathway to failing chemistry. From Shakeem's point of view he failed because he would not do the homework, and from his science teacher's point of view he failed because he did not learn enough chemistry. The contradiction is that Shakeem knew what he needed to do, had the resources to learn and do well, and opted not to do what it took to pass the course. He refused to be threatened with the loss of his job as a researcher and would not submit to the control of his science teacher, even though he was a black male for whom Shakeem had affection. It was not that Shakeem wanted to fail science, just that the social costs of passing were too great in terms of him losing status within his peer group.

A Fresh Start

Shakeem left Philadelphia at the request of his mother who wanted him to attend school in another city with a different set of peers. He kept in touch with me and described his school experiences in Atlantic City in the following way:

> I know that I have to graduate high school soon, very soon so I talked to the people I was supposed to talk to and got the grades that I needed to, to where as though, I'll graduate next year, rather than the year after 'cause we both know that I messed up, at City but that's in the past to me. When people ask me what grade I'm in, I don't hesitate to tell them the tenth grade and they say well you big and you got all that facial hair, why are you in the tenth grade, you look all old? I am old and I have no business in the tenth grade but I'm here because I messed up and what you should do is what you have to do, therefore you won't mess up and be in the same situation I am. . . . I mean I do the average thing that every other kid does in school, go to class, laugh and joke and stuff like that but when I see kids I hang out with and I associate with outside the classroom, they not going to class or they cutting class, I tell 'em like "yo" you gotta go to class man. You in the eleventh grade, you might as well keep going and it's like why stop now, why are you in the hallway cutting around if you don't, what are you here for? If you don't want to do anything, you cutting class all day, you might as well get a job because while you're cutting classes you're gonna eventually either graduate dumb or drop out early and get a crappy job so you might as well get a head start getting that crappy job or you can get your stuff together, you can go to class and you can learn and you can . . . Even if you don't learn as much as you think you should or you know you could, you could still get the grade to pass. If you go to class and average a "D," you'll still pass and get outta high school and you can get a job because you graduated high school. It's like there's, of course there's a step after high school, that's like the minimum to get a job now you need is like a college degree, if you want a good job but if you don't even have a high school diploma, what are you planning on? . . . I'm going to summer school this year and take Chemistry and next year I'll be a senior and I can graduate.

One year prior to his high school graduation Shakeem was adamant about what he would and would not do in relation to college application. However, on his return to Atlantic City he did not have ready access to people for whom college application and entrance ever was a topic of conversation. Further, he did not have a computer in his house or access to one in his neighborhood. To send e-mails prior to graduation he had to sneak on to a Web mailer during one of his classes or go to a public library that had computers available to the public. Hence, although Shakeem knew how to use computers and in many senses was highly literate, he had very little access at school and no access to computers in his home. Although he could and did go to the public library during its open hours, access necessitated the use and expense of public transportation. The limited access to computers was a significant disadvantage for Shakeem in comparison to most of his peers, making him more reliant on human networks to get the information he needed to do well at school, prepare for college entrance exams, and apply for college admission and financial aid.

> I didn't really think about this kind of stuff unless I'm around y'all. Seriously. And these are things that I need to think about. I need to know about all the programs, things like that. When I'm in Jersey it's like, a lot of people they say, we'll look into it and they don't really have time and I'll give them the number to call my house when they find the information because I don't have access to a computer. We have computers in our school but they're for when we have class and we use the computers for that class and there's a bus situation. I can go to the library but I really don't. That's probably what I need to start doing, looking at books and things about college and stuff. I really need y'all around.

Shakeem followed the course he laid out for himself and graduated, making a minimal effort to pass his final two years of high school in Atlantic City, making straight Ds to accumulate the credits for a certificate that was virtually worthless in terms of gaining college entrance or obtaining a good job. But, as is evident from his opening e-mail message to me, he could not erase his academic record. The high school diploma got him exactly what he predicted would happen when a high school graduate with poor grades seeks employment—minimum wage work.

Looking Back

Shakeem was focused on graduating from high school, which he succeeded in doing. But he had no plan beyond that. His mother's goal was to get him away from Philadelphia where peer pressures seemed to be a constant distraction that prevented Shakeem from accumulating enough credits to move beyond tenth grade. So, the social networks he had developed with university people, adult friends who created opportunities for him to build new skills with digital media and computers, were no longer as readily available. Although our research group maintained contact with him, we could not be as proactive as we felt we needed to be. For example, because he had relocated to a somewhat distant city we did not set Shakeem up with SAT preparation software and we did not make available to him high-speed Internet resources and video editing tools—as we did for his peers who were student researchers. Yet we stayed in touch with Shakeem and provided what support we could via telephone and e-mail. In addition he continued his roles as researcher and teacher educator, visiting researchers from our research team who had relocated to urban universities in cities such as Baltimore. Even though his social networks in Atlantic City supported Shakeem's learning, he did not get strong encouragement to prepare and apply for college entrance.

When many of his peers were receiving counsel to prepare for college Shakeem was remediating failed classes. It is not that the school didn't provide students with opportunities to learn about and gain access to college. Shakeem did not avail himself of the opportunities because of his refusal to conform to the rules and pass his classes. In this regard his participation in school was similar to Tyrone's and Nicole's, who both had the tools to pass any of the classes they took. Consciously or unconsciously they opted out. At the margins because of their race and their positions in social space, the three cases in this study used their agency to fail high school, at least initially. Then the system dealt them a curriculum that was so evidently not what they needed to improve their social lives. Perhaps they recognized, as Nicole certainly did, that what they were offered was not worth much effort because it was unchallenging and analogous to counterfeit currency.

UNSETTLED ISSUES

In this final section I bring the focus back to Philadelphia, where Shakeem earned the status of at-risk and failing student. Based on his video ethnography it is evident that Shakeem was at ease in his neighborhood and had an extensive social network. Conversations with his older cousin are similar in form and focus to many conversations we had with Shakeem. Her focus during one such conversation was on family and Shakeem's involvement with her children. Shakeem was playful and teasing in his interactions with her, showing a great deal of empathy and connectedness. Similarly, he spoke in a very gentle and kind way to children and to his grandmother. In these interactions there was no sharp humor and certainly no profanity in his speech. He also attended church and it is assumed that he spoke there in ways that were acceptable to the preacher and the parishioners. The question arises as to why Shakeem did not code switch more often in school. When he interacted with the principal he was pleasant and respectful and he was usually that way with me, once I had established my credentials as someone to be respected.

So it is evident that Shakeem knew how to code switch in and out of the school and he could address individuals and groups of individuals in ways that were canonical, clear, and articulate. For example, he made a fifteen-minute presentation at an international ethnography forum in the presence of eminent scholars from around the world, speaking to issues about his lifeworld, including his school-related practices. A key question then is why Shakeem did not use his power discourse to benefit his learning and especially his grades in his classes. Perhaps it was mainly to do with power; he would not allow his teachers to control him, even when it was in his best interests to do so. Also possible is that Shakeem had a status hierarchy that structured his interactions

---

Textbox 6.3

Voice over: I joined a lab group to discuss what a small group had learned from an experiment it had completed. Shakeem and another African American youth were interacting with me when Shakeem suddenly glared at the other youth and quietly told him to shut up. I am not sure what the youth said, but he repeated it and Shakeem shouted to him, "Shut up!" Apparently the youth repeated his utterance and Shakeem shouted again, this time twisting the collar on his shirt, beginning to choke him. The youth began to choke and Shakeem continued to twist the collar. I became alarmed and reached out to pull Shakeem's arm away. "Don't worry Doc. I got ya back." It was clear to me then that as a person Shakeem respected, I was not to be disrespected.

with others. I was struck by his use of street talk with some of the younger female researchers, his disrespect for most of his teachers, and his flawless mainstream talk when place and status required it. It seems possible that Shakeem's use of language was part of a campaign for respect, where respect can be earned by disrespecting others. One explanation is that upstaging others, except for those with exempt status and in sacred places, was relentless. Even though Shakeem knew he had to do well at school he lived the necessity to maintain and elevate his status within his social class.

It is difficult to imagine how discussions with his grandmother or the younger siblings and relatives would ever swing to education in any deep way, although it is easy to imagine that many of the people Shakeem interacted with might urge him to try harder to succeed at high school, do a better job with his homework, and even attend school regularly, arrive on time, and behave himself. But when and where would interactions occur about college preparation? Shakeem has an educational level that exceeds what others in his family attained, and even though family members clearly value education, Shakeem's goals to attend college so that he can get a job as a businessman and earn money to support himself and his family were not grounded in details of how to pursue particular pathways. Outside of the home there seem to be few resources to access conveniently—most families in the neighborhood struggle to make ends meet, do not have computers and access to the Internet, and library resources are some distance away.

Social life in his neighborhood provides Shakeem with opportunities to learn what needs to be done to succeed in the neighborhood. The capital he accrues through participation equips him to be successful in his neighborhood. When he travels to school, either on foot or via public transport, he learns to make the transitions successfully, stay out of trouble, and get to school. Life within the school partly resembles life in the streets because so many of the participants are much the same as the peer group Shakeem interacts with in the streets. He knows how to interact successfully and build social networks with youth in the school. However, the adults are another matter since they belong to a different social class.

In the school adults want control over students. Efforts to control him breach Shakeem's habitus of interacting fluently in a teasing and light-hearted way, sharing turns at talk, and using pauses as resources for interspersing witty commentaries. Shakeem's teachers usually do not like his attitude and playfulness and want to shut down his tendencies to participate using overlapping speech, move about the classroom, and inject humor into his interactions with others. The distinctiveness of Shakeem's ways of being in his neighborhood, streets, school hallways and lunchroom, and in the research lab are not welcomed in most classes and in interactions with most adults in the school building. Shakeem's free-wheeling style of talk, spontaneity, sarcasm, poetic expression, and verve are out of place and these are central to the core of Shakeem's identities in most fields of his lifeworld. His tendencies to rap and use metaphor and profanity also are shut down in most classes. Because so much of what Shakeem does is deemed inappropriate, his desire to get involved in central ways cannot occur with the degree of fluency that is characteristic of Shakeem's expressive individualism.

A striking difference between the neighborhood and the school is that social networks are fluid across age in the neighborhood whereas in the school the adults often oppose the formation of open social networks, preferring to remain isolated in order to retain control over students. Hence, Shakeem's efforts to interact informally with teachers were often rebuffed—regarded as inappropriate and potentially threatening to their power over students. In contrast, within the research groups we sought to minimize power differences based on status markers such as being a teacher or a professor. Not surprisingly, Shakeem seemed right at home and interacted fluently with peers, teachers, and professors. However, the teachers and some professors felt awkward and persisted in using titles such as doctor and professor with an expectation that others would use them too. Even though we agreed on open forms of dialogue and to drop titles there was a tendency from some teacher researchers to retain them.

How might Tyrone, Nicole, and Shakeem have fared if the curriculum was built around central features from their neighborhoods? In Shakeem's case this might have been possible to a greater extent if he had attended his neighborhood school, where it is possible that adults working in the school were from his neighborhood. This was the case at City High where, for example, Embry was a nonteaching assistant since the school opened more than thirty years ago. He has assisted with student discipline and behavior of several generations of students and still lives close to the school. Also, Officer Pauli, a school policeman, was a student at City High when it opened and he grew up in the neighborhood. Unlike Shakeem, Tyrone and Nicole grew up in the neighborhood close to City High and they knew some of the adults in the school; but like Shakeem, they did not adapt to mainstream school culture. A common factor seems to be their determination to be themselves, no matter what it takes. Their identities would not permit them to be controlled by schema they rejected. Although they knew about the achievement ideology, their practices aligned to a greater extent with the core ideology of urban youth—that interactions should at the very least acknowledge and maintain status and be respectful. If passing school necessitated a loss of status or accepting the disrespect of others, the costs were not worth it. From this perspective school was a place for creating and using social networks, to build friendships, and to socialize. Many of their friends did not come to school and they could achieve their social goals outside of school—hence it is no surprise that attendance at school was often not a priority.

Although the three cases I use to explore relationships between social class and urban science education all involve failure, I could have chosen differently to show successes. Elsewhere Rowhea Elmesky and I have explored the ways in which the expanded roles of urban youth led to success and pathways to college (Elmesky and Tobin 2005). In this chapter I wanted to explicate some major contradictions to highlight the salience to urban education of teachers and students learning how to align their cultures to create environments where alienation seldom occurs and learning thrives. Here I do not present the culture associated with the social lives of urban, African American youth as inferior. On the contrary, their culture is well suited to the youth being successful in their neighborhoods. I acknowledge the importance of these youth code switching, as they are able to do, building power discourses of mainstream America and, in so doing, reproducing canonical knowledges—thereby expanding their agencies to the extent that they can realize their dreams of a better life. If this is to happen, teachers must learn about the youth culture that characterizes students like these African American teenagers from West Philadelphia. Unless teachers are accepted as "my teacher" and know how to initiate and sustain successful interactions across boundaries of social class it is unlikely that the goals of students and teachers will align to benefit the learning of urban youth. When cultural misalignments predominate, negative emotions can swell and create conditions in which urban youth feel disrespected and oppressed (Tobin in press). Efforts to enact successful interactions will necessitate careful attention to conventional wisdom on who has control in urban classes. For students like Tyrone, Nicole, and Shakeem the costs of being controlled far exceed the benefits of academic success.

ACKNOWLEDGMENTS

The research in this book is supported in part by the National Science Foundation under Grants REC-0107022 and DUE-0427570. Any opinions, findings, and conclusions or recommendations expressed in the book are those of the authors and do not necessarily reflect the views of the National Science Foundation.

NOTES

1. Son is used metaphorically, not biologically, as a metaphor that shows strength of relationship and responsibility.

2. A school-within-a-school, typically consisting of about six teachers and 180–200 students.

3. I use present tense throughout this section even though it is now six years since these events occurred.

4. Nonteaching assistants patrolled corridors and guarded the school entrance, assisting school police to maintain order.

5. Term used in lieu of small learning community.

6. In a school that is highly tracked, SET was one rung above Opportunity. Initially designed to attract students with an interest in sports and business, the small learning community changed its name from Sports, Entrepreneurship and Technology (SET) during our research. The name changed but the students were the same.

REFERENCES

Anderson, E. (1999). *Code of the Street: Decency, Violence and the Moral Life of the Inner City*. New York: W.W. Norton.

Elmesky, R., & Tobin, K. (2005). Expanding our Understandings of Urban Science Education by Expanding the Roles of Students as Researchers. *Journal of Research in Science Teaching* 42, 807–28.

Seiler, G. (2002). *Understanding Social Reproduction: The Recursive Nature of Structure and Agency within a Science Class*. Dissertation Abstracts International, AAT 3043953. Philadelphia: University of Pennsylvania.

Sewell, W. H. (1992). A Theory of Structure: Duality, Agency and Transformation. *American Journal of Sociology* 98, 1–29.

Tobin, K. (in press). Aligning the Cultures of Teaching and Learning Science in Urban High Schools. *Cultural Studies of Science Education*.

———. (2005a). Building Enacted Science Curricula on the Capital of Learners. *Science Education* 89, 577–94.

———. (2005b). Becoming an Urban Science Educator. In W. M. Roth (ed). *Auto/biography and Auto/ethnography: Praxis of Research Method*. Rotterdam, The Netherlands: Sense Publishers.181–203.

Tobin, K., Elmesky, R., & Seiler, G. (eds). (2005). Improving Urban Science Education: New Roles for Teachers, Students and Researchers. New York: Rowman & Littlefield.

CHAPTER 7

The Challenge of Equitable Access to Arts and Museum Experiences for Low-Income New York City Schoolchildren

Lynda Kennedy

New York City is rich in museums and cultural institutions of every type, many with strong education departments. The last two decades have brought a paradigm shift in the field of museum education, which has become solidified as a specialized profession. This shift has come in part from the recognition that in order to receive public and private funds, museums and cultural institutions must show that they support and enhance the school curricula. Museums must evaluate their education programs, prove their effectiveness for teaching subject matter, and clearly state their program goals, along with how they connect to state learning standards. It is ironic that at a time when museum educators have become adept at writing curricula and drawing connections between collections, programming, and the needs of the classroom, that concern over performing well on standardized tests has caused many New York City school principals to limit or eliminate access to art and cultural institutions—doing away with field trips or even classroom visits from museum education staff.

In 2001, the federal government passed the No Child Left Behind Act (NCLB). Though the arts were articulated as a core subject in NCLB, the emphasis on accountability for English language arts and math (under the law, these areas are tested from third grade through eighth grade) has led to a reduction in arts instruction and visits to museums. After hearing from teachers and administrators across the country that the arts, including exposure to art in museums, were being sacrificed to make room for the subjects for which there are standardized tests, Secretary of Education Rod Paige wrote a letter to superintendents which was then posted on the U.S. Department of Education site (July 2004). In it, he writes that he finds the notion that NCLB has caused diminished arts programming disturbing and goes on to list funds that may be used for arts programming—including visits to museums and cultural institutions. The issue is not that there are no funds that *may* be used for arts programming, the issue is that there are few funds that *must* be used for arts programming. Even in New York City, where Project ARTS (Arts Restoration Through the Schools) funding *should* have been used for arts programming, those funds became discretionary at the school level, and in many cases were not used for the arts programming for which they were intended, but not mandated. The result was "children in some parts of the City have arts education for ten hours a week with frequent visits to museums and performances while other students receive little or no instruction in the arts whatsoever" (Committee on Education 2003, 10).

Unfortunately, the reality is that school administrators are concerned about the pressure to perform under NCLB and are channeling available resources into programs they believe prepare students to achieve on standardized tests. Though it may have been the furthest thing from what was intended by the creators of NCLB, as Stan Karp (2004) writes, "The new law's unmistakable message is *if it's not on the test, it's not worth knowing*" (6, italics his). This is particularly true in schools that are labeled "under-performing." According to the Campaign for Fiscal Equity (2003) "under-performing" often correlates with schools that have the poorest economic resources. It is in these schools that limited funding can mean that curricular choices are seen as either/or rather than both/and. Unfamiliar with research on the positive impact of arts and museum experiences on student academic performance—much of which is available through the Arts Education Partnership Critical Links Web site, www.aep-arts.org/cltoolkitpage .htm—administrators at these schools believe *either* they must spend money and time on getting tests scores up through targeted drill and test preparation in English language arts and mathematics *or* they include the arts and field trips but risk the failure of their school. This is not by any means an exclusively New York City problem. A recent national survey given by the Council for Basic Education (2004) showed that in schools with high minority, low income populations, 36 percent of principals had cut arts education and 42 percent were considering cutting arts programming in the future in order to make more time for test preparation. This widely held view of arts instruction—one that sees the arts as distracting and detracting from "important" subjects and visits to museums as taking time that is more needed elsewhere—could not have come at a worse time for New York City school children as it has only been in the last ten years that advocates for arts instruction have begun the slow reinstatement of the arts into schools from which they had been completely cut after fiscal difficulties in the 1970s.

ARTS AND MUSEUM EXPERIENCES AS AN INTEGRAL PART OF A QUALITY EDUCATION

In a presentation at *Learning and the Arts: Crossing Boundaries*, a meeting for education, arts, and youth funders held in 2000, Elliot Eisner of Stanford University stated, "The curriculum of the school shapes children's thinking. It is a mind-altering device; it symbolizes what adults believe it is important for the young to know . . . It tells the young which human aptitudes are important to possess." If we want all children to grow up to be participants in our cultural institutions—to be lifelong learners—then we must send the message that, by their inclusion in the school curriculum, the arts and museums are important. Beyond encouraging students to appreciate them, the arts and museum experiences are acknowledged as having multiple benefits, which is what allows arts instruction to be included as a core subject under NCLB. In addition to personal development, the fostering of confidence, problem solving, and self-expression that the arts allow a student, studies have shown that involvement in and exposure to the arts can impact on student performance in tested subjects. This is achieved not only through complementary skills (reading and comprehension in drama, observation and categorization in visual art, counting and pattern in music) but also through the engagement and motivation of students (Catterall 1998; Catterall and Waldorf 1999; Dupont 1992). Other studies show that an early involvement with the arts and arts institutions is an important contributing factor toward improved socialization and community involvement as well as academic skills (Chorus America 2003).

INEQUITY IN ACCESS TO ARTS INSTRUCTION AND CULTURAL INSTITUTIONS

As shown by Anyon (1980) in her "Social Class and the Hidden Curriculum of Work" and Fine (2004) in "The Faultlines of Racial Justice and Public Education," there is often an extreme difference in instruction and facilities between public schools in low income areas and those in more affluent areas. Though there are many societal causes of instructional difference, differences in access to facilities, cultural resources, and materials generally come down to finances or a lack thereof. Students in schools in low income areas are then more likely to face an opportunity gap when it comes to the arts and exposure to museums in spite of a per capita allotment of funds across New York City through Project ARTS.

Projects ARTS was created by the Department (then Board) of Education of New York City in 1997, with its first funding allocation of $25 million being distributed in 1998. In fiscal years 2000 and 2001 the funding had been raised to $75 million. For the fiscal years 2002 and 2003 the funding was lowered to $52 million, which works out to $47 per student for arts education. This $47 is intended to not only provide arts instruction to students (in art, music, dance, *and* theater) but also professional development for staff, curriculum development, trips to cultural institutions and museums, a district arts coordinator, equipment, and resources (Committee on Education 2003). In fiscal year 2004, the allocation was raised to $67.5 million, which is still woefully inadequate to provide a quality arts and museum experiences for New York City children. The cost of buses alone would eat up a large chunk of that allotment.

Public school parents in more affluent areas have organized to pick up the funding slack for their children. For example, PS 158 on the Upper East Side of Manhattan has a Parent Teacher Association (PTA) that provides funds for enrichment programs, including art, circus arts, poetry, the Harkness Ballet, contemporary dance, the National Dance Institute, music, and band (www.ps158.org/). Other Upper East Side Schools like PS 6 and PS 77 have PTA Web sites on which one can make tax-deductible donations on line. The fundraising committee for PS 6 states, "We ask each family to contribute for each child who attends the school" and includes a link to the "Family Gift" registration form (www.ps6pta.org/fundraising.aspx). On the PS 77 PTA Web site (www.lowerlabschoolpta.org/pta.asp) their call for volunteers includes asking for parents to join the grant committee who will "research and apply for grants according to the priorities determined by parents, faculty and administration." An example of a PTA fundraising budget from the Midtown West PTA for FY 2002–2003 shows a total of $107,304—$40,504 of which went to the music program and for teacher art supplies. As the enrollment of the school is 367 students (www.insideschools.org) each student is receiving roughly $110 extra toward arts instruction. The Midtown West PTA budget is small compared to that of schools like the Hunter College Elementary School, whose PTA fundraising goal for 2004–2005 is $400,350 and also asks parents to contribute $250–$350 toward their child's classroom fund to be spent on specific teacher requests (hceshunter.cuny.edu/pta/fundraisingoverviewworksheet.doc). Clearly, schools with parent networks that can give time, money, and expertise are able to channel more funding into enrichment experiences for their children. Because of the extra funds, paying for museum admission visits from museum staff and bus costs is not a problem at these schools. More important, enrichment experiences such as museum visits are considered important and time is given to them during the school week. It is no coincidence that these schools are listed on the "Inside Schools" Web site— run by the organization Advocates for Children—as being "notable" and their test scores are exceptional.

RECOMMENDATIONS

Simply saying something is important does not make it so. Giving a title to an initiative and creating a committee does not guarantee implementation. It is wonderful that the New York City Department of Education has developed "Blueprints" for arts education that encourage exposure to museums and cultural institutions, but without funding for trips, or museum educator and teaching artist visits to schools, the Blueprints will go no further toward exposing public school students in economically challenged areas to the arts and the museums that celebrate them. As long as teachers and administrators feel pressure to focus only on English language arts and math, without understanding that participation in and exposure to the arts contribute to success in these areas, equitable access to arts education and museum experiences for low-income students will continue to be problematic.

In their 2003 report the Committee on Education recommend increasing the Project ARTS budget over five years to meet the $700 per student annually that they recommend spending on art education, increasing the staffing of qualified teachers in all of the areas of the creative and performing arts, providing adequate facilities, and allowing more flexible school scheduling to facilitate meaningful arts instruction—allowing for trips, for example. Their recommendations are good ones, but may be unreachable at the present. A budget increase is particularly problematic. As shown by the case brought against the State of New York by the Campaign for Fiscal Equity, the New York City Department of Education is already seriously underfunded in all areas (Report and Recommendations of the Judicial Referees November 30, 2004). The report goes on to state that "inadequate physical facilities, excessive class sizes and overcrowding in New York City Schools" adversely effect the students' opportunity for a "sound basic education," (12) leading to the conclusion that increased funding for facilities for arts instruction—dance studios, music rooms, or equipped art rooms, let alone regular museum visits—may not be attainable in the near future.

ENLISTING PARTNERS TO MEET THE CHALLENGES OF EQUITABLE ACCESS

New York City itself provides a myriad of resources and support for quality arts instruction and integration. Many of the City's museums and cultural organizations already have long-standing, successful relationships with New York City public schools. Indeed, when the arts were cut from the City's education budget, it was these institutions and organizations that stepped in to provide arts programming for students and professional development for teachers. Based on a yearly survey of their members, the New York City Arts In Education Roundtable, a professional organization for those involved in arts education, estimates that cultural institutions in New York City raise funds for $102 million worth of educational programs for public schools annually. (NYCAE survey results 2002–2003) The Office of Arts and Special Projects of the NYC Department of Education has built on this relationship with the City's cultural institutions by inviting representatives to contribute to the development of the curricular Blueprints for the arts. In addition to the New York City Arts in Education Roundtable, there are many other professional organizations that can provide advice and support to administrators in New York City—the New York City Museum Educators Roundtable, the New York State Theater Education Association, the New York State Alliance for Arts Education, and the International Museum Theater Alliance—to name a few.

CONCLUSION

New York City public schools could provide many of the City's children with their best opportunity to be exposed to and participate in the arts. "Insofar as public schools undertake this mission, each generation is better prepared to appreciate the arts and contribute to the process of sustaining them as a major domain of human accomplishment," writes Lara Chapman (2004, 12). If there is access, many of New York City's children will experience their first trip to a museum, a concert, a ballet, or a theater performance with their class. If they have access, the first time they find a means to express themselves may be through paint or song or the violin. When we look to the future, to how these children will grow up and perceive themselves and the world, we must ask ourselves if it is acceptable that some children are exposed to this "domain of human accomplishment" and some are not. Museums must continue their work of assisting in the raising of funds to provide arts programming for low-income students and professional development for their teachers. Museum educators must continue to publish reports of successful partnerships that spread the word to all school administrators that the arts and the cultural institutions that celebrate and educate through them are essential to the quality education mandated by NCLB.

REFERENCES

Anyon, J. (1980) Social Class and the Hidden Curriculum of Work. In *Journal of Education*.

Arts Education Partnership. (2002). *Critical Links: Learning in the Arts and Student Academic and Social Development*. www.aep-arts.org/cltoolkitpage.htm

Campaign for Fiscal Equity. (2004). *The State of Learning in New York: An Annual Snapshot with Comparisons of Select Counties Around the State.*

Catterall, J. (1998). Involvement in the Arts and Success in Secondary School. *Americans For the Arts Monographs* 1 (9). Washington, D.C.

Catterall, J., Chapleau, R., & Iwanaga, J. (1999.) *Involvement in the Arts and Human Development.* University of California Imagination Project. Unpublished manuscript.

Catterall, J. and Waldorf, L. (1999). Chicago Arts Partnerships in Education (CAPE) Evaluation Summary. In E. Fiske (ed.) *Champions of Change: The Impact of Arts on Learning*. Washington, D.C.

Center for Arts Education. (2004) The DOE Blueprint: Your Questions Answered. In *News from the Center* (Fall/Winter 2004–2005).

Chapman, L. (2004). No Child Left Behind in Art? In *Arts Education Policy Review* 106, (2): 3–17.

Chorus America. (2003). America's Performing Art: A Study of Choruses, Choral Singers and their Impact. www.chorusamerica.org

Committee on Education. (2003). *A Picture is Worth a Thousand Words: Arts Education in New York City Public Schools*. Report to the Council of the City of New York. June 11.

Council for Basic Education. (2004). *Academic Atrophy: The Condition of the Liberal Arts in America's Public Schools.* Report.

Dupont, S. (1992). The Effectiveness of Creative Drama as an Instructional Strategy to Enhance the Reading Comprehension Skills of Fifth Grade Remedial Readers. In *Reading Research and Instruction* 31 (3): 41–52.

Eisner, E. January 12–14, 2000. Speech delivered at Learning and the Arts: Crossing Boundaries. *Proceedings*. Geraldine R. Dodge Foundation, J. Paul Getty Trust, and the John D. and Catherine T. MacArthur Foundation. Los Angeles.

Fine, M. et al. (2004). The faultlines of racial justice and public education. In *Echoes of Brown: Youth Documenting and Performing the Legacy of Brown vs. the Board of Education*. New York: Teachers College Press.

Honig, M. and Hatch, T. (2004). Crafting Coherence: How Schools Strategically Manage Multiple, External Demands. In *Educational Researcher* 33 (8): 16–30.

Inside Schools. www.insideschools.org

Karp, S. (2004). No Child Left Behind the Test. In *Rethinking Schools* 19 (1): 6–9.

New York City Arts in Education Survey results 2002–2003. www.nycaie roundtable.org/docs/nycaiesurveyresults02-03.pdf

Paige, R. (July 2004). Letter. www.ed.gov/policy/elsec/guid/secletter/040701 .html

President's Committee on the Arts and the Humanities & Arts Education Partnership. (1999). *Gaining the Arts Advantage: Lessons from School Districts that Value Arts Education.* www.pcah.gov

Robinson, K. Speech Delivered at Learning and the Arts: Crossing Boundaries, *Proceedings.* Geraldine R. Dodge Foundation, J. Paul Getty Trust, and the John D. and Catherine T. MacArthur Foundation. January 12–14, 2000. Los Angeles.

Shankman, N. (2002). *Arts Education in the New York City Public Schools.*

Supreme Court of the State of New York, County of New York: IAS Part 25. Report and Recommendations of the Judicial Referees. Campaign for Fiscal Equity Inc. et al. (plaintiffs) against The State of New York, et al. (defendants). November 30, 2004.

Part IV

CLASS AUTOBIOGRAPHY, EDUCATIONAL INSIGHTS

CHAPTER 8

My Daughter, Myself: Class Reflections through the Parent-Race-Gender Lens

Aaron David Gresson

Sitting in my neighborhood Starbucks on the first Wednesday of the New Year I pen these words as a young black father and daughter leave the coffee shop in this middle-class suburb of Baltimore—she's a "brown-skinned" youth with "nice hair"; he is also brown-skinned, dressed in suit, Brooks Brothers overcoat, cap, glasses and bow-tie— probably a minister, certainly an intellectual. I had only glanced at them when they first came in the cafe; he had gone to order coffee and she stopped to speak with a young white male cartoonist working at the table across from me. I had been struck by her ease in conversing with him; she obviously knew him as indicated by the ready give and take between them.

It was both uncanny and fortuitous that this daughter and father should have appeared here as I began this essay on myself as a classed creature. I had been thinking all day about what and how I would speak on my class experiences as a fifty-eight-year-old? What ripples from the streams constituting my memories of the past would I draw upon to weave a story of my "class"? Shirley had asked me to write because of my stories, to relive some of the moments I had shared with her and Joe: growing up and going to school in the segregated South, shining shoes for poor white sailors outside of the USO in Norfolk, conversations with my gifted mother, a domestic worker with an eighth-grade education but world-class wisdom and compassion.

Where do I begin? How does one recall and give ordered meaning to memories more like a dream than reality? A timeline can be a useful, if decidedly truncated way of giving contextual meaning to events and aid understanding as a dynamic, evolving, and, at times, contradictory process. I was born in 1947 in Norfolk, Virginia. A Virginian like Thomas Jefferson, I shared some of his eighteenth-century understanding of my ancestry and my place in mid-twentieth century United States. Jefferson believed enslaved Africans to be inferior humans even though he saw their humanity and their genius. His life, like my own, was shot through with racial contradictions. I saw these first in my parents.

My father was illiterate; my mother had eighth-grade education. He was a laborer, restricted from licensure as a bricklayer because these jobs were by law solely held by white men; my mother worked as a domestic in the homes of working-class Anglos and middle-class Jewish immigrants. In those days, she babysat, cooked, and did laundry all for $18.75 per week and carfare. Both sparkled brightly in their own way amid the pathos and pain of the semi-urban Southern neighborhood in which I spent my first fifteen years. My father would ultimately die in those streets, homeless among my peers who, through their alcoholism had become his. My manifest fate was to follow in their footprints.

And for years I did. I was a bright but disruptive, truant child; I shined shoes for sailors outside the segregated USO in Norfolk and did not have any plans for a life beyond what other black youth in my community dreamed: hard work, hard life, and hard death. Then came the 1960s, civil rights, Black Power, and the other movements against war, sexism, and social injustice. Through affirmative-action policies and practices I gained opportunities to study with privileged white males whose "great expectations" included elite postgraduate educations. I too began to dream and find doors open in the United States and Canada.

Over the years I have seen many other African Americans and minorities live similar stories of academic achievement and social success. Like me, they have attained degrees, academic and professional positions, and raised families in multicultural, liberal environments. And like me, they have seen the continuing, even intensifying widening gap between the haves and have-nots. The continuing educational gap and corresponding inequality of opportunities in the world of work clash against my personal story of attainment. And the relative demise of affirmative action, multiculturalism, and other so-called racial remedies remind me that Jefferson was not all wrong—at least, not yet.

Jefferson said that racial antagonism would continue to divide whites and blacks: whites would not abandon their supremacist beliefs and practices and blacks would not forget their suffering or overcome their "natural" inferiority. Race and education as an unfolding story of race in schooling and society describes the contradictory efforts to affirm and overcome Jefferson's reflections. In the following pages, I share my own understanding of this unfolding story in the context of my own evolving life as a racialized American male student defined by class, sexuality, gender, culture, and race.

MY FATHER, MYSELF

Among my earliest memories are those of my illiterate but brilliant father who best communicated with me when drinking or drunk: he would come in late at night—especially when unemployed in the winter—and take me from my bedroom—a sofa in the living room that I shared with my younger sister who still slept in her infant's crib at five. It was in this small room in a four-family apartment converted from a massive single-family home that he sought me on these wild and wonderful nights.

He would take me into the streets, to some friend's house where the broken, often drunken but hungry-for-discourse brothers sat and argued their pedagogies. How ironic it now seems: they were trying to make meaning—construct knowledge—with bits and pieces of their own grounded experience and the white man's "KNOWLEDGE." Jean Paul Sartre's words come to mind as I recall these times far into the past: "Once there was the white man who owned the word and ten thousand natives who had the use of the word" . . .

I was the native's son, the seeker of the word . . . only ten years old and in the fourth grade, but this man-child of the illiterate postbellum Negro had more than his father—he had words; he could read and write and he had a "gift of gab" or so the middle-class black women teachers told his mother. Less educated but streetwise griots—African American community elders—saw something else: they saw a preacher, perhaps a teacher.

And it was this gift of gab that his father wanted to share with his peers—not the child's beauty, his voice, his imitation of his mother's religious or spiritual proclivities, not any sexual or athletic prowess that might be lurking just below the surface . . . Just his Words . . .

My father, you see, was proud of my education, my learning, my willingness to stand there before him and these other battered, wounded black men, forgotten sons of another land and time, and speak like Jesus before the wise men in the temple. Out of the mouths of babes, says the Bible. I was a mere child but in my father's eyes, I was his personal and racial pride: I was a learner; and education back then, even now, remains the key to changing "class" for African Americans and poor people in general.

MY MOTHER, MYSELF

Unlike my father, my mother was that "Black Woman" less fictional-ized yet more characteristic of the "essence" of Black Womanhood. She was a survivor. Shaped by racial realities, she had evolved at the time of my birth into a hotbed of contradictions: She was "Afrocentric" before most of us knew what it meant; she was fiercely positive about black achievements and abilities; she was energetic and thrifty and cre-ative: she took my sister and me regularly to the Goodwill or thrift shops. But not just for clothes or household items: she bought us books to read and even once found an old metal chest that we painted red and used as the library to house the books that we shared with other kids in the neighborhood. She loved learning. Yet, she was marked by oppres-sion too.

A mixed racial woman, she looked like a Native-American woman — my father called her his "Yellow Woman." Dark-skinned himself, he was fiercely proud and possessive of her; she worshipped him in a naïve, girlish way much of her life despite his failures and their ultimate divorce. Her father had been a "White Indian" from the Carolinas, where her mother also hailed from. She told me that her mother, a deep chocolate woman, never married him because he referred to her first son as his "nigger."

Contradictions like these infected her, giving her a level of ambigu-ity that often seemed cruel and even more often lent to her tremendous humanity, her capacity to read and reach people far beyond the racial confines of the Old South we grew up in. On her mother's side, she came from a long line of aristocratic African Americans who had been teachers and entrepreneurs in northeastern North Carolina. Poor by white people's standards, her family shared the middle-class values, pretensions, and aspirations that most Americans did during the early twentieth century. Education was crucial for African Americans as well as whites during these times. She conveyed this to me, despite the poverty and "colonial education" forced upon minorities before the 1954 Supreme Court decision, Brown v. Board of Education.

It was also in her ambiguous and contradictory style that she prodded me to pursue education despite my manifest destiny of destitution and death. My mother once told me that my father had "a photostatic mind"—she meant he had a great memory; he could take a picture with his mind, and recall things. For her, in her eyes, this man, her first and eternal lover, might have been a lawyer had he not been born poor, black, and *unlucky*.

MY DAUGHTER, MYSELF

Unlucky. Could this be the meaning beneath all meanings of "class?" This possibility occurred to me earlier today when I reread a study on race, class, and language development. The findings seemed strangely familiar to me: both white and black youth from the middle classes received better and earlier linguistic stimulation and training than those from poorer backgrounds although early schooling experiences seemed to narrow the gap. I recall that I immediately felt a pang of guilt, fear, and despair at relearning what seemed so evident to me and millions more who had never conducted or read the research on race, class, and *luck*.

My immediate pang of guilt was due to my being a father separated from my fifteen-year-old daughter. My daughter's mother and I were not married when she was born. Although she lived with me as a child, she has known the broken home experience of so many American children of the past four decades. I never intended for my child to be without the constant love, protection, and guidance of her father, it just happened that way. So she has only faint recollections of the people, places, and things I shared with her as a toddler: the shared trips to conferences and guest lectureships at various universities; the time she spent in my education classes at Penn State where my student teachers fawned over her, passing her from one to the other student.

She only faintly recalls these times. And so I feel guilt. But I feel something more: fear. She spent Christmas with us this year and we had a good time. She is growing up so fast, so bright, so eager to be out there—learning and living her dreams. I tried to teach her as much as I could in the one week we spent together. It always seems that way: so much I want to tell, teach, give her and so little time—for me at least. She shared with me, during one moment, how she understood what I meant when I said that I had failed to give her mother—who had been my student at Brandeis University decades ago—as much "muscle" as she would need to make it outside the ivory tower and the working-class Pittsburgh community she had grown up in.

I talk often to my daughter, and other minority youth with great expectations, about "muscle." Others have called it family resources, "cultural capital," and connections. I call it muscle. It has also been called "class." My daughter and these other kids have brains, ambition, and hunger for success. But they don't always have "muscle." When they do, lay people have called it "a gift" or "good luck"; social scientists and educators have taken to calling it "resilience."

Whatever it is called, it is important. And my daughter's mother knows this because we have talked about its place in my daughter's developing life. My daughter told me that part of her reason for spending more time with me these days is that her mother wants her to learn from me, to develop this muscle, this resilience. Can I give it to her? I have previously thought so; the literature on African American achievement says that a father or fathering figure can be so very important for a female child—it seems that the literature says this is so across the board.

So, why am I frightened by this prospect of fathering, of helping my daughter realize her dream of attending Oxford and Princeton? Class. . . .

Yes, it's class. I know these institutions; I have visited them—even spoken at them. But I am not "their kind." And I'm not sure that I can help my daughter to become their kind. Maybe this is what marks my class—the failure to have turned my own achievements—degrees, books, connections, cultural capital—into the self-assurance and "insider knowledge" that she will need to be successful in these environments. And maybe my fear is due to knowing that her sex—female—affects the odds of my improving her choices and chances to realize them. But I am trying.

Last summer when she visited me, I took her to the Eastern shore of Maryland. We crossed the Chesapeake Bay Bridge and lunched on the shore at one of my favorite restaurants, Hemingway's. She was still thinking of Oxford as her first choice then. I had been so proud the day she called me to ask if I knew anything about study abroad. I reminded her that I had degrees from Waterloo and Toronto in Canada. I encouraged her to explore possibilities of study at Oxford despite my own reservations about the wisdom of this. On this day, while lunching at Hemingway's, I decided to gradually introduce some of the "class facts" beneath my fears for her great expectations and dreams. I told her that I wanted to show her one of the earliest American colleges, one unknown to many people.

Just down the road from Annapolis, on the Eastern shore, was the historically black college, the University of Maryland Eastern Shore. A small campus, this school was founded in the 1880s for African Americans living in the Maryland, Delaware, and Virginia region. This school has a rich tradition of service to the African American community. I wanted my daughter to know about schools like this, but I drove north toward Wilmington, Delaware, rather than south on route 50 toward Salisbury and the Virginia state line. I was heading to Chestertown, Maryland, and Washington College.

Named for George Washington, Washington College was chartered in the eighteenth century. I discovered it on one of my frequent trips between Philadelphia and Annapolis. Situated in the riverfront town of Chestertown, Maryland, this tenth-oldest college in America was the first to be chartered in the New World. Richly endowed and created under the auspices of the founding father, this exclusive school exudes its pedigree. It exudes class. It was this class that I wanted my daughter to feel firsthand.

It worked. We happened to be there on the afternoon after Convocation, the first day of winter term. Parents, students, administrators, and faculty casually walked around the central quad. Mostly looking at the various buildings and campus sculpture, only a few even acknowledged our presence even though we were only two of four nonwhites on the campus. The other two African Americans—both young female matriculants—looked straight ahead even as we passed them walking toward their new dorms with suitcases in hand.

We both felt it—*class*. My daughter turned to me as we made our way back along the winding roads across farmland to route 301 toward Annapolis. "I see what you mean . . ." is all she said. Later, on another visit, she shared that she had thought alot about what I had said and she had seen and she was considering Berkeley as a possible alternative to Oxford. Only fifteen, her thoughts about schools and careers are likely to change much over the next four years, so I don't worry too much about leveling her ambitions or destroying her spirit. But I do see how my own struggles with class, and past and present, birthright and achievement, influence my relations with my daughter.

"CUTTING CLASS"—THE MIXED BLESSING OF EDUCATIONAL ALTERNATIVES

I got the idea for this chapter's title from a book I read many years ago by Nancy Friday, *My Mother, Myself* (1997), a minor cause célèbre on middle-class white women and their mothers. Interested in gender issues, I had been drawn to it because of a study I was doing on black women and their racial commitments. One of the ideas I got from Friday's book was the close tie between mother and daughter. It seems to me that fathers too have such ties to their daughters; perhaps this is part of the nonpatriarchal meaning of the Greek tale where Athena is borne from her father's—Zeus'—head.

My daughter's growth into class—her life between her parents' race, class, and gender stories and those she is creating day by day in her own worlds—differs from my own. But we share class—our differences and positions notwithstanding. Stuart Hall wrote in his essay on ethnicity, difference, and identity: "Only when there is an Other can you know who you are." One meaning of this statement for me is that I have been and became a classed person through repeated collusions with real or imagined others.

My despair at the idea of my daughter's class is linked to memories of these collusions during which I co-constructed myself. I recognize that I have never been truly lower-class nor am I now truly middle-class: back then, there were things that I did and said that got me into trouble with whites and blacks—I didn't know and remain in my place. And now, often voluntarily, to avoid confrontation I assume a position or place incongruous with my "social class" rank. This happens not only but especially in the South when I move back and forth through highly racial and classed environments.

For instance, during New Year's my girlfriend and I spent several days in a new home I built outside of Myrtle Beach. On New Year's Day, we headed toward the ocean to find a spot for brunch. I wanted to show her a part of North Myrtle Beach, called the Shag Capital of America, where people come yearly to take part in a fifties-style dance. It is a historically "redneck" (read "lower working class") area of the Grand Strand making up this vacation spot in northern South Carolina. We passed a spot on the oceanfront that looked like the wrong kind of place to eat in if one is being sensible; but I felt like being "a middle-class American" and walked into this place out of the past where all eyes stared at us, never speaking, just gazing. After ten uncomfortable minutes where waitresses carefully avoided our eyes, we left unserved, and found our way back to the main drag where we belonged.

2005 . . . no—2006 . . . Things still have not changed. I found myself apologizing to my mate from the North, somehow I felt responsible for the experience—even though I knew better. Colin Powell, Condoleezza Rice, and Oprah notwithstanding, I knew my fifty-eight years of experience told me to stay away. But "class" had blinded me momentarily. As a child growing up in the South I would never have made that mistake whatever anyone might have said. But becoming "middle class" meant giving up so much of that time and place.

For the most part, I have not given it up; this is my shame and my pride. My shame because it means I have "essentialized" the nonessential; my pride because I know it's not essential and have remained relatively whole, compassionate, and hopeful even when I act less than I might. I have not become "middle-class." I dwell in the same in-between place as my daughter.

But I did not know that until I saw her "Otherness." This otherness—this marginality as American sociologist Robert Parks spoke of as he reflected on the Jew in diaspora or the immigrant in a distant land—has been renamed "the margins" and "the borders" by critical scholars. It has always existed. It is a source of both pain and promise. Few of us truly like being on the outside looking in, but most of us appreciate the freedom from constraint of custom, habit, and expectation. These are the twin poles of my daughter's class existence. I share these. So have many constructed into "blackness."

Many years ago, the well-known family therapist and social work professor Elaine Pinderhughes wrote about the confluence of three traditions or ways of being for African Americans: African, traditional middle-class American, and oppressed victim. Her observations made sense to me then, as they do now. It seems from the start my own trajectory toward middle-class success and respectability was bound up with traversing these triple "roads" toward destiny. As the first African American baby delivered at Norfolk General Hospital in 1947, I was classified by these three traditions. The segregated South of my birth was merely the broad outline of the context in which I achieved *classed self*. From the perspective allowed by Pinderhughes formulation, there were at least three dimensions to this achievement.

Cutting class and African culture. Because I no longer fly (that's another story), I spend a great deal of time traveling through various towns and communities in North America. On these often long, repetitive trips I frequently find myself zoning out, like the lone traveler on a snowy night from Robert Frost's poem, as I pass homes, shops, schools, and community centers of all types. What strikes me at these times is the essential *groupness* of human beings: we need to belong; most of us will do just about anything to belong; and culture—as values, beliefs, traditions, and artifacts—help us hold it together in this vast uncharted and unknown world. African culture—whatever its origins and fictions— has done this for me and millions of African Americans.

The comfort, the knowledge, the affirmation of the group has been a strong force in my pursuit of knowledge and schooling. The things that black men and women—and, yes, some white ones as well—have said to me over the years have been critical in my resilience, my hunger to achieve, to be recognized, to be affirmed.

As a child, this often meant that I hooked school; I did not go. I "cut class." This is the irony—one made all the more profound by educational research—that speaks to the fact that schools were not, and often continue to not be, places designed for education that will affirm the best in one. When the curriculum and pedagogy begin with assumptions of worthlessness, they invite one to cut class.

In this sense, then, "cutting class" is a powerful metaphor for the simultaneous resistance to learn the values, beliefs, and ways particular to a social class and the affirmation of agency and psychic investment in an alternative class or groupness. This seems so profound to me now because I intuitively knew and enacted these things when I stayed away from school so much as a child. I was not the handsomest, the richest, or the strongest. I lacked "class" in my class. So I sought "class" outside of school.

Cutting class and "middle-class American." And yet, even in this, one can see the profound truth that liberatory spaces exist or can be created through oppressive practices: When I would stay away from school for weeks at a time, watching daytime television at home or roaming the streets, I was being "remembered" by my teacher. My mother would tell me the tale that added to my enhancement as a student even as I cut class: "Your teacher told me that it was a shame that you are always out with the Asthma. But she said it way okay because when you came back, you were so smart that you still caught up and passed the class."

My teacher affirmed my "brains," and, constructing an image of a sickly youth—which I sometimes was—she redefined me beyond the behavior problem and classroom clown to some Robert Stevenson–like prodigy whose academic prowess could not be conquered by illness. My mother, again showing her own tremendous humanity, chided yet blessed me as she retold my misadventure over and over to anyone who would lend a sympathetic ear. I did not gain support for my truancy through her actions, but I did gain a sense of myself as learner, thinker, and "smart." I also learned the basis for bonding with my father through her actions.

Cutting class and "victim." My mother, fully realizing that I had hooked school, showed typical middle-class maternal pride as she revealed to my father those misbehaviors that affirmed for him that I was growing into "black manhood"—deviant but smart. My father was born in 1912. He was a hustler, a dude, a gambler, and, some said, a killer. I accepted him—good and bad—as I accept the white man—mostly bad, some good. I knew that my life was shaped or affected by whites in powerful ways: I saw this when the police, all white back then, would raid our apartment in search of my father for something he had done—more than once, he had beaten up his white childhood friend for whom he worked as laborer. This white man had told my mom that "Aaron is my best worker, and friend, but I am not going to let him beat me up and get away with it." He often put my father in jail for the weekend and let him out and back to work during the week.

CLASS, SCHOOL ACHIEVEMENT, AND THE MARGINS

This "dance of agency" with the white man was a routine part of my parents' and my own life growing up. As a child of color, a heterosexual male, raised in the Baptist/Pentecostal tradition, I was *classified* to live on the margins, to see, understand, and chose from the margins. In recent years, much has been written about the power accruing to those who live beyond the inner sanctum and its peculiar powers. But the vantage of the margins was understood long ago; within social science, Robert Park's studies of Jews and human migration identified the Steppenwolf, the pariah, the Marginal Man, as one whose peculiar place or position afforded a particular kind of knowledge as fact, perspective, and paradigm.

As I look back over my memories of cutting class, I recognize the margins and places I dwelt as the sources for my love of learning and my affirmation in pursuing new knowledge. Now, as I revisit my earlier fears for my daughter as she pursues her own academic adventure, I realize what I fear most is not her attendance at elite schools but her lack of experience with "cutting class." It is this experience of working from the margins to create both ways of knowing and seeing and being that constituted the architecture upon which my own lifelong learning and struggle for survival has been built. It is also why even as I have achieved, I have remained "declassified" in important ways, ways that preclude my giving my daughter the "class" she will perhaps need at the schools she is working so hard to gain access to. Perhaps before she finally arrives there, she too will get the chance to "cut class."

CHAPTER 9

Readin' Class: Droppin' Out

Eric J. Weiner

DROPPIN' OUT, PART 1

The quest for class consciousness puts us in a state of perpetually *becoming*. Developing consciousness of class is a never-ending process that takes detours through the past, comes round to the present, imagines a future that has yet to be, then detours again into the past (not necessarily in that order); it is a cyclical process characterized by a hostility to repetition and redundancy. In this essay, I write about my own process and do not claim an objective stance, which I believe is implausible within the parameters of historical narration.[1] This is not to say that what you are about to read is a lie or fabrication, deceptive vocabulary in the context of intro- and retrospective narration. As the character Scarface infamously said, "I always tell the truth, even when I lie." Or, as Halldor Laxness's character the Bishop, in his latest novel *Under the Glacier*, tells his companion Embi, "Don't forget that few people are likely to tell more than a small part of the truth, let alone the whole truth . . . When people talk they reveal themselves, whether they're lying or telling the truth . . . Remember, any lie you are told, even deliberately, is often a more significant fact than a truth told in all sincerity."[2] The only claim I make is that the moments that I discuss are as I think I remember them, as they have been told to me, and as I have interpreted various familial narratives that have been passed down over the years.

I have left more out of the narrative than I include, a natural consequence of the nonfalsifiable attributes of retrospective, first-person accounts as well as the impossibility of recalling everything that might or might not have occurred over a lifetime of overlapping events. Try not to get too hung up on the antipositivistic nature of my narrative, for as Kincheloe rightly asserts "there exists no final meaning that operates outside of historical and social contexts."[3] Be grateful that I refuse to make arrogant claims to knowing definitively. I only know contingently; that is, my knowledge comes from a complex matrix of sociological, cultural, psychological, anthropological, historical, pedagogical, communicative, linguistic, affective, and political spheres, all circulating around, in, and through the stuff we call "reality." In spite of this collection of interrelated "lenses," there will undoubtedly be blind spots. Nevertheless (or because of this), I hope the story I tell gives the reader a sense of my own struggle to understand "class," and given that we are, as Carol Gilligan points out, "individuals-in-relation," I also hope my struggle will teach you something about how class works in your own life as well.[4]

Because social class is intimately tied to other sociological categories of personal and group identification, like race, ethnicity, gender, sex, and sexuality, it is almost impossible to discuss one without implicating the others. Nevertheless, differing contexts ask for different kinds of critiques, just as different kinds of critiques produce specific kinds of knowledge. When analyzing and interpreting social things, we must never reduce what we see as the effect of only one social force, like racism or sexism. But that is not to say that we should stop analyzing social events for how race or class or gender or sexuality get played out around, through, and on a historically contingent "axis of power."[5] I have tried, in my retrospective narrative, to pick events and relationships in my life that bring attention to the salience of class struggle and class identity. This is not to say that other forces were not at work, simultaneously shaping my consciousness not only about class, but about race, sex, and gender as well.

Please take note as you read that my narrative is not simply an exercise in egocentric exposition. I have tried to theorize the narrative as I tell it, to get beyond the experiential in an effort to complicate what I think I know by thinking about the process by which I have come to know it. In an effort to disrupt the false dichotomy between theory and practice, or in this case theory and knowledge, I imbricate theory throughout the text.

It is employed as a mirror upon my narrative, as well as a spotlight, high-lighting various words, phrases, events, and feelings that I identify as having importance. This does not mean that the work of theorizing this text has been done for you. On the contrary, I have left untheorized—sometimes intentionally, most times unintentionally—many ideas within the text. More to the point, it is your job as a reader to theorize these narrative moments, as well as to retheorize those moments that I have theorized. As a critical reader, you must infiltrate, interrogate, and disrupt the text, not only to discern what I may mean, but to also give the text *meaning*. Although the author might in fact be dead, the text is always being rewritten every time it is read.

Coming to Class Consciousness: Are We There Yet?

By pressing our ears hard against the pregnant belly of the future, we honor and speak to the courage and grace of the dead. My story therefore must begin with my grandfather, Samuel Barrish, born into a poor Jewish family of six sisters in the last decade of the nineteenth century in Slutsk, Russia. Arriving on Ellis Island in 1902, he was six years old and could only speak Yiddish and Russian. As the only male in the family, he was forced to drop out of school when he was thirteen by a tyrannical father, so that he could help provide for the family. His father helped secure him a job in a bleach factory, where he worked until he was sixteen or seventeen. At twenty-one he joined the army to fight in World War I. Coming back a sworn pacifist, as well as a budding socialist (he would NEVER cross a picket line), for the next twenty years he made his way down the eastern seaboard from New England to New York City, finally settling in Philadelphia. Sam had various jobs, but he had an affinity for fixing things, a curiosity for technology, and a passion for smoking—cigarettes, pipes, cigars—until, at forty, the veins in his legs grew cold and stiff from, the doctor said, the nicotine in his blood. So, he quit at forty, substituting hard candies for nicotine, figuring, I am told, that blood flow was more important to living life than a set of pearly whites.

He married my grandmother, Florence, a year before he gave up smoking, when she was twenty-seven, a budding old maid according to her family at the time. Unlike my grandfather, my grandmother was born in the United States and into a bourgeois family. Her father owned a successful corner store in a working-class neighborhood in Kensington, Philadelphia (they were one of only two Jewish families in the neighborhood, which was inhabited primarily by Irish and Italian immigrants). They also owned a horse and buggy that they would ride down Broad Street to get ice cream on Sundays. Her clothes were custom made, while his were made to resist the daily grind of earning a wage.

Florence and Sam were married happily for the next fifty-six years, until he died at age ninety-six. They raised two children, one (my mother Rhoda) who graduated with an undergraduate degree in communications from Temple University, the first Barrish to graduate from a four year university. My aunt Debbie, the older, married Dick, a man with a short left arm, who drank gallons of vodka in between making what we called "good" money. Together they are only notable for the cruelty they exacted upon their two adopted children, one of which they violently disowned and the other which they physically abused in their million-dollar Boston suburban home, the colonial on the corner, with the green shudders and quiet shades. Before my mother and her sister stopped communicating, I remember visiting their home, and watching my aunt Debbie kick my cousin Elizabeth down the center hall staircase. My heart still beats hard as I recall her, an adopted baby from Asia, screaming fearfully as she tried to control the speed of the fall.

Unconscious of it at the time, watching this kind of violence within the comforts of wealthy suburbia, made it much more difficult, I would imagine, to believe the dominant social narrative that claims that white, wealthy people are more civilized, reasonable, and adhere to a value system that is somehow better and at odds with working-class people and poor people, who we learn, from the same narrative, have "different" values, are rude, uncivilized, and operate almost primarily in the realm of the corporeal and primal. Consistent with the ethos of the ruling classes, silence was one of the most salient dimensions of the household violence, as no one ever spoke publicly (and only whispered privately) about the events that took place in that house. Silence, in this context, is a powerful privilege of class that assists in the perpetuation of the mythologies that it creates for itself.

Florence's brother owned Tioga Electric, an electrical appliance and furniture store in Kensington, Philadelphia, which sold and repaired radios, refrigerators, washing machines, and the like. He hired Sam, who eventually became, not a "worker," my grandmother was sure to correct, and my mother remembers vividly, but a "store manager." Florence and Sam had one of the first televisions on their working-class block of row homes and people would come over to watch Milton Berle, after which they might play gin rummy or pinochle or sit on the stoop sipping hot tea with milk. He worked six days a week, and four nights for the next forty years at the store. He bought a modest row home, owned a car, played golf on his day off at the urban county course, which was a short mile from his home, and put his youngest sister through teacher's college in Fall River, Massachusetts. He would send Florence and the girls on vacation to Atlantic City in the summer, while he would stay home and work, meeting them on the day he had off from the store. He also bowled a fair game, and it is rumored that he could run three racks of balls on the pool table as a younger and smokier man.

In terms of class, my grandfather epitomized how muddled the category of social class can become in capitalist societies, especially after Henry Ford introduced the world to the assembly line and the banks introduced workers to credit.[6] Samuel was a Jewish man who had an eighth grade education, spoke Yiddish and Russian (lost the Russian) as first languages and English as his second (although the concept of ESL or bilingual education was still a long way from the reality of immigration), as a child was very poor, worked sixty hours a week as an adult (not sure how much as a child), and enjoyed sporting activities characterized by camaraderie more than competition, excellence more than winning. He dressed and ate simply, was unimpressed by wealth and extravagance, read voraciously, and was liberal in his attitudes about race and ethnicity.

This meant he believed that everyone, regardless of race, should have the same opportunities to pursue what has come to be called the American dream. A liberal stance should be differentiated from a "critical" attitude about race, which argues that differences in experience, culture, language, and history based upon race and ethnicity cannot and should not be ignored when discussing the issue of opportunity. My mother still jokes that she held a stereotype that African Americans were all good at math until she was in college, because my grandfather had hired an African American man to come to the house and tutor her in math, a subject that she struggled with as a young adolescent and he obviously felt ill-equipped to teach. Interestingly, my grandfather's investment in socialist ideals did not, for him, conflict with what he understood to be the American dream. For him, the promise of the dream, the promise of *H*america, depended upon a strong and vibrant public sphere.

My grandfather, however socialist his political sympathies were, still owned a modest row home on a beautiful tree-lined street in northeast Philadelphia. He paid off the mortgage in five years, saving a significant, if not monumental amount of money over the course of his lifetime, enough to allow my grandmother to die peacefully in her own apartment under the watch of a private twenty-four-hour home attendant. My grandmother never collected a salary a day in her life. He owned many different cars, the first a Model A Ford, the last one a gold 1976 Pontiac, which I happily inherited, after he became too old to safely drive. He could afford to send my grandmother, mother, and aunt to Atlantic City each summer, where they stayed in one of the fancier hotels near the boardwalk. He also managed to buy my grandmother three fur coats over the course of their lives, which, upon her death, were given to the African American woman who had kept her clean and comfortable in her dying months. Although this kind of opulence was not something that was important to him, it was extremely important to my grandmother. Florence was more materialistic than Sam, never letting him forget (although not with mean intent) how if he just invested in Levine's Furniture store on the boulevard, where they knew the owners, they would have been "comfortable" (even though, to my knowledge, my grandmother was never uncomfortable a day in her life). In spite of my grandmother's angsting over the "Joneses" (in this case the Levines), he was still able to afford, in his retirement, winters in Florida.

In light of all of these social dimensions, Sam was not quite the working-class subject he might have been if he had worked as a unionized factory laborer. He also wasn't quite a member of the bourgeoisie either. He was neither an owner, nor a "worker" in the Marxist sense of the word. Historically, my grandfather was living out a more complex reality than the struggle between the proletariat and the bourgeoisie. He represented a new breed of worker, one that emerged from a confluence of social forces.

In the 1920s, consumer society coincided with Fordism.[7] According to Aronowitz, Fordism was "perhaps the most effective deterrent to the development of class politics in the 1920s."[8] The Ford Motor Company, as is well known, developed the self-moving assembly line, which made work unbearably repetitive, but maybe more important, wrenched away control from the workers over the pace of their work. The assembly line also made mass production a reality of capital relations. "Mass production entailed mass consumption."[9] So Ford, according to Aronowitz, convinced banks to extend credit to consumers.

The extension of credit was no less than revolutionary in how it shifted emphasis from production to consumption. As such,

> . . . work was seen as a means to the end of buying more goods, as activity that came to fill up workers' free time. The wheels for the shift were greased by the expansion of the credit system, once reserved for business and professional people who could put up property as collateral to secure their loans . . . With the mass automobile and the one-family home came a vastly expanded highway system that enabled millions of Americans to spend more time on the road.[10]

Along with mass production and the emergence of a consumer society, the 1920s introduced "a new industrial bureaucracy of managers, engineers, and administrative and clerical employees in large and medium corporations."[11] Arising from this new credit system and production technologies were banks, consumer finance corporations, and retail establishments. In combination with the steady flow of new immigrants and rising minimum wages, there was a boom in educational jobs.[12] Aronowitz marks these developments as the impetus for the creation of a "new class of white collar employee tied closely to corporations and to local governments."[13]

Indeed, my grandfather, in some important ways, seems to have been an effect of this confluence of social forces. He represented a new class subject, whose political affinities were with the plight of traditional workers and other oppressed people, but who, materially, and in some regards culturally and intellectually, was aligned with this new class of workers. From him, I acquired a deep sense of justice. This is not to say that I had any conscious understanding of "class" when I was with him, but rather I began, I think, to sense the power of a socially just heart and mind. By treating everyone we came in contact with respect and kindness, from store owners and gas station attendants to his golf buddies, the disrespect and cruelty that was all around us, but remained invisible and silent, not because it was not there, but because I had not yet learned how to see and hear it, became more apparent to me. When the familiar becomes strange, as Henry Giroux[14] has said, it signals a transformation of consciousness; it marks a moment of cognitive and affective disruption.

My father's side of the family represents another category of social class, not easily placed on the grid of economic indicators. I never knew my father's father. He was, it is said, a bad man. What this meant exactly, I never found out. I did learn that he was a small-time mobster. And my father, Burt, was a small-time bag boy. He left my father and my grandmother, Ann, when my father was about thirteen. She eventually, and some might say ironically, remarried—a Philadelphia police officer.

Pop-Pop Izzy was a large man, who would fall asleep in the high backed chair after dinner every time we went to their row house for dinner. When they came to the suburbs to our house for Thanksgiving, he would inevitably commandeer the black leather recliner in the family room. I still remember holding his blackjack, the leather tightly wrapped around the slim mass of lead cracked and faded, I imagined, from too much use. For its size, I was amazed by its weight and equally fascinated and horrified as he showed me how a quick rap on the back of a crook's head with the blackjack would put him down. Such a weapon seemed at home in my father's childhood home, buried in a drawer smelling softly of old playing cards and keys. In Willow Grove, however, such a tool seemed as foreign to me as a Septa bus pulling up to my driveway.

I was surprised to learn that like my father's father, Izzy ran a numbers racket in the basement of their home. My father, the story goes, came home from high school one afternoon to find his mother in handcuffs, the FBI scouring the house, and Izzy absent, on his police horse fighting crime no doubt. The feds let my father go to his room, where upon opening the closet door he found a man hiding. He handed the man his coat, and quietly shut the door.

This reality was completely unknown to me as a child. But I can't help but feel that it informed my sense of class as I got older in some nebulous way, if only through my father's determination to not simply leave that life behind, but to erase it from historical memory, through a total investment in rewriting his working-class subjectivity. From working-class musician to hyperconsumerist and real estate capitalist, his materialism was both exciting and vacuous. Unfortunately, the "swindle of fulfillment" that Ernst Bloch so aptly applied to consumerist longings, shaped my father's new subjectivity in a way that left him lacking a sense of social agency. When you are swindled, the bag that you are left holding contains the cynicism of a sucker, the social cancer of hope and possibility.

When the two families would get together—my mother's and father's—class distinctions became more apparent to me, even as a child. Again, I didn't have the language to name what I saw in terms of class, but I did recognize the different ways, for example, that my Great-Aunt Bev (my father's aunt) and Florence spoke to each other as well as strangers like waitresses, bus drivers, or just another person trying to get through a crowded restaurant (When a tall red-haired woman pushed her way in front of both Florence and Bev as we made our way into the diner, Florence said, "Excuse me," enunciating the hard "c" for emphasis. Bev, on the other hand, stated clearly, for everyone within ten feet to hear, "Red haired BITCH!"). Florence, as I've said, embodied a bourgeois ethos—proudly identifying herself as a "lady," who every week went to get her hair done and where she would gossip with the other "ladies." Bev, on the other hand, embodied the scrappy ethos of a life lived working. If Bev had a problem with something Florence was saying (or anyone else), she would just come out and tell her. Or, if sitting at the same table in-legs-reach, and Florence was saying something that Bev thought she should not, Bev would kick her under the table to shut her up. Florence would try to ignore the kicking, going on in a contained tone, until eventually she would tell Bev to, *please*, stop kicking her.

As a child this was all terribly amusing. But in thinking back, it was class that was shaping the interaction between these two women. At the time, all I think I knew was that Bev was stronger than Florence. I admired Bev's ability to ignore what people like Florence said was inappropriate. I was able to do this because my grandfather, as well as my father and mother, never said anything derogatory about Bev. She was admired for her individuality, smarts, humor, and toughness. She used profanity when she was angry, took the bus to the McDonalds in center city to meet her friends for coffee until she was well into her eighties, and at four feet six inches tall, would never back down if challenged. My mother, father, and grandfather saw significant value in this kind of cultural expression, a mode of expression I have come to understand as class-based.

What I believe is of significance in this reflection is not that I recognized the differences in how my grandmother and Bev interacted, but that Bev's way of mediating the world was valued by people, like my grandfather, that I respected. The respect that I had for him transferred to Bev. It is important to make a distinction here between respect and tolerance. My grandmother tolerated Bev, although sometimes barely. My grandfather, father, and mother respected Bev. The difference is one of power and privilege. Those who tolerate difference often have put themselves in a position where difference signifies a variation on a norm. The norm signifies the manner in which those who tolerate do something, say something, and/or think a certain way. Those who tolerate difference fail to see how normalcy is an effect of power; nothing is normal, it is only determined to be so by those who have the power to make those kinds of determinations. Once normalcy is defined, then all other ways of being in the world are labeled as different, different from what is deemed normal. In some contexts, like many versions of multiculturalism, we are then encouraged to tolerate difference, although rarely does anyone ask you to tolerate normalcy. Maybe this is why I now find normalcy intolerable.

Not surprisingly, my mother embodied my grandfather's sense of justice (my aunt Debbie, in case you are wondering, we unofficially diagnosed as simply, yet dangerously, mentally disturbed). My father embodied a capitalist sensibility. This is not to say that he was not concerned with issues of justice, nor is it fair to say that she was not concerned with capitalist endeavors. They both embodied the liberal notion that a strong democracy would lead to a just world, and strong capitalism would lead to a comfortable one. Neither of them questioned, as far as I can tell, the contradiction between the need for social equity in democratic systems on one hand and the inequities that are in-herent to a neoliberal capitalist system on the other. This confluence of ideological forces gave birth to a new class subject, one that was dif-ferent than my grandfather's, my grandmother's, or Bev's, yet contin-gent on them nonetheless.

This new class subject was college educated (my father, like my mother, was the first in his family to graduate from a four year univer-sity), and sub-urban in its orientation to the single-family home, "su-per" markets, the *necessity* of automobiles to get to work and play, and the burgeoning strip mall developments. Residential developments with names like Deer Run Estates or Willow Highlands, in which iden-tical, "modest" split-level homes lined streets with names like Green-wood Lane, Lookout Drive, and Red Barn Road, attracted this new class subject, who had never seen so much space or trees or quiet.

Into this world I was brought from a Philadelphia hospital where I was born, the vestiges of urban life ephemeral in suburbia. My sister, only four years later, by contrast, came into the world in the suburban hospital just three miles from our home. From this world, I measured, evaluated, judged, experienced, hoped, struggled, failed, succeeded, loved, hated, fought, laughed, thought, cried, and learned. It was a world of comfort and privilege, yet I did not know what comfort and privilege was until I was much older. It was a world of safety, security, and whiteness, yet I did not know what these things were, either, until I was old enough to venture beyond the confines of what James Gee calls my "primary discourse."[15]

According to Gee, a discourse is the way we use language, think, and act that makes us a member of a meaningful social group. Our primary discourse comes from our families. Everyone has a primary discourse regardless of what kind of family someone has. But because our pri-mary discourse is acquired, as opposed to learned, we are unaware that we have a discourse specific to our familial/cultural location. Only when we move out of our familial location might we get a sense that the way we use language, act, and/or think is not the same as the way other people, who have dissimilar primary discourses than ourselves, speak, act, and/or think. In many cases, it takes a long time before people re-alize that their primary discourse is a discourse; that is, a historically and culturally specific way of thinking, using language, and acting.

Many people, because they live very isolated lives, rarely socialize with people who do not share their primary discourse. As a consequence, when they are introduced to someone who has a different primary discourse, it might be described as weird, funny, strange, different, stupid, ignorant, intelligent, or twisted. For example, if you speak Standard English as part of your primary discourse, and your students speak Black Vernacular English (BVE) as a part of their primary discourse, will you, as a teacher, be able to "read" their use of language productively, or will you read it as a deficiency?

In my suburban neighborhood, most of the kids shared a similar primary discourse, although I soon began to feel differences between what I was acquiring/learning and what most of my friends were acquiring/learning. The most significant difference was not the way I used language, the way I dressed, or the things I did in the neighborhood, but rather the way I thought and the activities I was involved in outside of the neighborhood. I was introduced at a very young age to urban culture. This included going to jazz concerts as a young boy, modern museums and art galleries, theater in New York City (on and off Broadway), and a range of restaurants from the elegant to the home grown. I was also encouraged to play sports generally reserved for the wealthy, like golf, tennis, and skiing. The neighborhood kids who I was friends with generally didn't do any of these things. Mike, my best friend until he moved out of the neighborhood at thirteen, played football, never saw a theater production, rarely ate at restaurants, never went to New York City, Washington, D.C., or Boston, and, as far as I can remember, never stayed in a hotel, rode in a cab, took a subway ride, or listened/saw a jazz performance. We were as close as two young boys could be, but we were developing different discourses of class, and as we headed into our teens we grew apart for many reasons, but one major one being the fact that we began to embody unique class subjectivities. Looking back it would seem easy enough (normal enough) for me to have elevated my experiences and diminished my peers', but my grandfather's and mother's deep sense of respect for people who might have class knowledge dissimilar to my own had the effect of opening up worlds for me that might otherwise have been closed down, even with the same experiences. Conversely, Mike never dismissed me or my developing class subjectivity, although by the time we roamed the same high school halls we were strangers, looking at one another across a long expanse of class distinctions. I think the mutual respect held, but it was not enough to make us friends as we were when we were kids, as we were before we had definitive, yet different class identities.

Paulo Freire talked about the powerful nature of "epistemological curiosity," by which he meant the tendency for people to explore the world beyond their immediate world with a sense of wonderment unhinged from the nasty delineations of negative judgment and prejudice.[16] This is the kind of curiosity I had about discourses other than my own. Do not misread this, I valued my own discourse, but also was intensely curious to learn about other discourses. I had not yet begun to think critically about my discourse, but surely my curiosity about and respect for other discourses paved the way to thinking critically about my own.

Most important, I developed an *admiration* for discourses that emphasized the body and physicality; these filled a gap in my own developing discourses. I wanted to be like my friends who were adept at fighting, and I would watch as they never backed down from any confrontation, whether it would leave them hurt and bloody or victorious. But "watch" is the key word here, as it suggests that most times I was a voyeur, never really a part of this discourse, but seduced by it nonetheless. My friends, like Mike and Craig, who symbolically filled Mike's shoes in my high school years, operated in a world where street smarts mattered more than book smarts, physicality more that intellectual creativity. Yet both were intellectually creative and intense readers. Similarly, I possessed a certain degree of street smarts, much of which I learned from them, and a degree of physicality, although mine was more bravado than anything else. But my fluency in other cultural and political discourses was growing at a much faster rate than my fluency and involvement in Mike's and Craig's discourse.

Part of this is due to the fact that my parents sent me to a rather elite private school in the beginning of the seventh grade. This move, against the backdrop of what I have been discussing, is one of the most salient moments in the continuing process of my coming to class consciousness. Although I knew I was different from some of my friends when it came to the "urban" experiences that I was having, I had no way to anticipate the level of wealth and privilege that permeated Germantown

Academy. Like my curiosity about other secondary discourses, the dominant discourse of power, privilege, and entitlement that informed the attitudes and dispositions of Germantown's faculty and student body had a certain mystique and appeal for me when I first encountered it.

The grounds of the school were a tapestry of playing fields, tracks, and tennis courts, like I had never seen. The arts building, accented in glass and steel, was donated by a wealthy alumnus. For most classes, we sat around conference tables and discussed history and literature or attended presentations on topics like the Enlightenment, slavery, and democracy in the large lecture hall. Classes were no larger than fifteen students, while the "Mothers' Committee" made sure that our dress adhered to a strict code of what they considered acceptable attire for students of our stature: no jeans, no sneakers, shirts with collars for boys, and for girls, no dresses too high above the knee (the shock and awe that reverberated through the school when I showed up in black motorcycle boots, camouflage cargo pants, black leather jacket, and a Led Zeppelin concert shirt with a collar sewed into it still makes me smile, as it, technically, broke no rules). The library was a carpeted room, brightly lit with large wooden tables and high-backed chairs with the school seal and name engraved into them. On the first day, we would get a "credit card" that we would use to buy books, lunch, sporting equipment, or anything else that they sold in the bookstore, future training for the consumer culture that we were poised not only to participate in, but to shape and develop. More than preparation for the Ivy League, it was the Ivy League. With all this, it might be surprising for some to learn that I was downright grateful to have been kicked out at the completion of the eleventh grade, three years after they were considering my expulsion for the first time.

I soon realized that no matter how I dressed or used language, I would never be an accepted member of Germantown Academy's academic community. Although I tried, I could never get over the degree to which my peers not only felt entitled to their privilege, but easily ignored what I was beginning to consider the "real" world. For the next three years I muddled about in this environment, learning many things about the discourse of the ruling class, but growing more resistant to its values every year.

Like other discourses, however, elite class discourses are fractured, meaning they are underdetermined; that is, they are not foolproof in their capacity to envelop the minds and bodies of those who are subjected to their rules and strategies. There were a handful of students at Germantown Academy who came from significant wealth and privilege, but nevertheless resisted the rules of the dominant discourse. All of us, for one reason or another, were expelled from the graduating class of 1985. This kind of purging also goes on in public institutions by relegating the "at-risk" kids to special education, tracking them so that they are contained, or simply by creating conditions of learning that are so horrible, no one in their right mind would want to keep attending. But in private school, they simply have the right to kick out those who fail to get with the program or, in academic-speak, resist the hegemony of the dominant discourse.

At Germantown Academy, the dominant discourse, perpetuated by students and teachers alike, was characterized by a number of ideas. The most prominent for me at the time was their enormous sense of entitlement. In Jonathan Kozol's book, *Savage Inequalities* (1991), freshman high school students from impoverished public schools in New York City, commenting on well-funded public schools, sum it up like this: "They get used to what they have. They think it's theirs by rights because they had it from the start. So it leaves those children with a legacy of greed. I don't think most people understand this."[17]

The "legacy of greed" that this freshman student so eloquently points out is not necessarily explicit in the discourse. It's not like the students would walk around discussing how greedy they were, nor did they openly admit to being greedy. Their greed, and the validation of that greed, emanated from the new books that we bought every year; the long oval tables that we sat around as we learned, like young business executives or diplomats, where we could find ourselves in historical narratives, canonized literature, and philosophical arguments; the new uniforms that we purchased so that we could participate in sports like golf, tennis, track and field, football, baseball, field hockey, lacrosse, hockey, swimming, wrestling, and soccer; the credit cards that empowered us to purchase the necessities of private-school life; and the freedom to choose elective courses that we thought were interesting. Manifested in the practical activities of everyday school life, greed comes to signify, not an unpleasant attitude or disposition, as it might in working-class discourses, but instead is buried in the belly of entitlement, driving these students to not only want more, but to believe they *deserve* it; deserve more knowledge, more power, more wealth, more beauty, more capital, more authority, more, more, more . . .

By the time I was sixteen, I felt completely alienated from the faculty and the students. I was labeled the "bad" kid, cutting classes, smoking cigarettes at the deli across the street during lunch, getting in fights, dressing "differently," and getting high before, during, and after school. I actually began to believe it! I internalized the constant criticism and explicit doubt about my potential that the teachers and students would express. I struggled with a combination of anger and fear; anger over what they were saying, and fear that they were right. I still remember vividly a skirmish that broke out in the lunchroom between me and what seemed to be the entire football team, although led by one particularly large boy in the grade ahead of me. The feather earring that I had put in my ear at the coaxing of a friend earlier in the day was so offensive to the table of football players that they felt compelled, as I walked by their table, to woof "fag!" "What, motherfucker," I said as I stopped in front of the table, staring down six or seven apelike boys, trying to swallow the fear that was slithering up my throat and down my legs. The biggest got up, and nose-to-nose in front of one hundred students, we stood until a teacher came and broke us up. The fight to come was the talk of the school for many days, keeping me up just as many nights, but, alas, never materialized because . . . who knows, the toughest in private school, generally speaking were, I believe, never as tough as they pretended.

I often thought how the scene would have played out if Mike or Craig were in my shoes. The answer is simple: They would have punched him in the neck and face right in the lunchroom, and to hell with the teachers or the consequences. Both Mike and Craig asked me, quite directly and somewhat confusedly, why I hadn't done just that. In fact, after I was kicked out of Germantown, I went to the local public school for two months as a senior before dropping out for good. While there I reconnected with Mike on the first day of school, who later that day laid some adversary out on the stairs on the way to class who he heard was going to jump him and his friends after school. No questions, no words, just quick, painful, and definitive retribution.

I am not advocating violence, but I do want teachers to see that privilege exacts a symbolic violence upon those that it ignores or positions as different and/or undeserving, just as we tend to use an enormous amount of resources on controlling incidences of physical violence. From behavior models of learning and teaching to punitive "one-strike" zero-tolerance policies, our collective attention has been diverted away from the violence of greed and entitlement and toward controlling the bodies of our students. By controlling the body we simultaneously legitimate the environment of ubiquitous greed and entitlement so evident in neoliberal capitalist systems.[18] The French intellectual Michel Foucault clarifies this process when he writes:

> First of all one must set aside the widely held thesis that power, in our bourgeois, capitalist societies has denied the reality of the body in favour of the soul, consciousness, ideality. In fact nothing is more material, physical, corporal than the exercise of power. What mode of investment of the body is necessary and adequate for the functioning of a capitalist society like ours? . . . One needs to study what kind of body the current society needs . . .[19]

In terms of class interests, could it be said with some confidence that what type of body a society needs will depend upon whose needs are to be met by that society. In the context of Germantown Academy, elite society needed bodies/minds that would be able to lead the way into the future of a globalized, capitalistic system, to shape future generations of capitalists, and to imagine a future defined by the needs of corporate and private interests. Even in the United States, we are not natural-born capitalists, but instead have to learn the Discourse of neoliberalism. Future stock brokers, bankers, lawyers, judges, real estate developers, and entrepreneurs were being groomed for colleges and universities, the next step in formalizing the legitimacy of their entitlement and greed.

In the context of many public schools, even those in suburban communities, bodies are being prepared (and there are always exceptions) to perform well in positions that suffer from a lack of worker autonomy; that is, the degree to which a worker controls the conditions in which he/she works. From issues of time to the realities of pay, these bodies/minds are being prepared to meet the needs of a society that demands a large degree of docility. It is important that these bodies/minds do not lead, for if they did it might not be in the direction that the elite would want them to go. Those bodies/minds that resist and rebel, the future of leaders of oppositional struggle, are often labeled as "problem children," "undisciplined," or just plain "bad."

I was the "bad" kid in private school, but Mike was the "bad" kid in a suburban public school (the "bad" kid in the poor urban school has his/her own unique situation). The discourses of class that defined each version of bad were different in terms of what constituted unacceptable behavior, appropriate knowledge, effective skills, and possible futures. Who was "bad" was shaped by the dominant discourse of each school. But in both discourses there were people—students, faculty, and administrators—who embodied the "historically and socially defined discourses" of the particular institution of which they were a part.[20] As embodiments of a particular discourse of class, these people were authorized to define what exactly was "bad." In turn, alternative discourses of class were embodied by Mike and me, which resisted each of our school's dominant discourse. This resistance, as Paul Willis revealed in his ethnographic account of working-class boys in London, might have challenged the legitimacy of the school's dominant discourse and reinforced an alternative class-based subjectivity, but it also, especially in Mike's case, seriously diminished at the time our opportunities to develop a significant degree of social power and economic autonomy.[21]

After getting kicked out of Germantown Academy, I attended the local public high school for two months before dropping out of school completely. Coming back to public school after going to private school for five years added a considerable degree of complexity to my coming to consciousness about social class and schooling. At Germantown Academy I was at the lower ends of the economic scale, and, by the time I left, was openly disgusted by the blind privilege of my peers. I was spending most of my time with Craig and a few other guys, all older, out of school, and as far away from the discourse of Germantown Academy as I could comfortably get. We spent most of our time just hustling to make a bit of money for life's necessities: beer, cigarettes, nickel bags of dope that we would cop on the street, and girls. Life was simple and characterized by an almost complete disregard for the future. This was my life in the eleventh grade, and as I made my way into twelfth grade, school was a place that I exclusively associated with intimidation and symbolic violence. To say I hated it would be an understatement. My first day at the new public school a teacher asked me if I "was set." I wasn't sure what he meant at first. But then it dawned on me that he assumed that I was wealthy and privileged like the other students at Germantown Academy. I was pissed. After all, I had learned to despise those students and their value system. The thing I was about to realize was that, in comparison to many of my peers at the public school as well as the friends I was spending most of time with, I was wealthy and privileged, and this was especially true in regards to Mike.

I admired Mike. When I saw him again in the first week of twelfth grade, the different lives we had been living for the last five years didn't stop us from warmly embracing and shaking hands, but it did prevent us from becoming daily friends. We hung out occasionally, but by this time our class identities were more solidified as well as distinct, even though we both had rebelled against similar bourgeois attitudes and ideas. After high school (much of what I write about Mike's life after high school is all hearsay and speculation because I have not spoken to him in twenty years, although not only do I think about him often, he unexpectedly, I am told by my mother, who lives in the same house in which I spent my youth, knocked on her door two years ago, two daughters in tow, asking after me), he went into the navy. He then got into construction, I am told, which would be the same field as his father—who left him when he was quite young—and two of his four brothers. From what I hear, I do not think life has been easy for him.

After I dropped out of high school, I passed the state's GED test, and entered Temple University in Philadelphia. Even without a real high school diploma, and all the trouble, I was still expected to apply to college. Moreover, it was generally assumed, at least by my mother, that I would be able to get in. This is a different dimension of privilege and entitlement; it's indicative of what Pierre Bourdieu called cultural capital.[22]

A person's cultural capital comes from how valuable their ideas, thoughts, language, and actions are in the larger sphere of power and authority. Even though I did not adopt the discourse of entitlement and greed that dominated Germantown Academy, and actively rebelled against it, I still embodied certain aspects of ruling class and bourgeois culture that could be "read"—and would be read positively—by people in the admissions office at Temple, for example. My writing skills could be mistakenly read as a sign of intelligence. My body did not admit to any physical violence. Manipulated by years of braces, my teeth were straight, white, and all in attendance. For the interview, I dressed "up," putting on a silk tie which corresponded nicely with my shoes. I spoke not only Standard English, but I spoke it in a dialect that was soothing to the ears of my interviewer. And I had learned how to flirt in an acceptable manner in any number of contexts, interviews with attractive admission's counselors being one of them: Never vulgar, always smart, confident but not arrogant, enthusiastic for learning (about her), eye contact, make her laugh without trying too hard. But equally significant was my sense of entitlement. I felt this implicitly, although would have denied it at the time. There was something that was planted inside of me that encouraged me to believe, in spite of my academic failures and disappointments, that college was a place for me.

I also had not rebelled against the ruling class discourse to the point that I dismissed out of hand all the cultural activities generally reserved for the ruling class. I liked playing golf, although I had to caddy so that I could play for free. I enjoyed the theater, fine dining, jazz clubs, expensive cars, and elegant hotels. I wasn't willing (or able), in my rebellion, to completely reject the things that gave me pleasure (however ephemeral) simply because they were associated with ruling class life.

My social interests were fractured, my cultural capital was contingent on my fluency in multiple discourses, a sense of entitlement, and my association to bourgeoisie life, yet my political and intellectual commitments were becoming more invested in trying to understand and eradicate the inequities that I not only saw in the streets, but that I recognized in my own life. I was getting numerous second chances, while many of my friends seemed only to get one, and the one that they got, I began to recognize, was stacked against them before they ever sat down to play. When I was washing dishes or making cheese steaks for work, for example, it was always temporary (even when it lasted for many years), and I seemed to know this as I know my name. When my friends would get jobs like this, or I would talk to the other workers in the kitchen, the temporary aspect of the job that indicated a different future for me, was often absent for them. This is class privilege, plain and simple.

I quickly dropped out of Temple University, and moved to Colorado. I spent the next seven years learning about class as well as other social things, much of it on an old 1983 BMW motorcycle, which took me coast to coast through and around the United States and Canada. Obviously, the story could go on, and maybe that is an important point to make about narratives; the beginning and end are left arbitrarily up to the author. No doubt I have other salient moments I could share with you concerning my becoming conscious of class, like the meaning of my first (but not last) tattoo, or my sudden realization as I searched for a job in Colorado that I had no functional job skills besides washing dishes and bussing tables. But this would belabor the point of the narrative. It is now time to explore more deeply the complex relationship between the individual and the social in the context of becoming conscious of class.

DROPPIN' OUT, PART 2

A Sociology of Class

My narrative presumes that we are not born conscious of our social class, although we are certainly born into a particular social class, which even conservative commentators, like David Brooks of the *New York Times* now admits has an affect on a person's ability to move up the economic ladder.[23] Although my narrative of class consciousness concentrated primarily on my individual and interpersonal experiences of class, class is a social phenomenon which refers, from a Marxist perspective, to a worker's relationship to production, while others use it to describe income level or one's cultural power, which might or might not include income. In all cases, since at least the beginning of modern capitalism (although certainly precapitalist societies had a hierarchy of culture and knowledge shaped by access to and/or possession of power), there has never been a classless society. As soon as "capital" — cultural, economic, social—becomes a means by which societies organize their *power relationships*, class becomes a prevailing marker of difference. As a marker of difference, class shapes our attitudes about one another in terms of authority, knowledge, power, intelligence, beauty, and success.

But in modern capitalist societies like the United States, class takes on the added burden of representing a *fluid* marker of difference. In other words, the dominant narrative about class in the United States tells a story of class as a space and place that one moves through as opposed to a space and place in which one gets stuck. Class, from this perspective, is a powerful marker of the utopianism of capitalism's promise, and is often dismissed as a consequence by capitalists as being unimportant to understanding social phenomena, like success in school, professional advancement, or even the development of knowledge.

The American dream is the most popular of these narratives, passed down like scripture from generation to generation as well as pushed across national borders, seducing many people from other countries who grow up believing that the United States is a land where class, if it exists at all, is made fluid by hard work and determination. If you fail, explains the scripture, you have only yourself to blame, because opportunity, like fruit on the ripest trees, is readily available to those who "pull themselves up by their boot straps." What the scripture ignores, yet Billie Holiday brought to the collective unconscious as only her voice could, is the fact that some trees bear a strange fruit/Blood on the leaves blood at the root/Black body swinging in the Southern breeze/Strange fruit hanging from the poplar tree.[24] Pulling up on your boot straps will not loosen the noose around one's neck; it just might tighten it.

Developing class consciousness in the "fractured" social reality of today's neoliberal workforce necessitates that it should be developed around a conception of power and not salary, job title, or job skills/responsibilities. Breaking into the *unconsciousness* of class—beyond the muddled category of middle-class—is made increasingly difficult given the hegemony of the consumerist myth of free-market equality. In this context, class identity is exchanged for consumer power. Consumer power presumably erases the need for class struggle and the formation of class movements. Although economic status does have significance in the reality of consumer power it does not guarantee the formation of class interests. Making invisible the salience of class in everyday life, the appeal to the utopia of consumerism hides the fact that

Professional and managers do not mingle much with service or industrial workers, immaterial workers of all sorts are rarely in the company of blue-collar workers, and none of the above socialize with the poor, working or not. In sum, black or white, there is little blending of people from sharply disparate economic backgrounds. They inhabit different neighborhoods, even in the suburbs, where once social scientists purported to discover class blending. Different socioeconomic groups attend different churches, increasingly send their kids to different schools, and have different forms of leisure-time activity. Professionals and business people attend classical music concerts, go to the theater, and until recently were the core of voluntarism . . . Working-class people and the professional/managerial groups do not share the same cultural tastes, even in popular music, which in the past two decades has lost its universal appeal (the exception seems to be teenagers, for whom hip-hop has become *the* popular genre).[25]

These divisive differences, under the hegemony of consumerism, are delegated to the cultural realm, just as they are elevated as important indicators of class character. This double move has two powerful effects on class consciousness. First, it minimizes the importance of labor in the organization and maintenance of cultural hierarchies. High culture and low culture are reinforced in ideological terms thereby suggesting that cultural values and interests are intrinsically better or worse and not, more accurately, expressions of power. Second, class formations are denied legitimacy because class interests—cultural—essentially replace power as the modus operandi of class solidarity.

For example, a unionized machinist might earn enough money to secure a mortgage, buy or lease a new automobile, and/or take family vacations each year. But it would be a mistake to say that his consumer power translates into class power. His influence over his work environment, not to mention his power to determine the worth of his labor, is seriously compromised by his lack of class power. Outside of his union's influence, he controls neither his time nor his product. He will have almost no authority over what he produces, how it is produced, and under what conditions it is produced. He has essentially exchanged class power for consumer power.

An African American female adjunct or nontenured professor has a similar relationship to the power she has to control her working environment as well as the level of autonomy she enjoys over her intellectual and pedagogical productions. Although the machinist works in a typically "working class" context, the professor does not. The professor, as a consequence, correlates her class with professional elites. But given that the professor must conform to the mandates of the state (if it's a public institution) and/or the directorate of the university, which includes chairs, deans, chancellors, boards, and presidents, her class location, in terms of power, is quite in line with the machinist. Both struggle for autonomy and freedom in relation to what they produce and under what conditions they produce. Time, for both workers, correlates to labor output. Although the professor's output does not fit comfortably into the category of surplus value, she is nevertheless a wage earner. Her wage, before tenure at least, is determined by market forces on one hand, and an ideological investment on the side of administrators and state directorates in logical positivism on the other.[26] This ideological investment articulates with the larger, more inclusive ideology of technological rationality, which Herbert Marcuse explains has become, under the pressure of monopoly capitalism,

> the "correct" attitude toward instrumentality. . . , the correct logos is *techno-logy*, which projects and responds to a *technological reality*. In this reality, matter as well as science is "neutral"; objectivity has neither a telos in itself nor is it structured toward a telos. But it is precisely its neutral character which relates objectivity to a specific historical Subject—namely, to the consciousness that prevails in the society by which and for which this neutrality is established. It operates in the very abstractions which constitute the new rationality—as an internal rather than external factor.[27]

Within this epistemological matrix, the professor must produce a product that satisfies the criteria of both, which is especially impossible if she is in education or any of the other social sciences.[28]

In both examples, the workers struggle for dignity under the purview of an official directorate. Both share the burden of time as well as the lack of autonomy in terms of what they produce. Both, we might guess, circulate in different cultural spheres reinforcing the notion that they have little at stake in the common struggle over their labor. And most significantly, both have little power over the conditions in which they work. As Kelley points out,

Institutions of higher learning are by no means above exploitation or resistance, and the rules of the game are determined by the flow of capital. Thus unions are critical for defending university employees from corporate downsizing—a lesson few full-time faculty want to acknowledge. Beyond the obvious issues facing low-wage workers at universities, few of my colleagues recognize that they are about to be caught in the crisis themselves, especially with the elimination of tenure just around the corner, the hiring of casual labor to teach undergrads, and the reliance on academic stardom as the first wedge in the creation of a two-tiered faculty.[29]

As a reward for their powerlessness and/or "working class" alienation, the machinist, adjunct professor, computer programmer, store manager, etc., are recognized as members of the new consumer "middle-class": Buying power replaces class power. Consumption replaces direct political action and is the new civic agency. The laboring consumers share a power of recognition on one hand, and the powerlessness of being recognized on the other. Having authority over neither, both are celebrated as representative prizes of the capitalistic hunt. They are both recognized, in part, by how they are represented, and neither has enough power to represent themselves or their interests in the public/private sphere. Challenging this project pedagogically is complicated by the fact that the historicity of the consumer "class" is made invisible by the authority of monopoly capitalism.

Consumerism today, however, is markedly different than consumerism in the early twentieth century. In terms of class consciousness, the most significant change in consumer culture is the advent of globalization. Although as difficult to historically mark as it is to define with any accuracy, "globalization," according to Zygmunt Bauman, "is about what is happening to us all. The idea of globalization refers to von Wright's 'anonymous forces,' operating in the vast—foggy and slushy, impassable and untamable—'no man's land,' stretching beyond the reach of the design-and-action capacity of anybody's in particular."[30] Using many historical examples to support his point, Aronowitz argues that "Globalization may be read as capital's counterattack against the constraints on its power won by labor movements throughout the world, including the United States."[31] In both cases, globalization, in economic and political terms, translates in our current historical juncture into the widespread integrated, interdependent, and inequitable distribution of capital and labor. The "third" world is directly implicated, as a consequence, in "first" world affairs and vice versa. More than just the objects of imperial power, the "third" world becomes the "semi-skilled" and "unskilled" labor force for the "first" world's rabid consumption of goods, fuel, and food. By describing the work of some laborers as "unskilled" or "semi-skilled," notice how the language of capitalism diminishes the importance of the work that they do, while simultaneously legitimating the low wages that they earn.

Consumers, however, are kept ignorant, for the most part, of the "who" and "how" of production. "First" world consumers experience the material world in terms of relative cost *to them* while enjoying the comfort of not having to ever ask, "Under what conditions was this produced?" Their relationship to production, especially in terms of manufactured goods and the workers who make them, is one of alienation (*Spaltung* and *Verderben*).[32] Consumerism within globalization severs the practice of consumption from the mechanism of production. It is as if the clothes, shoes, cars, dishwashers, etc., have magically appeared in the nearest Wal-Mart or Disney store. The anonymity of production hides the "foggy and slushy" intimacy of globalization; it makes invisible the dirt, grime, heat, exhaustion, violence, and brutality of the reality of neoliberal capitalism as it is experienced and as it was fought against in developing and developed nations throughout the globe.

If this kind of information became part of a public pedagogy people might begin to ethically reflect upon not only the relationship between their consumption and the reproduction of poverty and the destruction of the planet, but begin to recognize *their own* class powerlessness in the eyes of those, who in economic and maybe political terms, are much worse off than themselves. Revealing the invisible mechanisms of production through education will not automatically produce resistance, just as critical schooling will not, alone, bring about a critical consciousness about the conditions in which so many throughout the globe work. But by combining the two there is an opportunity to forge meaningful connections among workers through a critical reading of power.

Coming to class consciousness along the axis of power in the era of globalization means, in part, recognizing common struggles across different geopolitical, economic, and cultural contexts. "First" world consumerism short circuits class formation by making invisible both inequitable relations of power *and* the relation between consumption and production. This invisibility alienates workers from one another, just as it alienates consumers from other workers and the process of production. By intervening into this alienating dynamic, we might be able to begin to recalibrate our relationships to each other and global finance.

None of this is to suggest that resistance by workers is not currently going on, nor is it to say that we are all dupes of a Weberian iron cage-gone-global. But incremental reform should be distinguished from the formation of class power and class struggle. Resistance is occurring every day, but it is most often characterized by incremental reform in the service of specific identity interests or it is the fractured rebellion that we witness every time the WTO has a meeting. These movements of reform and rebellion are vitally important in terms of what they mean in the context of oppressive apparatuses. In other words, they give evidence to the fact that domination is, as Theodore Adorno said, leaky. They might, in fact, be "creating history without much preparation and setting new conditions for political struggle."[33] We will only know, of course, retrospectively and even then our knowledge will be animated by the long shadow of partiality. Nevertheless, it would be a mistake to confuse these instances of political consciousness as *class* consciousness.

The difference is significant when we consider the former as an acknowledgment of power, but the latter as an acknowledgement and awareness of an oppressive capitalistic structure. Class consciousness, in this context, is the awareness of a specific and historical social structure that organizes labor along the axis of power. As such, class formations should be developed around the common albeit historical experiences of powerlessness that occurs *across* economic indicators, labor typologies such as blue collar/white collar, and educational levels and *through* cultural "difference." Class struggle, then, can be fought in the classrooms and the shop floor, in the computer lab and the kitchen, in the laboratory and the library. Likewise, it is fought through the modalities of black liberation, sexual justice, and gender equity.

If my "middle-class" students were taught to evaluate their class position in terms of their power to control their work and mode of production as opposed to how much they consumed, they might begin to feel a sense of connection with others who struggle with similar levels of powerlessness. Moreover, if they were to understand their relationship as consumers to the producers of what they consumed, they might begin to feel a certain level of responsibility for changing the conditions in which "third" world laborers often work. As it stands, they often feel intimately connected to people who do, in fact, have control over many aspects of their working lives. This leads them to form alliances—if only at the affective level—with people whose class interests might be antithetical to their own.

Against dominant U.S. dogma, class is a complex socio-economic-cultural-political force; it defies easy description and changes over time. What was true about class thirty years ago might not be true today. What is true today might not be true thirty years from now. Historical accounting can help us see *how class works*, although it can also blind us to the power of class struggle and class formations to change social and political space, depending upon the perspective from which histories are written[34].

Sociologists often discuss the relationship between work and class by identifying our work (what we do to earn a living) and the places that we do our work as somehow relevant to determining our place on the grid of economic indicators. From this perspective we get abstractions like the labels middle class, upper-middle class, lower class, etc. What do these labels tell us about the people who supposedly occupy them? Does it tell us how much they earn? If so, who determines how much earnings make a family of four, for example, poor or lower class? Who decides how social goods are distributed to each class? How much power does each of these classes have in the political process? If they have different degrees of power in a democracy, can we really say with certainty that we live in a functioning democracy? What do these labels tell us about the cultural interests of each grouping? Do the "middle class" have the same political interests as the ruling class when it comes to health care? Does this kind of graph tell us anything about cultural capital, that is, the authority a person has in a given context? Do these categories potentially hide more than they reveal about the interests of each class? How do these labels dehistoricize social class, making it a grouping of sociological categories that we move into and out of depending upon the amount of money we make? How do these labels obfuscate some of the most salient dimensions of class, namely the role class has played in the struggle for a more equitable distribution of power in capitalist society? In these struggles, class gains not simply historicity, but the power to transform space—social, political, cultural, and economic.

By saying that *class works*, following closely in Aronowitz's footsteps, is to say that it *does* things, shapes things, disrupts, challenges, intervenes, and transforms the future, just as it can rewrite the past. Class, as we will see below, is a powerful force in the history of social change and is organized around fractured social, political, cultural, and economic interests. What role will it play in the future of social change? What role, as (future?) teachers, will class play in the decisions you make in terms of the curriculum you develop and/or teach and the pedagogical strategies you employ? Indeed, how will your own "coming to consciousness" about social class affect the process by which your students develop their own class consciousness?

Toward a Pedagogy of Class Consciousness

For the remainder of my discussion, I will address two pedagogical dimensions—Historical Memory and Utopian Thought—of thinking about class in terms that recognize it as a historical force that works to transform both individual consciousness and social space.

Historical Memory

History should be taught not only across disciplines, but must be reclaimed and rewritten by those marginalized and victimized by the prerogative of the victorious. Historical memory, in its official guise, is the clearest articulation of hegemony. Rewriting, reclaiming, revising, and interrogating should become the pedagogical tools of historical excavation. We need to be leery of those who would encourage our consent to give up these democratic practices in light of the attack on the World Trade Towers on September 11, 2001. Quoting Walter Benjamin, Aronowitz writes, "The tradition of the oppressed teaches us that the 'state of emergency' in which we live is not the exception, but the rule.

We must attain a conception of history that is in keeping with this insight."[35] History should be about cutting, not covering; it should be resurrected as a form of critical consciousness, where the past is re-aligned to a future that we can imagine, feel, and anticipate with great excitement and hope.

A significant part of Aronowitz's work over the years, and more recently Robin D. G. Kelley's, is comprised of trenchant historical accountings of class struggle and class formations throughout the twen-tieth century.[36] These historical narratives are organic, meaning that one action is explicitly tied to many others, and vice versa. Their methodology resists and rejects severing history into parts: people, events, sayings, documents, wars, moments, etc. Severing history into separate and distinct parts is a tool of domination, perpetuating social myths through exclusion and celebration. Instead, they rewrite domi-nant historical narratives, trenchant accounts of struggle, success, power, and courage. The historical narratives that these men write are most notable for how they resurrect the long-buried narratives of those who fought but lost the power necessary in a winner-takes-all world to tell their own stories. In this retelling, life itself is relived in a way that rejuvenates the present and infuses the future with its most radical qual-ities: uncertainty and possibility.

For example, Aronowitz rewrites the official history of the New Deal by showing, in incredible detail, the undeniable tenacity of labor to fight for "industrial democracy" in spite of caustic governmental resistance, AFL concessions on proportional representation, and the establishment of the National Labor Relations Act, the Wagner Act, and Social Secu-rity. Instead of reading the Wagner Act and Social Security as productive concessions to labor, Aronowitz sees these concessions as articulations of authoritarian political structures. These initiatives, from this perspective, restricted "labor's ability to employ a wide array of weapons to advance its interests . . ."[37] The power of Aronowitz's narrative is not found in the success or failure of these struggles, but rather in the animation and "rememory" of class struggle and class formation. Aronowitz writes,

> At the turn of the decade [1930], the state of the opposition offered few grounds for hope that corporate capital's domination of the workplace

and the political culture could be effectively challenged. Unions were on the defensive, and many had been reduced to shells. In response to increased pressure from southern employers to increase productivity in order to buttress sagging profits, textile strikes in 1929 at the large Loray mill in Gastonia, North Carolina, in Marion, North Carolina, and in Elizabethton, Tennessee, displayed a high degree of courage and militancy by southern textile workers, whom both experts and many union officials had believed to be docile and antiunion. The Marion and Gastonia strikes were assisted by Socialist and Communist organizers, respectively, and this gave employers, as they sought government assistance to defeat the strikes, the excuse to brand the walkouts a red conspiracy. Plagued by an avalanche of court injunctions, jailing of strike leaders, ruthless firings of union activists, the deployment of local and state police, and lack of support from the official labor movement, the resistance was overwhelmed.[38]

Both Hoover and Roosevelt were guilty of ignoring mass protests and Hoover went as far as firing, under the direction of Gen. Douglas MacArthur, on protestors. One year later, in March 1930, in two dozen cities, Aronowitz reports that "more than a million unemployed rallied and marched for unemployment insurance, immediate relief, and public funds for job creation; and in 1932 the Ex-Serviceman's League marched on Washington demanding the federal government make good on its pledge to pay a veteran's bonus that had been deferred since 1918."[39] Incredibly, these veterans—who fought for the United States, were fired upon by U.S. troops for demanding what was rightly theirs. Equally troubling is the fact that this history is rarely, if ever, invoked in our children's history books or in the national discourse about freedom and patriotism.

In response to labor's insurgency, the Wagner Act, introduced by Sen. Robert F. Wagner, and supported by the AFL leadership and Roosevelt, established a "framework for labor peace."[40] It effectively created a juridical framework from which labor, corporate ownership, and government could negotiate differences. Hoping to quell the recent acts of mass insurgency, the Wagner Act imposed a kind of administrative rationality on class struggle, thereby neutering what had become labor's most important weapon in fighting for industrial democracy, namely direct action outside the formal and acceptable parameters of juridical restraint. Aronowitz writes,

> AFL president William Green hailed the Wagner Act as "labor's magna carta"... While it would take more than two years for the Supreme Court to dispose of constitutional challenges to the law . . . the fact that the events of 1933–37 that shaped labor relations for the most of the remainder of the century occurred outside the framework of the law remains a hidden story save for a few radical labor activists, historians, and legal experts . . . [Green's] declaration about the significance of the law became the main story that was repeated by many of his industrial union adversaries, by the leading text books, and by historians of the New Deal. The workers themselves got little credit for the wave of organizing that preceded and followed the act. Despite widespread strikes and factory occupations in almost every major industrial center, the accepted narrative was that labor was flat on its back before the law's administration and unions grew only within the frame of the Roosevelt coalition and the New Deal.[41]

Kelley, in a similar "organic" vein, narrates the story of the American Federation of Musicians (AFM), who in the 1930s struggled to "bring back flesh" to the movies.[42] Contextualizing the historical, Kelley writes, "The strike itself represents a confused response to a series of transformations extending far beyond the employment of musicians."[43] Kelley is referencing the harsh reality of artists and musicians who were living in, what Walter Benjamin famously called, the age of mechanical reproduction. He writes, "Benjamin's interrogation is central to the entire history of music under capitalism, for efforts to 'rationalize' and perfect music making in a market-driven world have led to inventions intended to eliminate human error or to capture flawless performances for posterity as well as for mass production and distribution."[44]

Within this context, the AFM's struggle, argues Kelley, was animated by a *lack* of solidarity with other unions and by a serious level of invisibility within working-class culture. Moreover, musicians never did, and still do not, occupy a place in the public consciousness as workers. More important, they often do not see their own work in working-class terms. It exists, for many, in that netherworld of creative production; neither inside nor outside of capital, marginalization feeds the myth of the tortured artist struggling for truth and beauty. Relating more to the entrepreneurial classes, musicians struggle to reconcile the need for collective power against their "natural" impulse of individuality. As such, "they straddle class lines and historically possess a kind of cultural authority that may belie their material class position."[45]

Thinking of musicians as workers is also muddled by the "signifier" *play*, which ironically describes their work.[46] Although the signifier "play," in the context of what musicians do, signifies the concept of work, it nevertheless is caught up in a powerful web of meaning, or, if you like, a meaningful web of power. Because the dominant public discourse categorizes what musicians do as play (i.e., the opposite of work), it is enormously difficult to disrupt the relationship between the signifier and signified. In plain language, for musicians to play is to work, but in the public imagination play is the opposite of work, or at least a dimension of leisure that is significantly different than work. "And yet," Kelley writes, "if we think about the work of making music and the context in which this work takes place, we cannot help but acknowledge the myriad ways musicians are affected by the whims and caprices of capital, the routinization of labor, and the often dehumanizing conditions of production."[47]

In the first decade of the twentieth century, musicians who earned their bread playing music for the movie theaters began to be replaced by photoplayers. Theaters that could not afford photoplayers started to use cue sheets, which essentially "told" the musicians what to play and when to play it. These standardizing inventions, Kelley argues, were put in place by movie houses, in the main, to quell the subversive activity of musicians, especially African American musicians who were accused of "subverting a film by engaging in playful musical signifying that would have horrified studio executives."[48] Interestingly, these standardizing tactics had an important pedagogical role in familiarizing the public's ear and eyes regarding the relationship between certain kinds of music and specific kinds of people. By 1920, "more specific guidelines for musicians, including explicit ideas about how to convey race, ethnicity and nature" appeared in the scene.[49]

Culturally, this is a significant moment for a couple of reasons. First, it is a move that essentially tries to "fix" meaning through control of the accompanying music. The meanings that are being fixed are those privileged by white, moneyed men. As such, what might be visually uproarious to the African American community might be a matter for concern by the ruling class. Because music often cues an audience's response to specific visual stimuli, by controlling it and those who play it, meanings get fixed over time. Second, the meanings being privileged were often dangerous stereotypes, reinforced through the musical gaze of Western composers.[50]

The imposition of this new technology primed the musicians for what was to come just a few years later, which was the emergence of sound-film technology. The slope was certainly slippery for the musicians of the 1920s, as they were ill-prepared to fight for a place in the era of mechanical reproduction. Moreover, as they were quickly becoming obsolete in the eyes of movie-house owners, their appeal to the public was built on the false and heady assumption that "flesh" was both irreplaceable on one hand, and desirable on the other. The public's need for live musicians it seems was belied by the dramatic increase in attendance after the musicians were replaced by technology.[51]

By 1930, according to Kelley, the AFM was struggling for legitimacy with only 14,000 musicians employed in theaters nationwide. Although some locals tried to fight against the tide of lay-offs and firings, in the end they were not able to save their jobs. The AFM was not done fighting, however. In 1928, at the national convention in Kentucky, amidst many alternative suggestions, Joseph Weber, the union president, chose against "union principals of solidarity," opting for a public relations campaign that would persuade the public that "music is dependent for its quality upon the mood of the artist."[52] Over the next ten years the AFM and specifically local 802 in New York City fought against the reality of mechanical reproduction not only through PR, but by conducting strikes and trying to form solidarity with organized labor. These actions were plagued by ideological problems such as the difficulty in getting people to see musicians as laborers as well as practical problems like getting musicians to strike and other union men and women to respect the picket lines that formed outside of movie theaters. In 1937, Local 802 ended their campaign against movie houses that used prerecorded sound. As Kelley reports, "An inauspicious ending to what had turned out to be a fairly inauspicious campaign."[53]

Kelley tells the tale of AFM as a parable, focusing on the pedagogical dimensions of historical narratives. He writes,

Embedded in this unremarkable campaign is the tale of what happens when working-class consumption of popular culture workers, in this case theater musicians. We might go one step further and say it's a story about the limits of solidarity—limits set by employees who are not seen or do not see themselves as "workers," and by working-class consumers whose own self-interest may actually clash with the demands of laboring artists. Finally, and most fundamentally, this is a story about technology and workers' control, and how utterly ill-equipped the union was to deal with the transformation of the *work* of art in the age of mechanical reproduction.[54]

Kelley concludes, not unlike Aronowitz, by identifying, at least cautiously, "the power line"[55] as one of the most important problems for the workers of the twentieth century. The power line is problematic for the sole reason that under capital's hegemony different kinds of workers are divided from one another and "taught" to evaluate their interests against the dubious mirror of "what" is produced as opposed to "under what conditions" they produce it. "When will we see," he asks, "musicians as workers and realize that wealth in the music industry is generated in the same way it was generated in the coal mines of Ludlow: through the exploitation of creative labor?"[56]

Resurrecting historical narratives from the ashes of historical memory is an essential element in obtaining class consciousness; however, it, in itself, is insufficient. As both Kelley and Aronowitz illustrate, a vibrant social imaginary is both an outcome and precondition of reading history critically. The apparent contradiction here cannot be remedied. However, if we perceive the process dialectically then the contradiction becomes only one moment in the move toward greater insight. The contradiction will always already be present in the development of historical memory, but it is only to be feared if it comes to represent the end, the period. Contradictions contain within them the dialectical potential for heightened consciousness when they are engaged pedagogically; that is, when they are broken into and broken through in the service of developing political clarity and utopian thought.

Utopian Thought

Pierre Bourdieu writes, "To conceive of a revolutionary project, that is to have a well thought out intention to transform the present in reference to a projected future, a modicum of hold on the present is needed."[57] This hold, according to Zygmunt Bauman, is made increasingly precarious given that "the ground itself . . . feels ever more shaky, unstable, infirm, undependable . . ."[58]:

> The state of precariousness . . . Bourdieu observes "renders all the future uncertain, and so forbids all rational anticipation—and in particular disallows that minimum of hope in the future which one needs to rebel, and especially to rebel collectively, against even the least tolerable present."[59]

Aronowitz argues that there is more than a crisis of hope plaguing the utopian project, but a crisis of the intellect which prevents a collective re-imagining of the future, a future substantively different than the present or the past.[60] I call this state of consciousness *imaginative inertia* and I believe it describes much thinking today by students, teachers, politicians, scholars, and intellectuals. Imaginative inertia is not, however, the inability to imagine any kind of future. Rather it describes a "dystopian" ontology, where "we can imagine the future but we *cannot* conceive the kind of collective political strategies necessary to change or ensure that future."[61] If we cannot think radically, then we assuredly will be unable to radically act. The word "radical," since the attacks on the World Trade Towers in New York City in 2001, has come to signify, for many throughout the world, action beyond reason and rationality. It connotes a fanaticism manifested in violence, death, and destruction. I am using it here, however, in its etymological sense "of going to the root of a problem."[62] As such, I would suggest that a radical imaginary be thought of as a tool of both reflection and projection. Only through creative and critical reflection does the possibility exist to examine where we have been, who we are, and why we have evolved as we have.

Within the educational context, it would mean, as Nicholas Burbules argues, "*to learn to question what one's 'education' has been* . . . [O]ne 'aim' of education should be to develop an ongoing capacity to reflect upon and question the sort of education one is receiving, or that one is providing to others—an aim that involves subjecting our educational aims to a relentless skepticism."[63] This relentless skepticism should not overwhelm what Giroux calls a "language of possibility," meaning that our critical deconstruction of the past and present must be rigorously matched by a commitment to conceptualizing and designing political and pedagogical strategies that can/might/should bring about the kinds of changes that are desired. Together a space is created "in which immanent critique and transfigurative desire mingle with one another."[64]

Although "improbable, but eminently possible"[65] in their realization, projecting ideas about what should be gives us a goal to fight toward, with the understanding that these goals should never blind us to the unanticipated effects of our struggle. Freedom, in this sense, is not a retreat from responsibility, but is rather its goal. Unfortunately, many on the Left and Right in education are often hesitant to think about freedom as anything more than the degree to which one can escape authority—governmental, educational, and/or pedagogical. Erich Fromm called this type of freedom "negative freedom" because it imprisons individuals within a social matrix of isolation, fear, and anxiety. As such, negative freedom undermines political agency because it attacks individual spontaneity, what he considered the pinnacle of positive freedom.[66] Negative freedom creates the conditions for a fear of authority by positioning authority as the opposite of freedom, while, at the same time, offering itself as the only hope for escape.

But instead of escaping into a world in which individual creativity, political agency, and social responsibility guide the creation of democratic formations, people escaping from negative freedom find themselves dependent on a new type of bondage. The repercussions of this cycle—negative freedom, escape into new structures of domination, dependency due to isolation and the denial of the spontaneous self, then a renewed escape from negative freedom into new bondage—causes a crisis in the educational and political sphere by delimiting political agency to those actions which denounce political power in the name of freedom, negative freedom.[67]

Negative freedom is the driving force behind dystopian thinking, creating imaginative inertia through the imposition of "social" fear. This fear causes paralysis—intellectual, political, and pedagogical—by rewarding docility and disciplining radical thought. The disciplinary mechanisms can be both subtle and frightening. From the Patriot Act to the seemingly innocuous policies associated with No Child Left Behind, freedom is what we are supposed to fear, while constraint will set us free.

CONCLUSION

Becoming conscious of class is a process that has a fuzzy beginning and no end. Schools are just one place in which we are socialized into thinking, speaking, and doing class in specific kinds of ways. In every society, there are always some students (and teachers) who resist and rebel against dominant socializing narratives of class. They are those people who recognize, for example, the hypocrisy in the idioms "freedom of speech" and "freedom of choice" because they know that their freedoms are more tied to their social, economic, and cultural power than to democratic principals. It is not enough to be free to speak, if those who are speaking do not have the power to create the conditions in which they can be heard. Likewise, it is not adequate to be free to choose if the choice about what choices can be made has already been made by someone else. This level of freedom is for suckers; it is for those who choose unquestionably between Coke and Pepsi, but never think about who decides what goes into the machine.

But we are not all suckers, nor do we have to be. Where does this resistance come from? When were the seeds of rebellion planted? My own narrative suggests (and you might come to a very different conclusion) that the seeds of consciousness may be planted generations before the soil is ever tilled. As such, archeological and genealogical excavation is called for in the development of class consciousness. They might be laid deep within the rich soil of consciousness during a shift in location, geographic disruption representing a time when we are made aware not only of "difference," but of our own "otherness" as well. In this context, we must become cartographers, mapping our travels so that we know where we have been, where we are, and where we would like to go. As good cartographers, we must leave our shores, or else risk mapping ourselves at the center of the world. Seeds may also be planted without notice, by a teacher for example who praises a student for creating a metaphor that runs against the grain of the dominant discourse. We must be prepared to respond to that which we cannot know, but which we know can arise when we least expect. We must be willing to act without guarantees, knowing that we might be wrong, but secure in the knowledge that we can change the course of our actions when we are.

But just because seeds are planted does not mean that they will grow. The fertility of our social minds and bodies depends heavily, if not almost entirely, upon the environment we create. Is it rich in resources? Does it offer positive and supportive attention? Does it value creativity, imagination, individual expression, cooperation? Does it support the development of democratic agency, which is the ability a person has to control their own life through democratic struggle and resistance? Does it name oppression/oppressors and create the means by which we, as a community, can struggle against it/them? Does it support a sense of social fairness, providing the most and best for those that have the least and worst? Does it allow for the formal desegregation of our schools, which are still segregated not only by race but by class as well? Once desegregated, have we created an environment in our schools that creates understanding between people with different experiences without legitimating the status quo? Does it nurture the kind of courage it takes to fight for what is right and against what it wrong? Are you prepared to help create this kind of environment?

NOTES

1. See Joe Kincheloe (2004). *Critical Pedagogy*. New York: Peter Lang, 27–30; Joe Kincheloe (2001). *Getting Beyond the Facts: Teaching Social Studies/Social Sciences in the Twenty-First Century*. New York: Peter Lang; Henry A. Giroux (1997). *Pedagogy and the Politics of Hope: Theory, Culture, and Schooling*. Boulder, Colo.: Westview Press.

2. Susuan Sontag, "The Report on The Journey." In the *New York Times* Book Review. February 20, 2005. 16–18.

3. Kincheloe, *Getting Beyond the Facts*, 29.

4. Carol Gilligan (1982). *In a Different Voice*. Cambridge, Mass.: Harvard University Press.

5. Aronowitz (2003). *How Class Works*. New Haven, Conn.: Yale University Press, 141.

6. Ibid.

7. Aronowitz, *How Class Works*, 67–69. For a critical essay review of Aronowitz's book see, Eric J. Weiner. (2004). In *Logos Journal* 3.4. www.logosjournal.com/

8. Aronowitz, *How Class Works*, 67.

9. Ibid., 68.

10. Ibid., 69.

11. Ibid.

12. Ibid.

13. Ibid.

14. Henry Giroux (1997). *Pedagogy and the Politics of Hope*. Boulder, Colo.: Westview Press.

15. James Paul Gee (1992). "What is Literacy." In *Becoming Political, Too*. (Ed.). P. Shannon. New Hampshire: Heinemann Press, 3.

16. Paulo Freire (1998). *Pedagogy of Freedom: Ethics, Democracy, and Civic Courage*. Critical perspectives series. Lanham, Md.: Rowman & Littlefield Publishers.

17. Jonathan Kozol (1991). *Savage Inequalities*. New York: HarperCollins, 105.

18. Henry A. Giroux (2004). *The Terror of Neoliberalism*. Aurora, Ontario: Garamond Press. "Under the reign of neoliberalism," writes Giroux, "capital and wealth have been largely distributed upward while civic virtue has been undermined by a slavish celebration of the free market as the model for organizing all facets of everyday life." xv.

19. Michel Foucault (1977). *Power/Knowledge*. (Ed.) Colin Gordon. (Trans.) Colin Gordon et al. New York: Pantheon Books, 57–58.

20. James Paul Gee (1992). "What is Literacy." In *Becoming Political, Too* (Ed.). P. Shannon. New Hampshire: Heinemann Press, 3.

21. Paul Willis (1977). *Learning to Labor*. London: Press.

22. Bourdieu, Pierre (1986). The Forms of Capital. In *Handbook of Theory and Research for the Sociology of Education*. (Ed.) John Richardson. New York: Greenwood Press, 241–58.

23. David Brooks, "The Sticky Ladder." *New York Times*. Op-Ed., January 25, 2005.

24. See www.pbs.org/independentlens/strangefruit/

25. Ibid., 31.

26. Henry Giroux, *Pedagogy and the Politics of Hope*. Giroux explains the culture of positivism, "The central assumption by which the culture of positivism rationalizes its position on theory and knowledge is the notion of objectivity, the separation of values from knowledge and methodological inquiry alike." 11.

27. Herbert Marcuse (1964/1991). *One Dimensional Man*. Boston: Beacon Press, 156.

28. Noam Chomsky (2003). "The Function of Schools." In *Education as Enforcement*. (Eds.) K. Saltman and D. Gabbard. New York: RoutledgeFalmer, 25–36.

29. Robin D. G. Kelley (1998). *Yo Mamas Dysfunktional*. Boston: Beacon Press, 139.

30. Zygmunt Bauman (1998). *Globalization*. New York: Columbia University Press, 60.

31. Aronowitz, *How Class Works*, 27. Some of his examples include labor's success in preventing employers from arbitrarily firing worker, bargaining about technological innovations without labor input, and wage and benefit concerns, including the social wage. 27–28.

32. *Spaltung* is a German word out of the Marxist lexicon on alienation that means "division or cleavage." *Verderben* is another dimension of alienation meaning "spoiled or corrupt." See the Dictionary of Critical Sociology, heading "Alienation," www.public.iastate.edu/~rmazur/dictionary/a.html (accessed October 5, 2004).

33. Aronowitz, *How Class Works*, 230.

34. Aronowitz, *How Class Works*.

35. Ibid., 224.

36. See Aronowitz, *How Class Works*; Stanley Aronowitz (1998). *From the Ashes of the Old*. New York: Basic Books; Robin D. G. Kelley (1996). *Race Rebels*. New York: Simon & Schuster; Robin D. G. Kelley, *Yo Mamas Dysfunktional*. Of course there are many others who engage in resurrecting erased memories. See, for example, Howard Zinn (2003). *A Peoples' History of the United States*. New York: Perennial Classics; Howard Zinn (2003). *The Twentieth Century*. New York: Harper Collins.

37. Aronowitz, *How Class Works*, 80.

38. Ibid., 76.

39. Ibid., 77.

40. Ibid., 79.

41. Ibid., 80–81.

42. Robin D. G. Kelley (2001). "Without a Song." In *Three Strikes*. Boston: Beacon Press, 121–55.

43. Ibid., 139.

44. Ibid.

45. Ibid., 125.

46. Ibid., 124.

47. Ibid.

48. Ibid., 127.

49. Ibid., 128.

50. Ibid., 128–29.

51. Ibid., 130.

52. Ibid., 134.

53. Ibid., 151.

54. Ibid., 124.

55. Ibid., 155.

56. Ibid.

57. Quoted in Zygmunt Bauman (1999). *In Search of Politics*. Stanford: Stanford University Press, 172.

58. Ibid., 173.

59. Bauman quoting Bourdieu, 173.

60. Aronowitz, *How Class Works*, 224.

61. Constance Penley quoted in Henry Giroux. (1997). *Pedagogy and the Politics of Hope*, 223.

62. Martin Jay (1973). *The Dialectical Imagination*. Boston: Little, Brown & Company, 257.

63. Nicholas Burbules. (2004). "Ways of Thinking about Educational Quality." *Educational Researcher* 33 (6): 4–10. www.aera.net/pubs/er/pdf/vol33_06/03ERv33n6-Burbules.pdf (accessed October 6, 2004).

64. Nancy Fraser quotes in Henry Giroux, *Pedagogy and the Politics of Hope*, 224.

65. Aronowitz, *How Class Works*, 230–31.

66. Erich Fromm (1995). *The Fear of Freedom*. New York: Routledge, 220.

67. Eric J. Weiner (2003). "Paths from Erich Fromm: Thinking Authority Pedagogically." *Journal of Educational Thought (JET)* 37 (1): 59–76.

CHAPTER 10

July 12, 1977: The Journey to Class Consciousness Begins— A Rural White South Carolina Story

Randall Hewitt

I began my long journey to class consciousness a little after 2 o'clock, July 12, 1977. My Aunt Margret had just called my grandma, my momma's momma, to tell her that my daddy had been hit by a county trash truck. At the time, I could not have known the identity of the caller or the purpose of the call. I was simply taking advantage of the telephone ring to stand inside my grandma's refrigerator door and drink Pepsi-Cola straight from the bottle. I remember sizing up how long I had to stand there and drink by the nature of the conversation taking place in the front room. The caller must have asked for her by name because immediately after her initial "hello," my grandma declared, "This is Miriam," and I knew right away that I had plenty of time.

July in South Carolina can be hotter than a motherfucker and this particular Tuesday had been all that—not to mention certain and secure in its routines. Momma and Daddy had left for work well before daylight. My grandpa was out exterminating bugs. My little sister and brother were over at Uncle Ronnie's until the first shift let out at 5 P.M., and as usual I was left to roam the quarter mile between my house and my grandma's, which was at the top of the street. My daddy had left a list of chores that my little ass had better have done by the time he got back. He didn't leave a written list and didn't have to. When he told me to do something, I had better goddamn be listening. His command usually was underscored by a flick to the back of my head or, in more serious cases, lightning fast punches to any body part closest to him. I had long learned, by watching him interact with cops, teachers, door-to-door preachers, bill collectors, and anyone else for that matter, that the magnitude of his response to the world was always greater than the severity of the circumstances and could never be completely predicted. For example, I once heard him threaten to burn his own momma's house down because she refused to lend him $57 to have his water turned back on. And I knew from direct experience that he could easily snatch me up by my hair and slam me head first into the wall for eating all of the Cool-Whip or for clogging the toilet just as he could for not checking in on the severely neglected pit bull that he kept tied up in our shit-filled backyard. I loved my daddy but he was a ticking time bomb, a first rate son-of-a-bitch whose blind rage often rendered him temporarily insane and whose physical strength made him outright dangerous. Thus, my ability to listen keenly for mood and nuance developed in direct proportion to my fear of his volatile nature. So, when he told me the night before to wash the dishes, pick up the broken egg shells and tattered Kotex the dogs had strewn across the yard, cut the grass, don't eat the lemon pie, and be up at my grandma's by lunch, I had all this done by 8 A.M. and was killing serious time when the South Carolina Highway Patrol (SCHP) showed up in my driveway.

One—if not *the*—rule in our house was never do anything that evoked the law. I quickly turned on the mental scan to identify what I could have possibly done to bring it out. Nothing, except occasionally throw rocks at trains. I was a good boy, did what people told me to do, was taught to say "yes sir" and "no sir," played football in the fall and baseball in the spring. I didn't steal, didn't forge my grandma's checks or smoke her cigarettes, and didn't stay out past 9 o'clock at night. I came from hardworking people who prided themselves on the fact that they could outwork anybody anytime and took every opportunity to prove it—silently, of course. My people weren't loudmouths. They humbly struggled to make it to work every day, keep their clothes clean, put food on the table, and if they didn't have the latest model Pontiac in the driveway, they would, by god, this time next year, the Lord willing.

The officer didn't get out of his car but spoke to me through his passenger-side window. He asked me what my name was, where I lived, what my momma's and daddy's names were, and where they were at this hour. The nature of his questions made me suspect that he knew my parents left me alone every morning, and I certainly didn't want to get them in trouble. But he didn't seem urgent for my answers. I told him our names, that we lived here, that my daddy drove a gas truck for DeLaney Tank Lines, and my momma worked in spinning at Fiber Industries. I said that they would be home around 5:30 P.M., and for good measure, told him that I was staying at my grandma's, who lived up the street and who had sent me down to my house on an errand. He took down her address and told me to have a good day. Being a truck driver's son, I knew something about police jurisdiction. Furthermore, anytime something happened in our neighborhood, like when one of the teenagers stole a car or when momma and daddy got into fights with each other, it was the county sheriff that showed up, not the SCHP I waited until the patrol car eased around the corner and then headed for the safety of my grandma's house.

My grandma didn't go to bed on Tuesdays until around 6:30 in the evening. She worked six days a week on the third shift at Poe Mill and Mondays were her only days off. When I got to her house at 9:30, she was sitting at the kitchen table, drinking coffee and smoking cigarettes, and listening to George Jones sing "He Stopped Loving Her Today" on WESC. Any other day she would be in bed already. Any other day she would get home around 7:30 in the morning, fix my grandpa grits and toast for breakfast, and then go to bed until he came home for lunch. She would get back up just long enough to make him a tuna or egg sandwich, put some form of bean on the stove for supper, smoke another cigarette, and then go back to bed until he came home around 4:30. Sometimes, though, she would have to get back up to smoke another cigarette. She would sit in my grandpa's reclining chair, still drugged by deep sleep, sheer addiction taking care of the mechanics. Watching her in this state could be quite comical. She would sit there with her head and shoulders hanging just above her crossed knees, arms folded across her lap with the cigarette between her well-disciplined index and middle fingers. Then, as if prompted by a nicotine sensor inside her, she would lift at the torso just enough to slide the cigarette up and underneath to her mouth, draw hard and deep on the end, and then slump back over her knees only when the cells in her lower extremities gave her the go-ahead. Then she would hang there idling until the sensor went off again. And though there was great humor in this, there also was something deeply telling about her in it.

The fingers that held her cigarettes were crooked in the joints at the ends. In fact, the index and middle fingers on both of her hands were crooked, and light yellow calluses lined the edges of her index fingers, both thumbs, and the insteps of her feet. Since she didn't sleep with her teeth in, her face hung drawn and hollow, like it had something sobering to tell. She looked nothing at all like the mothers of friends from my football team or any of the female teachers I had known. Their faces were bright, tan, and clear, not lined with deep ruts or stained by years of cigarette smoke. Their hair was shiny, impeccably combed, and typically pulled back with a bow or bouncing around their shoulders. Their clothes were colorful, as if brand new, and always neatly tucked, never wrinkled and never lint-ridden. Their fingers certainly were not crooked and their finger nails were often were painted to match the color of their clothes. They smelled of perfume and sometimes of cinnamon, like they had been working on some craft project. Their teeth were brilliantly white and arrow-straight, and they would thrust these teeth forward in a smile in lieu of a handshake. And their eyes were fresh and attentive, as if they had just awakened from a long restful nap and were darting about to see if they had been missed. I had no way of articulating these differences to myself at the time but I felt them. These women, who were roughly my grandma's age, were hot shit and my grandma, slumped over as she was, unconsciously poised to take the fourth and final drag off the Pall Mall before going back to bed, was a shrunken hag. Sometimes during our midday encounters, I would grow ashamed of her and couldn't look at her. How could a person let all of the teeth in her head fall out? "Nobody gets this way for nothing," I would answer myself in disgust. This was her answer when I asked her why this one family at the laundromat always stank—as my daddy described it—like rotten ass. Sometimes, though, especially when she seemed the most groggy with sleep yet the most possessed to consume nicotine, her creaturelike presence stood out against the routine in my life and its story would take form. "Life will do these things to you, son." This is what my daddy would sometimes tell me when he was trying to explain why he beat up momma. He would hold me close to him, he would cry and I would cry. I didn't know for sure exactly what "things" he was talking about but I somehow understood and could accept that he was right. Somehow things just happened to him and all he could do was loose his shit. What kind of things happened to my grandma?

All she did was work and I had seen the place she worked. We kids went there several times a year, at Christmas Open House and at Family Appreciation Day. "Giving back to families my ass," my daddy would say, or, more to the point, "Fuck them son-of-a-bitches." My grandma didn't feel this way though. "Be thankful you get anything at all," she would say. She was proud to take us to where she worked. She had worked in cotton mills all of her life and had worked every job in the gray mill. She would parade my brother and me through carding, warping, drawing, and then to weaving. She was the third-shift supervisor in weaving but knew everybody on the first and second shifts because she used to be the supervisor on these shifts too.

From the outside, Poe Mill was like my school. It was a massive brick building, several stories high with long, hollow hallways and with big windows that were completely bricked up. Rows of large, loud machines lined the hallways from end to end and ran all the time. These machines were so loud that it was useless to talk to anybody, even oneself. After a while, the sound of the machines would drown out having any thoughts at all. My grandma would show us to everybody, and everybody would smile and then take out his earplugs just long enough to see what Santa Claus was going to bring us and then put the earplugs back in with a concerned look toward the machine. There were about four long rows of these machines on each floor and about three people to a row, all men. Some of these men would wink and say that my grandma was the only woman that they could work for. I guessed that I was supposed to be proud of this; my grandma sure was. I wondered why my grandpa didn't feel this way, though. He would take every opportunity to announce, "I ain't working for no woman." Sometimes my grandma would roll her eyes at him. Other times, depending on how fed up she was with him, she would say, "Well, if women can do the job as good as men, then I don't see nothing wrong with it." This was the same conversation they would have about black and Latino people, except my grandpa would call them "niggers" and "spics" and my grandma would remind him that he didn't need to be ugly about it.

The men watching the machines were busy hooking and stabbing at them and shuffling rapidly along their sections. My grandma said that she did the same thing as everybody else but that it was her job to make sure everybody else was doing what he or she was supposed to be doing. She said that her shift lasted for as long as I was in school each day and without recess. I thought hard about this.

I went to school because they made me, not because I liked it and wanted to go. "They" referred not only to my momma and daddy, my grandma and grandpa, my Uncle Billy and Aunt Betty, but also to some other authority beyond them, some other power that told them what to do. Besides, there was no Aunt Dot or Papa at school. Aunt Dot was my grandpa's sister and she, along with their daddy, lived with my grandma and grandpa every since they were married. Papa was a meat butcher at Dick Smith's Grocery, an old mill-hill company store. He came home cleaner than any slaughter-house butchers in our neighborhood. He also came home with big 64-ounce Coca Colas and bubblegum every night and would watch *Monday Night Baseball* with me. He would dip snuff and I would chew the bubblegum like it was Beachnut or Redman. My daddy chewed loose leaf but everybody else in my family, including Aunt Dot, chewed off a plug.

It might have been true that Aunt Dot hadn't worked a day in her life, hadn't worked enough to draw one cent from Social Security, but she was pure love. She would rub my head at night and tell me stories about distant relatives from Scotland and England, how they came here with nothing and hid in barrels to get here, how they picked cotton, and drove horse and buggies for the company store. She would play I Spy with me and sing me haunting songs of "poor, wayfaring strangers" until I fell asleep. Aunt Dot was tender to me, especially when I was sick, and thought that there was no one else in the world like me. I certainly didn't feel like this at school. I was just another member of the Blue Jays there, which wasn't the Eagles and may have well as been called the Buzzards. No one at school loved me like the people in my grandma's house, and I learned early that the way the world was talked about in school was not the way we talked about the world at home. In fact, I increasingly wondered if we were talking about the same world at all. "Ain't," "fixin' to," "bathum," "thoat," and all cuss words were not legitimate words at school and their use there put one in danger of a swat with the yardstick. A stove had a "burner," not an "eye," a point that I could accept but it seemed that none of my teachers could grant

me the fact that some people used "eye" or "head" in place of "burner."
The people and characters we read about in the Blue Jays reading group
had to learn responsibility in saving their allowances and in making
good choices. My daddy said that my allowance was scattered along
the road in the form of a bottle return and that I shouldn't spend it all
in one place. When I told him that other kids got allowances for doing
chores, he said that other kids don't get ass whippings for not doing
what they are told either. He said that he didn't have the money to give
me every time something needed to be done and that I had better watch
my smartass mouth. "Not everything up at that school house is worth
listening to," he would say. He didn't have to tell me that.

Mohawk, Saratoga, and Concord meant nothing to me. I knew Greer,
Appalach, Reidville, and Sugar Tit. These were the places I fished,
pulled potatoes from the ground, watched dirt-track races, ate homemade ice cream, and swam in creeks. These were places where real
wars took place: where the Dobsons fought the Thaxtons for illegal al-
cohol and pot routes; where whites and blacks sometimes shot at each
other and other times killed a hog or sang in the choir together; where
religious nuts held political office or fought for the souls of heathens
like my daddy's, who would turn his dog loose on them if they pissed
him off enough. I hated the bottomless math packets, partly because my
teacher couldn't get around to me often enough to help me, partly because my momma told me that I was dumb at math, which made me
ashamed to ask for help, and partly because I couldn't get them finished
due to my frozen fingers. Since my daddy and momma left for work
early, I was at my bus stop by 6:30 every morning and the bus didn't
pick me up until 7:55. Math worksheets were the first things we did
when school started at 8:25. Most mornings from late November to
mid-March, I had no control over the pencil until about 9 o'clock because the tub socks over my hands couldn't hold the cold off at the bus
stop. I would try to hold the pencil for a little while and then say "fuck
it." This attitude, of course, would always get me in trouble with Ms.
Doolittle or Ms. Harrison. They would tell me that I had better finish
my work or they would have to write a note to my daddy. There was no
use in complaining about it to my daddy. "Everybody's got a fucking
problem," he would say, "and you had better learn to deal with it
quick." Math in particular didn't concern him. What he wanted to know

was whether or not I was doing what my teachers told me to do and was behaving myself. In fact, my daddy came to my school only five times, one time at the beginning of each elementary school year. He made it clear to both me and my teachers that he wasn't concerned about what reading group I was in, what math level I was on, or how big the words were I could spell. He was concerned with my behavior and my behavior only, he would say, widening his eyes in seriousness and nodding his head once in warning.

Momma would always get pissed off when my daddy went up to the school. She said that his behavior made us all look bad and that it would be her who would have to deal with my problems at school whenever they came up, not him. My daddy didn't know jack shit about math, momma would say, and remind him that he wouldn't have graduated high school if it wasn't for her. He never disputed this charge as a wrong against him, never verbally or physically snapped back at her for saying this like he did when she threatened to go on welfare or ask grandma for the rent money. Instead, deep hurt and shame washed out his usual snarl and he wouldn't talk to her for days. Momma would just let him pout but he wasn't simply pouting; there was a fierce determination in his silent resentment, in his every movement, from the way he ate his pimiento cheese sandwich, which he would make his goddamn self, to the way he backed out in the car to go somewhere. Then at some point when we were alone, he would tell me that he wanted me to do good in school so that I could get a scholarship for college. He said he didn't want me to have to wear dirty tub socks on my little hands and scratchy-ass coats two sizes too small for me. He didn't want my kids to suffer through earaches and stomachaches with half-ass, homemade remedies and not be able to see a real doctor. He wanted me to get a good education so that I wouldn't have to worry about buying a burger if I wanted one or fixing the car when it needed it or hiding from bill collectors every time I turned around. He wanted me to get a good education so that I could take care of my kids and do so proudly without putting up with any shit from some candy-ass boss who didn't know the first thing about the very job he was commanding me to do. My daddy wanted me to do good in school because he loved me, but what he took to be good and what Ms. Doolittle, Ms. Harrison, and the rest of the Eagles knew to be good were two different things.

I also knew that my daddy wanted me to do good in school out of some deep regret, out of feelings of personal failure. He refused to be dominated by anybody and sending me to college meant that he would have proven every one of them motherfuckers wrong. I took "every-body" to mean Ms. Doolittle and Ms. Harrison, who seemed to look at me and everyone else from the mill hill with pity. It often included Mama, who sometimes saw my daddy as a lazy bastard who couldn't keep a job for more than three weeks. It certainly included my grandpa, who looked down on my daddy because he came from cotton pickers and because he was a "nigger lover." And it may have included my grandma, who didn't directly say that my daddy was a bad man but her feelings about him came out when she claimed that people who sup-ported the unions—and my daddy did—were people who couldn't do for themselves. She was proud that she could do for herself. She let it be known, too, that by the time she was fourteen years old, she was raising ten of her own mother's children plus going to school and work-ing herself. If a woman, with all she's got to do, can make it without somebody else speaking for her, surely a man can do it, unless there's something wrong with him.

Of course, when I walked into my grandma's house at 9:30 on Tues-day morning, July 12, 1977, neither one of us could have known that there was something already wrong with him, at least in the sense that Aunt Margret would call about a little more than four hours later. Nei-ther one of us would have substituted his name for one of the two unidentified victims making WESC's news update every thirty min-utes. Neither one of us would have pictured his face entangled in the fiery wreckage spilling over the corner of S. Church Street and Camp Croft Road and blocking traffic. It would not have crossed our minds to place him amidst, not to mention in the care of, the SCHP, emer-gency workers, and Hess officials gathered at the scene. By this time of day, he was probably already in Mt. Mitchell or Fletcher or Mars Hill. By this time of day, he was resting his big left arm in the driver's side window. He'd be singing Statler Brother songs over a mouthful of tobacco juice and pushing the Mack as hard as it could go. Besides, my grandma and I both knew he worked for Delaney Tank Lines, not Hess. So, when the newsman mentioned Hess for the third time that morn-ing, any slight doubt either one of us may have had about him being involved was directly dismissed, and we instantly became gawkers of an experience my people knew all too well.

Work-related accidents often were woven into the stories I had heard men and women on the mill hill tell each other time and time again. We all knew these stories in some form or fashion, and they were told almost like gossip, almost like warnings. For example, Ms. Cole's son, Max, used a pair of uninsulated pliers that he got from the first-floor gang box at Victor Mill and was electrocuted while trying to fix a warping machine. Butch Lister and Larry Brannon also were severely shocked while trying to do similar things, all within a nine-month period. Jerry Slaton out in warehouse was run over by a forklift and killed, and he had four little kids and a wife to feed. Of course, everyone knew about the endless severings and disfigurings in consequence of people putting their hands, arms, and heads into the machines to relieve line snags. According to my daddy, the head mill honchos always would respond by saying that no company official authorized the victim to take such and such an action and thus was in violation of company policy when injured. Daddy said that his response would be, "Alright then, every time the smallest thing goes wrong, tell them motherfuckers in the front office we ain't doing a lick of work until the problem is fixed." My grandma said that she wouldn't put up with that; she wanted people who would work, people who could do for themselves and not complain all the time. This would really piss my daddy off. He accused my grandma of always putting the company's problems back on the worker. "What about all that cotton dust and lint those poor bastards suck down every time they take a breath for eight hours? That ain't their fault. What about the gasoline drivers the company doesn't want to give life insurance to? That ain't their fault either."

Regardless of whose fault it was, all of us knew and accepted the fact that every job has its own particular hazards. As a tank driver my daddy risked jackknifes, dangerous fumes, and explosions. I had heard the story of Lemar Drummond hitting black ice one night coming back down the mountain from Boone, North Carolina, the rig running over the guardrail and falling 130 feet before blowing up. I had heard my daddy tell Momma about how some guy named Lumpkin flipped his truck at Reidville Circle, pinning his arm underneath, and how he was yelling at bystanders to cut off his arm before the tank could blow up and kill him. And while I had the idea that these sorts of things could happen to anybody, my daddy included, my daddy was such an onerous son of a bitch that I unconsciously wagered he could kick life's ass itself and then be home by sundown to see if I had done the things he had told me to do before he went to work. My daddy was my world and everything else was merely a satellite concern.

In fact, right after my grandpa left at 12:30 on this particular Tuesday until my Aunt Margret's call, I practiced like hell for this world. My brown Free Spirit bicycle became a Mack single cab pulling dangerous cargo along the familiar corridor stretching from my grandma's house down to mine. I drove in the spirit of the great freight haulers I knew of and with keen awareness of their legendary feats in the face of everyday troubles. I drove heroically in light of the WESC reports about the Hess wreck. Another fallen brother of the road, a goddamn shame, simply a goddamn shame. But life had to go on. I had too many stops to make, too many mouths to feed for it not to. At some point during my runs, I pulled out of my grandma's terminal heading south and saw the red and blue rack of a squad car backing out of my driveway a quarter mile down the street. It wasn't the SCHP this time. Their cars had single blue bubbles on top. Two forms of law at my house in one day definitely meant something was going on, something far more serious than any kid-mischief I could have been involved in. I quickly turned my bike back into my grandma's driveway and, unbeknownst to me at the time, would never pretend or desire to drive a truck again.

My Aunt Margret's call came as I was running up the kitchen steps to tell my grandma about seeing the law at my house. I could see her turning the corner into the front room as I topped the steps and knew that it was useless to come in hollering my news. Nobody just interrupted my grandma while she was on the telephone. She wasn't going to have that and the flyswatter she had tethered to her this time of year served as the physical deterrent. Plus, I needed to take care of some physical needs of my own and would have drank the Pepsi bottle dry had I not heard concern and disbelief in the "what?" she gave the caller. Next I heard "intensive care" and "Spartanburg Memorial," then, "Has anybody told Sandra?" When my momma's name was mentioned, I knew right away what the call was about. It suddenly made sense why the law had been at my house and I knew my daddy wouldn't be back that night and possibly for many nights to come. I quickly put the Pepsi bottle back into the refrigerator without any concern for how much was missing and hurried into the front room to see for myself if what I had heard this time was right.

My grandma's face didn't carry the alarm that her voice initially did when she first answered the telephone. She looked alert and calm as she parroted the names of people and their telephone numbers back to my Aunt Margret. If my daddy was the most emotionally volatile person I knew, my grandma was the most stable. She had kept the same job at Poe Mill for twenty years. She paid her bills—on time—and never had her telephone, water, or electricity cut off. At least as long as I had been alive, she bought groceries every Friday morning and washed clothes every Sunday afternoon. She often would tell my momma, always in the presence and, seemingly, for the benefit of my daddy, that it didn't take her too long to learn that her actions have consequences. She said that she learned real early that if she wanted to live a good life, she couldn't quit every job just because somebody said something cross to her. My grandma simply didn't let things upset her, not even my daddy.

For example, when I was seven, I took out a .357 caliber handgun that my daddy kept in his chest of drawers and accidentally shot it inside the house. Normally, my daddy would have whipped me for not doing what he told me to do, which was "don't touch the gun," but this particular time, he gave me the option of a whipping or playing midget league football. Playing football didn't seem to have anything to do with not following my daddy's directions. This option didn't make sense to me at all and the ensuing events associated with it were just as strange and illogical as the option itself.

By midday a full set of football pads sat in my closet, along with a new Riddell helmet that my daddy got for himself. Weeks passed without one mention of me shooting the gun or of football. Then, one Saturday around noon, I was up at my grandma's house watching *Fat Albert* when my daddy came in with all of the equipment and said, "Put your stuff on, boy, let's go." He had laid out a wooden board in my grandma's backyard and was standing at the end opposite me with his helmet on and a wad of tobacco in his mouth. He then threw a football to me and told me to run at him as hard as I could, which I did. His forearm knocked my facemask into my throat and the entire impact lifted me slightly upward and then snapped me to the ground flat on my back. At first all I saw was green and would have puked from the horror if all the wind had not been knocked out of me. Then my daddy was standing over me screaming, "Get up, get your fucking ass up," tobacco juice dripping into my facemask and then onto my face. My momma and grandma came outside immediately. My grandma picked me up and held me close to her chest and took me into the kitchen. From the kitchen window, I could see my momma and daddy fighting in the yard, momma crying and calling my daddy a stupid son of a bitch and my daddy crying himself and shoving Momma off of him. At some point right before he snatched open the kitchen door, I heard him say, "He's got to learn that when the wolf comes to the door, he'd better eat the son of a bitch." And then the commotion came inside the kitchen.

My daddy ordered my grandma to put me down so that I could go home. My grandma said that I wasn't going home with them today. My daddy yelled, "I said he's coming home, goddamn it." Without a flinch at all and without breathing heavy or raising her voice, my grandma told my daddy, "I told you he ain't, so you can go on and pitch your fit somewhere else." She wasn't going to have that kind of carrying on in her house. I stayed with my grandma for the next three and a half days after this, wrought with a dread and shame that, little did I know, I would only start to be released from four years later when my Aunt Margret called to report the accident to us.

My grandma could tell by looking at me that she didn't have to tell me about my daddy, but she did anyway, in the same straightforward but not unkind way she probably told fellow weavers around Christmas time that they were being laid off. Aunt Margret had said that the official news from the hospital was a "wait and see," "too early to tell" situation. She also said that the county trash truck ran the red light and hit my daddy between the cab and the tank as he started across the intersection. I didn't know what to do next or how to act or what to think. Contempt for the trash man immediately washed over me. Anybody who would stoop to picking up other people's rotten shit all day was a drunk, a criminal, or a moron and couldn't do anything else with himself. My daddy didn't deserve this low-life shit. I tried to keep myself from feeling this way by thinking of the families that had to deal with a similar situation but nothing came to me. There wasn't one story

CHAPTER 10

about them that I knew of. I then tried to picture what the trash truck driver's people were doing, if they knew, what they were feeling. Again, contempt trumped empathy. What kind of people would get themselves all mixed up with a trash man anyway?

My daddy would have busted my ass if he thought I felt this way. He once gave me a whipping for talking back to Coach O'Neill because my daddy thought I thought I didn't have to listen to black people. "People who ain't got a pot to piss in nor a bed to slide it under don't have the luxury of holding anything against anybody." My daddy said that he didn't give a rat's ass what color a person was, what that person did for a living, or if he had horns coming out of the top of his head; I had better listen to this person and be respectful. He said I wasn't going to be a bigot like my grandpa was. But I hadn't talked back to Coach O'Neill because he was black. I talked back to Coach O'Neill because his "keep jersey tucked even after the game" policy was unfair. My daddy had me all wrong, but I didn't dare say anything. It simply didn't matter to him what my motives and intentions were most of the time, and I had already learned that telling him what I thought or how I felt most often made matters worse. He once whipped me because Ms. Cole accused me of breaking the windows out of her back shed. Sobbing hysterically, I tried to tell him that I didn't do it but this only infuriated him more because he thought I was lying to him. When some older boys admitted to blaming me, he said that he should knock my head off just for associating with them. On another occasion, I came home crying because Johnny Waldrop, the neighborhood bully who was every bit of fourteen years old in the fifth grade, kicked me in the stomach at the bus stop. My daddy said that the world is a harsh place and didn't want to hear that candy-ass shit. He told me that the next time we catch the little bastard out, I was going to bash his head in. Some time goes by, maybe a month, my daddy saw Johnny Waldrop coming down our street on a bicycle. My daddy came around back while I was playing with toy dump trucks and made me go out with a baseball bat to hit Johnny. I couldn't do it, though. Too much time had passed. I guess I didn't harbor the deep-seated hatred toward Johnny necessary to "coldcock him" like my daddy wanted me to. Terrified, I tried to explain this to my daddy, but my feelings were no match for the explosive disgust he directed at me. I was simply a yellow-bellied pansy-ass who would let the world just shit all over him, and my daddy wanted nothing to do with that. So, it was this kind of terror, shame, and inadequacy that I started to feel free from once my grandma reminded me, by way of calling Uncle Billy, that it didn't look good for my daddy. I sat down to wait on her to make a few telephone calls and was immediately swept off by a flood of maybes and what ifs.

Maybe, if my daddy was paralyzed, he couldn't work and then Momma finally would see what it means to have the burden of keeping us all alive. Maybe, then, she would love him more or at least feel sorry for him. She couldn't belittle him for quitting his job and for making her go on food stamps. Maybe, then, he wouldn't feel so bad and wouldn't beat his head against the wall and threaten to kill himself. Maybe if he was just maimed or crippled, he could work at Uncle Ronnie's Trader's Den or run the cash register at Uncle Charlie's Package Store. Since the wreck was the other man's fault, maybe my daddy would get insurance money that would help him pay off those goddamn overpriced living room and bedroom suites that Momma got suckered into all because she wanted to be blue-blooded. I then wouldn't have to answer the telephone every time it rang and lie and tell the Benson Furniture man "the Hewitts don't live here anymore."

If my daddy got some money, maybe he could buy a new Pontiac and then wouldn't have to shoot the old one because it wouldn't start and then walk off to leave me standing in the cold, crying and wondering if he was ever going to come back again. And then I started to think, what if my daddy didn't come back this time?

What if I didn't have a daddy at all? Momma could finally marry somebody like Kevin Brown's dad, Ted. Ted was a purchasing agent and worked in an office at Homelite. He got basketball tickets to all the great rivalry games between Clemson and South Carolina, Georgia and Georgia Tech because, as Kevin said "his dad was a very important person who people just loved to wine and dine." It was true that Ted looked important, and so did Kevin. Ted wore a different suit every day and never was dirty, even on the weekends. Kevin never wore anything else but Levi pants that Ted ironed for him everyday and Izod shirts with collars. Momma said that you wouldn't catch people like the Browns putting their kids in high-water Toughskins and stain-ridden t-shirts. She always said this in a way that made it seem that my daddy didn't take good care of us. She also said that Ted spoke calmly and convincingly like a person with class should. My daddy said that Ted was self-righteous and it was more like he was a cross between a politician and an insurance salesman or a preacher. It was also true that Ted never got upset at anything, which is what I thought Momma secretly liked about him. Kevin once told Momma and me that there wasn't a "be seen and not heard" rule at his family's dinner table. There certainly was at my daddy's dinner table: it was "shut up and eat." Kevin also said that his dad didn't get mad at him when he was afraid to stand in the batter's box after being hit in the head with a wild pitch either. Momma and I both knew that Ted didn't even care if Kevin called his momma "mommy," which was something my daddy had long since made me stop doing.

Sometimes, especially when we had to stay at my grandma's because my daddy and momma were fighting, Momma would compare my daddy to people like Ted and act as if my daddy didn't care about our feelings at all. But I didn't feel that there was anything special about the way Ted treated Kevin's feelings. For example, Ted wouldn't let Kevin ride the school bus even though Kevin constantly begged him. Ted said that he couldn't be too sure what went on inside a public-school bus and couldn't take the chance of Kevin getting mixed up with people who might be up to no good. He also wouldn't let Kevin drink sodas or eat candy and said that he cared too much about his son's health to ever have that poison in their home. This kind of care didn't make sense to me at all. Kevin had to eat peanut butter snacks every day after school made from real peanuts and with no sugar added. He also couldn't watch television unless his parents turned it on for him and then he always had to watch PBS. I hated having to go home with Kevin sometimes after school. His parents wouldn't let us do anything and what we did do seemed strange. Kevin and Ted liked to talk about school projects like it was fun. They were always working on some science project involving levers or building replicas of some museum that they had gone to see on the PTA-sponsored trips. Sometimes during these projects, Ted would tell Kevin that he could do anything he wanted as long as he put his mind to it. This was the same thing my daddy told me, except I knew that my daddy and Ted meant two different things when they said it. What Ted meant was that Kevin could become anything he wanted, like a doctor, a lawyer, or an engineer. My daddy meant that I could overcome anything, like being afraid of a baseball and Johnny Waldrop, doing poorly in school, or simply being poor.

Sometimes Kevin and Ted would talk about places and people they had seen together while watching *Meet the Press*. I liked this talk because it always turned into a personal listing of the top five favorite places in the world to visit. Their list included Hilton Head for golf and tennis, D.C., New York, and Paris for people, pleasure, and politics. I picked Myrtle Beach and the Blue Ridge Mountain Parkway, mostly because these places were all I knew, and Atlanta, of course, because my daddy said it had soul and Tommy Nobis. Ted and Kevin always looked at each other like they would talk later every time I gave my reasons for my favorite places. When they did this, I knew exactly what my daddy meant when he called them "fucking snobs."

But if my daddy didn't come back this time, Momma could marry someone like Ted, and we could move into a house where there was a real neighborhood name like Crestview Heights or Country Club Estates. People in these neighborhoods may have been "suits" or snobs, but they weren't tobacco-chewing lint heads forever caught in the endless struggle between making next month's rent and drinking up this week's paycheck at the local AmVets. The lives of the people who lived on the mill hill went nowhere and we all knew it, even if we couldn't admit it.

About forty-five minutes after Aunt Margret called the first time and right as I started to feel guilty for thinking my poor, hurt daddy was a mill-hill loser, she called back to tell us that my daddy was dead. Guilt and the excitement from the news made everything a confused, surreal mess. "Died on impact" was what the hospital told Aunt Margret this time. None of us could accept this. My grandma held me tight against her and said, almost in a proud way, "Your daddy sure was a fighter, son." She didn't have to tell me this. I flashed on my daddy pinned inside the burning cab, fighting, punching, clawing to get out. I bet he fought the fire itself, clutching at the throat of each flame, gritting his teeth and yelling his old, "Get off me, motherfucker." My grandma said that she was certain he fought like the dickens to live, to be with Momma and us kids one more time. I also knew this was right too, even though life with Momma and us kids sometimes pissed him off.

And it wasn't until a few hours later when I was in the Bi-Lo Grocery store that I began to feel just what kind of fighter I had lost. My Aunt Betty had taken me there so that I couldn't see the 6 o'clock news. I was looking at the prewrapped hamburger and steaks, puzzling over changes in form from life to death, and wondering what Coach O'Neill was going to say when he found out that the coach of his defense wasn't coming back next fall. And then standing right there in the meat section, I heard a very haunting song.

> Just a song before I go, to whom it may concern.
> Traveling twice the speed of sound, it's easy to get burned.
> When the shows were over, we had to get back home,
> And when we opened up the door I had to be alone.
> She helped me with my suitcase, she stands before my eyes,
> Driving me to the airport and to the friendly skies.
> Going through security I held her for so long.
> She finally looked at me in love, and she was gone.
> Just a song before I go, a lesson to be learned.
> Traveling twice the speed of sound, it's easy to get burned.

I couldn't make out exactly what this song was about, what it meant. But it was as if it was played for me. It was as if every last detail of my life came rushing into this moment. My daddy was a traveler, he loved me, he was burned, now he was gone, and I was alone. It suddenly dawned on me that my life had changed and would never be the same again. The seamless reality I had been living for eleven years was suddenly ripped to pieces, "here today, gone tomorrow." This concrete human being who I called my daddy, this thing that tenaciously and resiliently fought the life he both loved and hated, this form struggling to be proud of where he came from, what he was, but who also struggled against it, fought to overcome it, had simply just vanished, just evaporated like gasoline spilt on the pavement. And all I could do was ask questions.

I became flooded with questions about who he was and why he was the way he was. It was as if I had never really seen him, never reflected on who he was, until he was gone. Because my reality had been so profoundly altered, I began to reflect on what and who I was and where I belonged in the world. I became obsessed with questioning everything because if this could happen to me, then maybe nothing was as it seemed. I became a seeker and a searcher, longing for answers to fill the vast and lonely void that had so suddenly split my world open, leaving every emotion and every meaning raw and exposed. My intellectual journey since then has been one of attempting to understand and soothe the haunt that attached itself to me so strongly that day.

My education, both formal and street, has focused on the existential. In my own life and in my role as a teacher, it is the asking of these questions that has lead me to a better understanding of what to ask next. Educational philosophy as a life's work has been nothing more than a logical extension of my quest to make sense of where I came from and how it made me who I am. If my father gave me anything, he cultivated, albeit harshly and not without injury, an indefatigable drive. And for that I am grateful.

CHAPTER 11

Poverty of Mind, Poverty of Spirit: Breaking the Shackles that Bind

Nina Zaragoza

The brothers stand in a row one right in front of the other and for some reason in order of height. Each wears a white t-shirt, blue denim shorts, white crew socks, and black Converse sneakers. They are among the hundreds of children in the South Bronx who file through a community organization's site to collect needed school supplies. As they wait in line, I watch a young child sway from one foot to the next in rapid succession, another pull his little sister's beaded braid, and yet another lift herself off the ground by grabbing on to her grandmother's purse. The brand new tan and black backpacks stood upright already filled with:

- three traditional black-and-white marble notebooks
- a pencil case filled with five yellow number 2 pencils
- eight black Bic pens held together with a rubber band
- a brown wooden ruler
- a pink rubber eraser
- a clear plastic pencil sharpener
- a box of 24 Crayola crayons and
- four red, blue, green, and yellow pocket folders

And so the 2005–2006 school year begins for the children in our public school system but I have bowed out. I have resigned my third-grade special education position after more than twenty years of public school service in Miami and New York City. I am through beating my head against the wall of test prep booklets, beating my knuckles against DRA assessment kits, and trying to beat the system from within. I have broken out of the city-school walls and into the surrounding communities. These last years in New York City solidified my growing dismay. It saddens me not to work in a classroom filled with children, but it frees me to serve them instead as the education coordinator of a nonprofit organization. This organization devoted to youth development, works with youth outside of school by supporting their teachers with school supplies, providing resources for community-based after-school programs, and connecting with the children's families.

So why did I finally decide to leave the public schools? Why me, a professional educator that has always been passionate about my work and the students I serve? I woke up every morning filled with a joy and sense of purpose that carried me through and above most of the petty annoyances of classroom teaching: bulletin boards, lunch forms, not enough supplies, constant interruptions, and too much testing. While the more serious issues of poverty, low self-esteem, low achievement, and injustice in the schools pushed me to seek my Ph.D. in order to enter into teacher education, I never left the public school classroom. As a professor my projects were school-based and afforded me the privilege of continuing to teach children in the public schools (Zaragoza 2002). In fact, for the 1999–2000 school year I decided to teach full-time again as a Dade County public school teacher (Zaragoza 2005) and relished every minute. Totally energized in a classroom I felt like an artist at work as my students and I explored and grew in a structured and dynamic learning environment. Things changed, though, when I returned to the city of my birth.

At the district office in Brooklyn they can't quite figure out what to do with me. I have lengthy transcripts, varied qualifications, and so in their eyes I am totally overqualified as a classroom teacher. When I insist that I do not want a reading coach job the transcript evaluator introduces me to the district special education director who, after a brief conversation with me, dials the phone and says, "Hey, Rachel, I have someone here who I know you will want to meet . . . Okay, I'll send her right over." Within five minutes I sit on a bus bound for the red-bricked, five-storied school I would teach in for the next three years.

I feel exhilarated back in the city I left at eighteen. Old and new memories blend together and every experience, taking the bus, the subway, eating pizza and Italian ice on the corner, hearing Arabic, Spanish, Hebrew, and Korean all within the same neighborhood remind me of the diversity I always loved. I am home. The school has the same front steps that reach the office and auditorium on the second floor as my elementary school, PS 122. I walk up the steps and whisper to myself, "Wow, now I'm a NYC teacher!" I, a true New Yorker, always felt unless I made it in New York any other accomplishment was less. So, now, begins the big time!

I watch the children walking from the candy store and see myself. I see big sisters gripping little sisters' hands and feel my sister's hand. I smell Italian cookies baking and see my seven-year-old self in front of Jacobi's bakery under the subway trestle clutching a small brown bag filled with four anisette cookies. "So this is what it means to return home," I think, "to return to yourself." And I am home because when I see my students I see myself. When I teach my students I teach myself.

I teach in a self-contained special education classroom filled with twelve first and second graders and I wonder why. In Miami we serve special needs children in inclusion rooms or in general education rooms with support. Self-contained in New York—a city on the cutting edge? How strange. But, of course, I love my students and go beyond the labels the system uses to shackle them. I want to inspire them to break these shackles that bind and accept their freedom like I finally did in my high school years.

MEMORIES

The memory of Long Island floods over me. My stomach still tightens when I am forced to think about it. To this day, more than twenty years later, I cringe at the thought of traveling there. And I wonder sometimes why my mother moved us there—of all places. I guess even until the end she fought to turn that American dream into a reality. But we never did quite make it, the white picket fence, the backyard with a pool, and the house became, for me, symbols of death. She died in that house and the young girl that I was died, too.

As a single mother working three jobs trying to raise five children in Queens, my mother struggled. At one point, in order to survive, she put us all into foster care for a year. Obviously, we never owned a home and because our landlords always decided to sell the house we rented we moved every year or so. We usually stayed in the same neighbor-hood, though, so in my elementary school years I only had to switch schools once. My siblings and I held the distinction of not having the same name as my mother and I remember the dread I felt every time my mother needed to sign a form. I can hear the teacher call out even now, "Whose field trip form is this? No one has this last name. Oh, that's right, it's *your* mother, Nina, isn't it?" My face burned and my eyes lowered and I hoped that no one noticed.

I think we did pretty well in Queens, though. Even though my mother couldn't afford to buy me a Girl Scout uniform, ballet classes, or new clothes I made it through playing on the block, watching my brothers play handball, sitting on the stoop, sneaking off to Astoria pool, and winning school reading contests. My reading ability garnered me the recognition I needed to feel accepted in school. It also helped that I won a well-attended fight on the playground, and I relished my reputation as a fighter, "She's small but she's tough!" The move to Long Island changed that—for a while.

"I'm not moving out there with you. I'm staying right here!" My eighteen-year-old sister yelled and she did just what she said. She got married and stayed in Queens. I moved all the way to East Islip and for the next six years lived in a house that looked like everyone else's on the outside. So how did a poor single mother from New York City end up in one of the richest neighborhoods on "the island"? She sold her soul. Or so I thought, as a thirteen-year-old thrown into the town's mid-dle school. She made a deal with my father—if he paid the mortgage he could forget about paying any other child support. Thus began my battles at the grocery store, in the house, and in school.

I'm too hungry to eat just potato chips so I wait on the lunch line. But someone stands behind me. I pretend to forget something, leave the line, and come back so that I'm last again. I near the cash register,

"$1.50"
"Free lunch," I whisper.
"Speak up, honey, I can't hear you."
"Free lunch," I say a little louder.
"Oh right, Lopez, I just saw your brother. You hardly eat, honey, that's why you're so skinny!"

I hear someone snicker behind me. I walk away looking down, bangs covering my eyes, with the end strands of my brown hair brushing through the spaghetti sauce. So, to avoid the lunch line, for most of my school career in East Islip my lunch consisted of Wise potato chips and Yoo Hoo chocolate drink.

I couldn't avoid the grocery line, though. This day my mother sends me to the store with food stamps and I wait in line praying that no one comes behind me. I switch places.

"That's okay, little girl, go ahead of me."
"Oh, I forgot something."
"I'll save your place."
"No, no that's okay. You go ahead."

I walk down the endless aisles pretending to shop, waiting for the lines to shorten and cursing my mother. Cursing her for sending me and never my brothers; for bringing us here; for getting sick; for being poor and making me use these food stamps. How could she do this to us? In Queens it didn't matter if we had a car or not. Here we can't get anywhere without one and we walk a mile to a store. In Queens if we went to Catholic Charities for food and clothes, fifty other people lined up behind us. Here if we go we can get as many cans of disgusting ground turkey or blocks of yellow cheese as we want since it looks like no one else wants them. And in Queens we always had heat. Here we walk around the house with our coats because we don't have enough money at the end of the month for the heating oil. I hate it here.

"Hey, I know where you got those shoes and that dress too! My mother put them in the poor box at St. Mary's. Hey look at her! She has on my used clothes!" Just another great day at East Islip High School — where I hide behind my books and look beyond to the city. Where I read *A Tree Grows in Brooklyn* and know that someday I'll return to where I belong. East Islip High School where the guidance counselor never tells me I have the grades to go to an Ivy League college — where no one even tells me what that means. But I figure out how to fill out the financial aid forms and find out the farthest school to go to and still be able to get New York State money. My mother cries when I leave for Buffalo. I don't look back. Not yet. I actually end up traveling the world from Miami to San Francisco to Michigan back to Miami, and then to Russia before returning home.

EAST LANSING, MICHIGAN: GLEN CAIRN ELEMENTARY

When I entered Mr. Voigt's third/fourth grade classroom I immediately felt the energy and passion from both the teacher and his students. I worked with this teacher and his children (my son Michael included) for a full year as we guided young authors through the writing process to final publication (Zaragoza, Voigt, and Zaragoza 1996). Teaching and learning flowed in this classroom filled with beginning, in-process, and finished projects. Children and teacher moved in synchronicity within personal and community purposes as they accomplished the academic and social tasks at hand. Report cards had no numbers on them but consisted of narrative writing that celebrated the progress and strengths of each learner. These young writers, readers, mathematicians, scientists understood their goals as their work was embedded in true meaning and therefore displaying of state standards and assessment rubrics didn't monopolize any wall space. Instead, poetry, children's art, writing, and photos predominated and created a home where children's voices stood strong and honored. Because most of their parents worked as professors at Michigan State University, they were accustomed to this recognition and they blossomed.

When my Brooklyn College graduate students read of these children in Michigan they cannot believe this could be possible for their students in East New York. Most of these young teachers have never even experienced a room that could be so dynamic and alive unless, like a few of them, they grew up on Long Island, and then they remember their own education. But these memories don't carry them into their classrooms because their students come from other neighborhoods, other groups. They buy into "the truth" that the kids they teach do need highly scripted, highly structured mechanistic programs to learn. "Oh, my kids can't do that, Dr. Zaragoza. They can't choose what they write or read! That would be way too confusing! I can't even get them to behave!"

And the words they speak for these students they also speak for themselves. With these words they tighten the state shackles of No Child Left Behind and deny their children and themselves real authorship, genuine and purposeful reading, and work. The memories they might have had of a deeper, freer kind of teaching die and the standards, the test preparation, the constant rubricizing of even their bulletin boards live. In this world principals threaten "a letter in your file" if at 10:05 A.M. children's books are not opened to page 23 of the test prep booklet. Here reality overwhelms the memory and these teachers make no room for dreams or another kind of vision.

VLADIMIR, RUSSIA: THE AMERICAN HOME

Teaching in Russia for two years proved to be one of the most memorable and freeing experiences. Quite ironic, don't you think? In a private school for students whose families could pay, I taught English to both children and adults. We performed Langston Hughes poetry, connected to American movies and novels (*American Beauty*, *One Flew Over The Cuckoo's Nest*, *The Usual Suspects*, *Catcher in the Rye*, *Of Mice and Men*, *A Streetcar Named Desire*), and connected to contemporary music (Tupac, Eminem, Green Day, Linkin Park). The students and I drank in this invigorating work and relished every single minute of it as we spoke about deep personal and cultural issues and formed strong teaching and learning connections. In fact, these connections continue to bind us together as our memories transcend place and time.

At Brooklyn College the teachers I teach ask about strategies, topics to assign, behavior methods, and time-management tips. Into these conversations I try to weave in hope, encouragement, and support. I try to speak words into their hearts that will inspire them to go beyond the shackles and enter into the world of dreams and memories. They sometimes try to understand but most often they avert their eyes. They turn away with spirits weary and tired of the constant struggle to fulfill the system's demands and the needs of their students.

MIAMI, FLORIDA: LITTLE RIVER ELEMENTARY SCHOOL

Working in urban schools and special education for my whole career I initially wondered why we needed to continually struggle for everything.

We get less of everything: supplies, adequate school buildings, technology equipment, teachers with teaching abilities, and care. How appalling not to have a tape player (let alone a CD player), a sharpener that really sharpens, shades that shield the sun, radiators that turn on *and* off, and air conditioners in 90 degree weather. And as our children wear their coats inside during winter or sweat profusely in the summer, meaningless curriculum assaults their minds filling them with a tangible anger straining for release. Soon I realized, though, that the state had its plans and I decided to fight back with my own plans.

Our fifth graders grabbed the carefully placed worksheets from their desk and diligently started to work. Finally, what we had practiced for just this time was performed in front of the intended audience. The education auditors seemed impressed and so our rehearsals paid off as we were commended for the amazing control we had over our students and the wonderful learning that going on in our classroom. Little did they know that my team teacher and I had decided long ago that we would not let the mandated, mechanistic, scripted reading program *Success for All* eat away our time with our students. We had the nerve to offer them something that their middle-class cohorts took for granted — education that had some kind of meaning, education that enabled true engagement in a critical, high-level process. We had the audacity to offer real work that ignited a passion and hunger for learning.

At Brooklyn College many of the teachers I teach are not happy when they hear that I taught my fifth graders how to fight the system.

"But when you do this, you're teaching your students to lie! I can't do that!"

"What lies do we pass on to our students now?"

"What do you mean?"

"When every minute of the day is programmed, when every inch of wall is filled with preconceived standards and rubrics, when every discreet skill is measured on a scale of 1 to 4 what are we telling our students?"

"What do you mean?"

"What do these actions tell our students about learning?

Some of these teachers understand that what they do during the day has nothing to do with real learning and they feel exasperated by the lock-step schedule they must follow but see no way out. They tug at the chains but disillusion overtakes them. Others believe children will succeed with these methods and they work their fingers to the bone to move the "2s" to "3s" and the "3s" to "4s." In fact, under administrative orders some schools actually ignore the "1s" by not offering extra before- or after-school test prep sessions because as they say, "We need to concentrate on the children who will be able to move to the next number."

Either way, when seeds of passion for real learning try to grow in the hearts of our teachers, they fall on dry, rocky soil. This soil cannot nurture these seeds to fruition and they die. If some passion does exist, the cares and worries brought by the system extinguishes the fervor for real, genuine, deep teaching and learning relationships. This poverty of mind chokes our students. This poverty of spirit suffocates our students. They walk through a desolate, barren field filled with land mines waiting to take them out, already taking them out.

BROOKLYN, NEW YORK: PS 192

I refused to sell my soul. I offered and expected real and genuine work from all my students labeled "special education" and they met my expectations. They cultivated their own souls as they performed poetry and self-written drama productions to a live, "regular education" audience. I dared to try and break down the so-carefully-constructed walls that separate the haves and have-nots, the free and the enslaved, the boundless and the bound. I had the absolute nerve to challenge my students' placement in a self-contained room and wondered aloud at the injustice of it all.

I am not the only one wondering. Families are not blind to their children's plight in the public schools. They see their daughters and sons falling further and further behind, biding their time in a system that could care less for the future of their children. But families know outside the school walls other chains await. So they look for after-school programs, community youth groups, anything to keep their children in school:

Liz: I don't know what to do with him. He just wants to get his GED.

Juanita: Yea, my daughter did the same thing. She settled for the "Good Enough Degree."

Liz: But that's not going to cut it anymore. Now even a real high school degree doesn't get you much.

Juanita: True. Pretty soon you need the masters to get anything decent.

Liz: He just hates school. He wants out. When I ask him about his work he says he just does worksheets.

Juanita: My granddaughter says the same thing. The other day I heard her reading out loud in the children's group and compared to the others she sounded so behind. I'm really worried about her. She's in third grade and if she doesn't pass those tests she won't be promoted.

Liz: Tell me about it. They just pass up our kids and concentrate on other neighborhoods.

Juanita: It's a racist thing. Didn't you hear what Muriel said about her principal's attitude?

Liz: No.

Juanita: Well, Muriel went to talk about some of her students not doing their homework and calling the families about it and the principal actually said something like, "Why bother? Don't you know that in this neighborhood kids don't do their homework?"

Liz: Yea, like I heard someone else say once this system is set up so our children fail.

Juanita: Yea, they definitely don't want to lose their McDonald's workers.

Liz: I'm just praying my son makes it through. If only he would get a teacher that believes in him.

Juanita: Good luck with that.

Tragically many families have little faith that there will be that special someone in the schools to help nurture their children. They, too, have experienced a system that is cold and alienating, void of any comfort or hope and they desperately seek out mentors in their churches, clubs, and after-school programs. They watch their young ones turn into angry, hopeless teenagers lashing out or inward and pray for some kind of support—any kind of support.

BREAKING THE SHACKLES

And now my work focuses on helping community-based organizations provide this support and mentoring that our students rarely receive in the public schools. The program we've designed attempts to break the chains of educational oppression that ensnare the youth in our New York target communities who have met with academic failure across grade levels and/or across subject areas. Continual confrontation of such academic barriers causes a sense of helplessness and a cycle of "learned helplessness" (Peterson, Maier, and Seligman 1995) ensues. Students exhibiting such helplessness perceive their failure is due to a personal lack of competence and not circumstances that can be controlled (i.e., more effort). Therefore, they withdraw from the task attempted or refuse to attempt to address the task at all and sit "helplessly" by.

Sadly, many of our youth have, therefore, withdrawn from or lost their dreams to circumstances beyond their control, to the larger world that surrounds them, and to their own inner world of condemnation and self-hate. Our students need to know that they are allowed to dream and that their dreams will be protected. We must help them remember these dreams and inspire them to seek new ones. Perhaps, we can serve as "dream keepers":

The Dream Keeper
Langston Hughes

Bring me all of your dreams
You dreamers
Bring me all of your heart melodies
That I might wrap them in a blue cloud cloth
Away from the too rough fingers
Of the world.

Students given the tools to break through this cycle begin to view themselves as active thinkers and learners within the learning process. To accomplish this shift of vision other alternatives must be explored and while our program mirrors some of the structure of the literacy elements in the public schools (silent/independent reading, reading aloud, reading discussion groups, reading response journals, etc.), there are major differences in delivery so that students' self-confidence can be directly addressed and strengthened. This type of program incorporates student choice and therefore respectfully addresses the various strengths and needs of all students. Because students are allowed to make choices about reading and writing materials/topics and given access to high-interest materials, they become involved in meaningful work.

For example most of our students develop academic skills as they engage in script writing (this would encompass both reading and writing), role-playing, video camera use, songs for reading practice, and video-game/board-game instructions for reading practice. Also, as much as possible, these students are offered the opportunity to mentor younger children. In this way they bolster the skills/talents they possess and discover new ones. These activities emerge from ongoing projects that go far beyond the regular school fare offered to our urban youth.

PROJECT ORIENTATION

A project is work that needs to be completed over time and so requires a level of commitment usually not necessary for daily activities such as filling in a worksheet, finish reading one more chapter, etc. This type of commitment can be inspired in the students when they are allowed to choose what they want to create. Mentors need to have an active part in the decision especially if a group project will be agreed upon. Just as in other areas of literacy, the mentors' passion is a major key to success. Possible projects ideas include:

- original drama production that includes script writing, inclusion of music/dance, practice, and performance before an audience
- poetry recital that can include already published poets and original poetry written by students
- visual art exhibition including painting, photography, sculpture, documentary, personal logos, crafts, etc.
- cultural fair that can include research and presentation of information on a certain culture—their food, dance, music, etc., related to culture under study

- newspaper for a larger community
- individually published books
- group published book (i.e., anthology)
- work within the community with young children, senior citizens, local business owners

Projects usually connect all aspects of literacy into one meaningful whole, address a range of literacy skills, and can be adapted to any age group. Drama, for example, incorporates writing a first draft, revising, editing, publication (final script), and performance (oral development). Of course, the participants need to read the script as well. This is a powerful way to motivate students to acquire the skills they need for success for a number of reasons:

1. It is meaningful work and has a genuine purpose (i.e., performance).
2. Students want to complete the work because it is significant for them and they have had an active part in choosing the project.
3. Students are internalizing literacy skills because they are using them in a meaningful, purposeful context.
4. Literacy skills become relevant for the students because they begin to understand why they are important and how they are used in everyday life.

While community projects at first glance might not seem like literacy, when such projects are examined more closely the literacy connections become evident. For example, work with younger children and senior citizens could easily encompass reading/writing/performing activities. Also, projects with local businesses enable students to learn the financial literacy necessary for success in this area.

Working with others in their neighborhoods goes beyond specific literacy skills and encourages students to see themselves as connected to and responsible for a larger community. This type of responsibility enables them to:

- look beyond themselves to a larger vision
- have a positive influence on the community around them

- view themselves as community change agents
- understand that without them the community would be less.

Empowered students lead to vibrant, dynamic communities forged from the deep connections developed during real and revolutionary work. Students who help others and look beyond themselves begin to see themselves as change agents and confidence is built because they involve themselves in purposeful actions and affecting positive community change.

Because students play an active part in the choice of reading materials, topics written, and projects completed they become accountable for and foster their own success. Active students see that their actions do have a direct connection to their success and therefore the cycle of learned helplessness begins to break. Here, too, recognition of the mentors' assets occurs because of their active involvement in facilitating the agreed-upon decisions. When mentors and students are passionate about the work the whole community is inspired to continued growth. Because mentors participate in the same process as the students, they get to know each other through their personal learning choices and deep connections now denied to them in their schools emerge.

The community becomes a safe haven where members reclaim the support and respect inherently theirs. In this type of community members take the risks needed for further academic success. When success happens and students realize that they have played an active role in their own success self-confidence increases. Our educational design allows for such nurturing because of the philosophical principles it is founded upon:

- the creation and growth of a safe, supportive academic community
- personal connections that are committed and respectful
- all members as active participants in all academic areas
- decision-making power for all community members
- tasks that are meaningful and purposeful
- opportunities for all members to serve the larger community

Indeed, because most of our mentors have overcome similar obstacles, our students have living proof that negative cycles can be broken and that with support they themselves can break them. When given the concrete tools needed to succeed in college (i.e., exact process for choosing and applying for a college, financial aid, process for seeking academic aid, etc.) our youth will confidently use them to obtain the reality of their vision.

BEYOND DREAMS

When students work together with positive mentors in a supportive, nurturing community focused on academic, emotional, and community growth they are given permission to dream. During participation in our education model our youth grow into visionaries as they make academic choices, design purpose-filled projects, and serve in their neighborhoods. They become youth who play an active role in their own growth and the growth of others. They understand that their decisions and actions do have influence and make a difference. They become youth able to hope, to exert their power, and ready to make their dreams a reality. With something to accomplish and the confidence and skills needed for such an accomplishment, more of our youth will graduate from high school, look toward college, and beyond.

UNBOUND MEMORIES

And so now I look beyond the public schools toward their surrounding communities. I watch these young children of the South Bronx gather their brand new backpacks and supplies and I remember the freshness and hope of all my first days of schools, even the tough ones on Long Island and as a teacher in the New York City Public Schools. I use these memories to fuel my work and inspire others to break the shackles that bind, and reach beyond the "too rough fingers of the world" and reclaim the power, freedom, and abundance already within them.

REFERENCES

Hughes, L. (1995). *The Collected Poems of Langston Hughes*. New York: Vintage Books.

Peterson, C., Maier, S. F., and Seligman, M. (1995). *Learned Helplessness.* Oxford: Oxford: University Press.

Zaragoza, N. (2002). *Rethinking Language Arts: Passion and Practice.* New York: RoutledgeFalmer.

Zaragoza, N., & Dwyer, E. (2005). *Look I Made a Book: Literacy in a Kindergarten Classroom.* New York: Peter Lang.

Zaragoza, N., Voigt, R., and Zaragoza, M. (1996). Writing Can Be Lonely: An Introduction to Coauthoring. *Reading* 30 (2), 19–24.

It's a Class Act

Shirley R. Steinberg

Seems to me that Diane Ravitch, the Emily Post of American education, once mentioned we had no issues of social class in the United
States of America. We were exempt from the problems that plagued
countries like Great Britain and India . . . indeed, our anticolonial heritage had spared us from that nasty set of categories. Implying that class
should not be addressed in school curricula, she also has objected to the
use of social justice as a component in courses. Only occasionally, perhaps this once, do I wish that Ravitch was correct. If I made one of my
three wishes to the proverbial, mythical wish-granter, I would wish that
we did not have social class in North America. I would wish that we
were all socially equal and that each person was valued for his or her
own self, without attention to the socioeconomic sphere in which he or
she revolved. Ain't gonna happen. Ravitch has, like many other scholars in their upper-middle-class, trite ivory towers, declared that there is
no class, but have reinforced class stratification by this far too loud denial of class. So, her claim that there is no class is actually her silent
Munchian cry screaming "*classssssssssssss.*"

Milan Kundera in his genius, *Unbearable Lightness of Being* (1985),
names kitsch as the "folding screen set up to curtain off death" (Kundera, 253). His female character, Sabina, desires to be an artist in the
footsteps of her father. His art was considered kitsch, below the realm
of high art, an antibourgeois insult to what art truly was. Sabina attends
art school, which, of course, denies the existence of what is hidden behind the curtain . . . the kitsch, and eventually embraces kitsch within
her own identity (not her art) as she is eternally unable to disregard the

folded curtain set up to avoid the kitsch. She may leave her home and walk within footsteps of high art, but she cannot ignore the unacknowledged kitsch. Kundera goes on to describe kitsch: "[K]itsch is the absolute denial of shit, in both the literal and figurative senses of the word; kitsch excludes everything from its purview which is essentially unacceptable in human existence." Theodor Adorno defines kitsch as: "kitsch or sugary trash is the beautiful minus its ugly counterpart. Therefore, kitsch, purified beauty, becomes subject to an aesthetic taboo that in the name of beauty pronounces kitsch to be ugly" (Adorno 1985). Kitsch, consequently is the denial of shit. It is Ravitch's denial of class. Social class is the shit about which North Americans cannot discuss. If we do not discuss it, it does not exist. But . . . it does.

Now if a student or parent is part of the dominant culture, in our case, white, middle-class, probably Anglo, Protestant, male, and heterosexual, then Diane would not see class. It is just when those specs aren't met that class rears its head. So, in a perverted way, Diane could be right, there is no social class *if* one is in your own social class . . . sort of a class invisibility for yourself . . . but not for anyone else—and certainly not for those of "lower" or different cultures than the defined dominant culture.

Fast forward to a kitsch TV reference, an episode of *Big Brother*, a North American take-off of an international show. Good ole Howie gets evicted by his housemates. Now Howie is one of America's favorites, however, his housemates see him as *common, gross, disgusting,* and *a moron.* Howie is *crass.* He tells it like it is. He makes no attempt to hide his feelings. When he is evicted, he speaks to each person who voted him out and mentions that they betrayed him, that they lied, that they had no integrity. As he leaves the house, he tosses a member's hat off the set and disgustedly exits the door—a houseguest yells the ultimate irony after him: "That's it, Howie, you're a class act, real class leaving the house like that." Of course, the guest felt Howie had *no* class. That someone with class would have tucked it in, *been a man,* and not shown his anger and disgust.

Up to this point, for seven seasons, *Big Brother*'s guests are told they are evicted, stand up, sadly hug each housemate (many who voted them out), smile, wave, and bravely exit the set. Howie transgressed by showing his indignation, telling the truth, and calling out those that had evicted him. By doing this, he demonstrated a lack of class, he broke the rules of class, he was outspoken, he violated the Western cultural capital of keeping quiet, swallowing his opinion, and being a *good sport*. Even though he was lied to, manipulated, and insulted, he was expected to walk out *with class.*

Much like higher education, the above example reinscribes the notion that *if one has class*, one keeps a low affect. In our upper-middle-class world of academia, it is *not* appropriate to move the screen hiding the shit. We are expected to passively sit and nod, to never show bad breeding in our dislike of the dominant power structure. As teachers, we are expected by existing society (dominant culture) to preserve and promote the status quo. To keep things going as they have always gone and to make sure that our students goose-step in line with state or provincial guidelines, curricula, and *manners*. Good manners show class, breeding, and an ability to function *correctly* in society. When one displays a lack of class, thwarts the status quo, ignores what is expected, and shows individuality, this violation of the rules of class, indicate that she or he is *not* being appropriate—but being crass.

This book has discussed class in many ways: class in schools, families, cultures, society, and in theory. In every chapter, an underlying message seeps through: social class prevents individuality, sustains mediocrity, and disallows evolution, revolution, and social justice. As educators, it is our duty, our mandate, to violate the *rules* of social class. We are those that must step up to trespass, to transgress, to usurp the dominant and stagnant culture of social class. As we call out indignations to our students, our schools, our society, we create the *class act* of resistance. By resisting, naming, and changing that which is, which was, and what is destined by the dominant culture to be, we become agents of social change. With every thread of my being, I hope to emulate those agents of class transgression in this book, those agents in our schools, homes, and communities, to seek to name injustice, class inequities, and walk out of Big Brother's house being called a *class act* by those who think they are being sarcastic. I want to acknowledge the shit of class bias, the kitsch of North American society, and insist that the screen be torn down.

REFERENCES

Adorno, Theodor. *Aesthetic Theory*. London: Routledge, 1984.

Kundera, Milan. *The Unbearable Lightness of Being*. Trans. Michael Henry Heim. New York: Harper & Row, 1985.

Wawrzycka, Jolanta W. Betrayal as a Flight from Kitsch in Milan Kundera's *The Unbearable Lightness of Being* (267–80), in *Milan Kundera and the Art of Fiction*, Aron Aji (ed). New York & London: Garland Publishing Inc.

Index

capitalism, 12; capitalist society, 251; modern capitalist societies, 244; monopoly capitalism, 246
Card, Andrew, 136
Charlemagne, 122, 123
Chauncey, Henry, 57
child labor. *See* labor
Christianity, 32; Christo-fascism, 32; dominance of, 9; influences on, 6; fundamentalist Christians, 41, 51; theology, 139
civil rights, 212; civil rights movement, 71
class: class-related protests, 31; consciousness, 244, 248; deterministic class theories, 43; domination, 7; identity, 30, 244; illiteracy, 59; justice, 21; Marxist class analysts, 6, 98; membership, 21; middle-classness, 99; multilogical class struggle, 39; new class struggle, 34; oppression, 4, 25; oppression of dominant hegemonic power, 18; privilege, 242; ruling class, 242; solidarity, 19; struggle, 65; supremacy, 61. *See also* working class
colonialism, 34, 41; American colonialism, 8; anticolonial movements, 10; colonial domination, 7; colonial location, 60; European colonialism, 8; neocolonialism, 8
common culture. *See* culture
community-based organizations, 295
completion rates, 105, 106
consumerism, 247, 248; consumers, 248; consumer capitalism, 43;

consumer power, 244; consumer society, 229
Cornell, Ezra, 129
corporations: corporate power, 45, 47; corporate power wielders, 9; corporatist state, 121; privatization, 11; transnational corporations, 6, 14
Counts, George, 7
credit system, 132
critical enactivism. *See* theory
critical ethnography. *See* ethnography, theory
critical ontology. *See* ontology, theory
critical pedagogy, 16, 25, 27, 29, 47, 48, 54, 56, 71, 148; of class awareness, 16–65; modern learning theories, 165
critical theory, 25, 36, 71, 73, 90; enactivism, 44; ethnography, 71–91; ontology, 21, 45; pedagogy, 16, 25, 27, 29, 47, 48, 54, 56, 71, 148
critical unions, 47
Crowe, Cameron, 149
culture, 55; common, 39; cultural capital, 77, 241; cultural difference, 249; cultural literacy, 166; cultural studies, 148; dominant culture, 74, 88, 162; hip hop, 167; of power, 79, 89; of resistance, 79
curriculum, 86, 147, 152, 158, 165; antipatriarchal, 10; antiracist, 10; curriculum theory, 148; hidden, 110; state-mandated, 167

Delpit, Lisa, 150, 151
democracy, 3, 250

About the Contributors

Phil Graham is associate professor of management at Queensland University. His research interests include political economy of new media, discourse analyses, and the implications of a knowledge economy for large-scale social and institutional change.

Randall Hewitt is assistant professor of educational studies at the University of Central Florida. He teaches courses in the philosophy, history, and sociology of education. His research interests include pragmatism, critical theory, the reproduction of social class, and democratic education. His forthcoming book deals with philosophy and the foundations of education.

Lynda Kennedy has developed curricula, education, and public programs for the Cathedral of St. John the Divine, the National Museum of the American Indian, and South Street Seaport Museum, among others. For more than four years she served as education coordinator at the Lower East Side Tenement Museum and went on to serve as manager of teacher outreach at the Brooklyn Historical Society (BHS). Most recently, she has held the position of director of education at the American Museum of the Moving Image. Lynda is currently pursuing her Ph.D. in urban education at the Graduate Center of the City University of New York and consulting on projects involving the integration of the arts into core curricula.

Joe L. Kincheloe is the Canada Research Chair at the McGill University Faculty of Education. He is the author of numerous books and articles about pedagogy, education and social justice, racism, class bias, sexism, issues of cognition and cultural context, and educational reform. His books include: *Teachers as Researchers, Classroom Teaching: An Introduction, Getting Beyond the Facts: Teaching Social Studies/Social Sciences in the Twenty-first Century, The Sign of the Burger: McDonald's and the Culture of Power, City Kids: Understanding Them, Appreciating Them, and Teaching Them,* and *Changing Multiculturalism* (with Shirley Steinberg). His coedited works include *White Reign: Deploying Whiteness in America* (with Shirley Steinberg, et al.) and the Gustavus Myers Human Rights award winner, *Measured Lies: The Bell Curve Examined* (with Shirley Steinberg). Along with his partner, Shirley Steinberg, Kincheloe is an international speaker and lead singer/keyboard player of Tony and the Hegemones.

D. W. Livingstone is Canada Research Chair in Lifelong Learning and Work at the University of Toronto, head of the Centre for the Study of Education and Work, department of sociology and equity studies at OISE/UT, and director of the SSHRC-funded national research network on Changing Nature of Work and Lifelong Learning. (see www .wall.oise.utoronto.ca)

Allan Luke is professor of education at Queensland University of Technology. His published work on literacy and language, educational policy, and sociology has appeared in *Harvard Educational Review, Teachers College Record,* the *American Journal of Education, Australian Educational Researcher,* and other journals.

Carmen Luke is professor of education at Queensland University. Her academic work focuses on teaching and research in the areas of multiliteracies, media literacy, and cultural studies. She has published numerous books and articles on new technologies and cultural change, women in higher education, and globalization.

Natalie Mixon is a doctoral student and an adjunct faculty in the secondary education department at the University of South Florida and a social studies teacher at Walter Sickles High School in Tampa, Florida. She teaches and develops curriculum for advanced placement human geography, anthropology, and sociology electives in secondary social science education and has presented at state and national conferences. Her scholarly and research interests include exploring the link between social class, culture, and the phenomenon of social reproduction in the public school system using GIS technology and qualitative methods.

Shirley R. Steinberg is an associate professor at the McGill University Faculty of Education. She is the author and editor of numerous books and articles and coedits several book series. The founding editor of *Taboo: The Journal of Culture and Education*, Steinberg has recently finished editing *Teen Life in Europe*, and, with Priya Parmar and Birgit Richard, *The Encyclopedia of Contemporary Youth Culture*. She is the editor of *Multi/Intercultural Conversations: A Reader*. With Joe Kincheloe she has edited *Kinderculture: The Corporate Construction of Childhood and The Miseducation of the West: How Schools and the Media Distort Our Understanding of the Islamic World*. She is coauthor of *Changing Multiculturalism: New Times, New Curriculum, and Contextualizing Teaching* (with Joe Kincheloe). Her areas of expertise and research are in critical media literacy, social drama, and youth studies.

Susan L. Stowe is a doctoral student in the department of sociology and equity studies at the Ontario Institute for Studies in Education of The University of Toronto.

Kenneth Tobin is presidential professor of urban education at the Graduate Center of City University of New York. In 2004 Tobin was recognized by the National Science Foundation as a Distinguished Teaching Scholar and by the Association for the Education of Teachers of Science as Outstanding Science Teacher Educator of the Year. His research interests are focused on the teaching and learning of science in urban schools, which involve mainly African American students living in conditions of poverty. A parallel program of research focuses on coteaching as a way of learning to teach in urban high schools.

Nina Zaragoza is a well-known scholar and teacher. Once described by Shirley Steinberg as the best classroom teacher ever observed, Nina has been a classroom teacher, taught English in Russia, a professor, and is now working in a nonprofit organization in New York. She is the author of many articles and of *Look, I Made a Book: Literacy in a Kindergarten Classroom* and *Rethinking Language Arts: Passion and Practice*.